The Film Edge

EDITED BY **EDUARDO A. RUSSO**

The Film Edge

Contemporary Filmmaking in Latin America

> The Film Edge : Contemporary Filmmaking in Latin America / edición
> literaria a cargo de Eduardo A. Russo. - 1 a ed. - Buenos Aires : Teseo;
> Fundación TyPA (Teoría y Práctica de las Artes), 2010.
>   358 p. ; 20x13 cm.
>
>   ISBN 978-987-1354-71-9
>
>   1. Cinematografía. I. Russo, Eduardo A., ed. lit.
>   CDD 778.5

The Film Edge: Contemporary Filmmaking in Latin America is an abridged and revised edition of *Hacer cine. Producción audiovisual en América latina* © 2008 by Editorial Paidós and Fundación TyPA.

Translations from the Spanish by Heather Cleary Wolfgang.
The chapter "Father, Country" was translated by Francisco Ferenczi.

This book was made possible by the support of The Rockefeller Foundation.

© 2010 Fundación TyPA
www.typa.org.ar

Cover design © 2010 by Trineo comunicación
www.trineo.com.ar

© 2010 Editorial Teseo
Buenos Aires, Argentina

ISBN 978-987-1354-71-9
Editorial Teseo

Hecho el depósito que previene la ley 11.723

Para sugerencias o comentarios acerca del contenido de esta obra, escríbanos a: **info@editorialteseo.com**

www.editorialteseo.com

Index

Acknowledgements 9

About the Authors 11

Foreword 23

1. National Perspectives, Regional Projections 29

Building at the Margins:
Trajectories of New Independent Cinema
in Latin America. *David Oubiña* 33

Cinematic Production in Mexico
Under the Sign of Crisis. *Gustavo Montiel Pagés* 47

The Unexpected Rise
of Central American Cinema. *María Lourdes Cortés* 65

Cuban Cinema Beyond Strawberries
and Chocolate. *Luciano Castillo* 81

Father, Country. *José Carlos Avellar* 105

Peru: Films for After a War. *Ricardo Bedoya* 145

Mirrors on the Periphery. *Marcos Loayza* 159

Argentine Cinema: a State of Affairs. *Jorge La Ferla* 173

Memories of New Argentine Cinema. *Andrés Di Tella* 199

2. Singularities in Context..213

Luis Ospina and Colombian Cinema:
Independence or Resistance? *Mauricio Durán Castro* 215

Cristián Sánchez,
the Stationary Nomad. *Jorge Ruffinelli*................................237

Lisandro Alonso:
States and Mutations of Cinema. *Eduardo A. Russo*..........259

Riding the Storm. *Paz Encina* 275

3. Genres, Formats, Projects...287

From the Real to Reality:
the Creative Documentary
in Latin America. *Carmen Guarini*.......................................289

Forms of Audiovisual Observation
in Contemporary Latin American
Production. *Malena Di Bastiano*..307

A Few Reflections on Short Film. *Paulo Pécora* 319

The Mise en Scène of Early Short Films. *Daniela Goggi*.........331

The Audiovisual Arts in Argentina:
Possible Horizons. *Mariela Cantú* 343

Acknowledgements

This book reaches the reader after several gratifying seasons of dialogue surrounding its Spanish edition, *Hacer cine: Producción audiovisual en América Latina*. The support of the Rockefeller Foundation, and especially that of Joan Shikegawa, has been essential in bringing this book into being. I would also like to thank TyPA, and particularly Américo Castilla and Ilse Hughan, for their trust throughout the process that has resulted in this new, updated collection.

The contributors to this volume have provided, in addition to their knowledge of and passion for the cinematic traditions in question, their generosity of spirit and celerity in attending to the vicissitudes of collaborative work. I wish only to reiterate my appreciation and underscore how gratifying it has been to work with them on this new phase of the project. Central to the production of this volume, on behalf of TyPA, were the contributions of Joanna Levine and Violeta Bronstein, who worked on the project at different stages of its development, and the meticulous coordination of Fanny Rolland, who organized each step of the editorial process. With regard to the translation, I would like to draw attention to the expert work of Heather Cleary Wolfgang, who translated the Spanish text of this volume, and Francisco Ferenczi, who translated the article on Brazilian cinema from the Portuguese. Joanna

Sprout read all the translated articles and offered valuable suggestions about their final presentation in English. The merits of this book can be attributed to the harmonious collaboration of these individuals. As is often said, but is no less true here, any element that bears further scrutiny is my responsibility alone.

Finally, I would like to thank my two closest collaborators, my wife Alejandra and daughter Guadalupe, whose love and unfailing partnership strengthened the editor's modest reserves from day to day. To them, as always, I dedicate the fruits of this work.

Eduardo A. Russo

About the Authors

José Carlos Avellar (Brazil) is a film critic whose articles have been published in anthologies including *Le Cinéma Brésilien* (Pompidou Centre, 1987); *Latin American Cinema* (1997); *Cine Documental en América Latina* (2003); *The Cinema of Latin America* (2003); *Alle radici del cinema brasiliano* (2003); *Mujeres y cine en América Latina* (2004). His published volumes include the notable *O Cinema Dilacerado* (1986); *Deus e o Diabo na Terra do Sol* (1995); *A Ponte Clandestina - teorias de cinema na América Latina* (1996); *Glauber Rocha* (2002); *O Chão da Palavra – cinema e literatura no Brasil* (2007). A collection of his texts can be found on his official website: www.escrevercinema.com.

Ricardo Bedoya (Peru) is a lawyer and a professor at the University of Lima, where he teaches cinema and audiovisual studies and gives courses on Peruvian and Latin American cinema. He has written film criticism since 1973, contributing to *Hablemos de cine* and a wide range of other publications, including the academic journal *La gran ilusión*, which he also edited, and Peruvian newspapers like *El comercio*, for which he wrote a weekly column. He has published a number of books, including *100 años de cine en el Perú. Una historia crítica* (1992); *Un cine reencontrado. Diccionario ilustrado de las películas peruanas* (1997); *Entre fauces y colmillos* (1999); *Ojos bien abiertos. El lenguaje de* *las imágenes en movimiento* (in collaboration with Isaac León Frías, 2001). His most recent works are *El cine silente en el Perú y El cine sonoro en el Perú* (2009).

Mariela Cantú (Argentina) is a scholar of audiovisual arts and media with a degree in Audiovisual Communication from the National University of La Plata (UNLP); she currently teaches in the film program at the National Institute of Art (IUNA) and at the UNLP. She coordinated Antonio Muntadas's seminar, *Intervenciones Urbanas* at the Spanish Cultural Center in Buenos Aires (CCEBA) and participated in the colloquium *¿Un lugar bajo el sol?* organized by Nekane Aramburu in collaboration with the CCEBA. Together with Jorge La Ferla, she curated the *Muestra de Video Arte Argentino* for the sixth Tandil Film Festival and the video screenings for the ninth. She coordinated a session that brought Roy Ascott into dialogue with artists, scientists and professors at the French Alliance, as well as a number of conferences held as part of MEACVAD 07. Her editorial activities currently include the compilation of writings on audiovisual art and the organization of the ARCA video project (an online database and archive of Argentine video production).

Américo Castilla (Argentina) is a museum consultant and a specialist in Arts Management. He has directed the TyPA Foundation since 2004, and has also served as the Director of the Museo Nacional de Bellas Artes (2006-2007) and as the National Director of Museums and Patrimony with the Argentinean Ministry of Culture (2003-2007). For twelve years (1992-2003), he led the cultural programs of the Antorchas Foundation, where he designed and implemented far-reaching programs to incentivize innovation in film, theater, literature, music, dance, and the visual arts.

Luciano Castillo (Cuba) is a film critic and scholar and holds an MA in Latin American Culture. He is the Director of the media library of the International School of Film and Television in San Antonio de los Baños and editor of the magazine *Cine Cubano*. He has given lectures, workshops and film courses at different universities and educational and cultural institutions in Cuba, Colombia, Venezuela, Guatemala, Argentina, Spain, Canada and the United States. His published volumes include *Rita a tres voces* (1989), co-written with Víctor Gispert and Alejandro Meléndez; *La verdad veinticuatro veces x segundo* (1993); *Concierto en imágenes* (1994); *Con la locura de los sentidos* (1994); *Ramón Peón: el hombre de los glóbulos negros* (1998/2003) and *Diccionario de realizadores del cine latinoamericano* (1997) with Arturo Agramonte, *Carpentier en el reino de la imagen* (2000/2006), and *A contraluz* (2005). He is the co-author of *Conversaciones con Jean-Claude Carrière* (2004) and is currently working on two manuscripts: *Tambores en Calanda* and *La libertad sin fantasmas: Buñuel y Carrière*.

María Lourdes Cortés (Costa Rica) is an historian of Costa Rican and Central American cinema, a professor at the University of Costa Rica, a researcher at the Foundation for New Latin American Cinema, and the director of CINERGIA, an organization that fosters audiovisual production in Central America and the Caribbean. She is the coordinator of the Central American and Caribbean regions of Latin American Television (TAL) in Brazil. She has served as the director of the first school of film and television in Costa Rica (Veritas University) and of the Costa Rican Film Production Center. She has also won the Joaquín García Monge prize for her contributions to the diffusion of culture and has twice been awarded the Aquileo J. Echeverría prize for her books *Amor y traición: Cine y literatura en América Latina* (1999) and *La pantalla rota: Cien años de cine en Centroamérica* (2005). For this latter work she also received the Casa de las Américas' Ezequiel Martínez Estrada prize, awarded to the best essay published each year. The French government named her Knight of the Order of Merit in 2005; her most recent book is *Luz en la pantalla: cine, video y animación en Costa Rica* (2008).

Malena Di Bastiano (Argentina) holds a degree in Visual Arts and teaches the subject at the School of Fine Arts (UNLP). She completed a Bachelors degree in Cinema Studies at the Foundation University for Cinema (FUC) in Buenos Aires, Argentina. She currently teaches a variety of courses and seminars, conducts research, and collaborates on publications. She is also pursuing a master's degree in the Aesthetics and Theory of the Arts with a focus on the audiovisual, at the School of Fine Arts (UNLP), where she teaches critical analysis and the theory and language of the audiovisual arts. She is an instructor at the Film Observatory, a school for documentary filmmaking, where she coordinated the specialized journal *Docs, Observaciones de lo real*. Her selected publications include articles in *Cine Ojo: un punto de vista en el territorio de lo Real* (BAFICI), *Videoperfiles* (EFT) and the academic journal *Arkadin* (FBA-UNLP).

Andrés Di Tella (Argentina) is a director whose works include *Montoneros, una historia* (1995), *Prohibido* (1997), *La televisión y yo* (2003), *Fotografías* (2007), and *El país del diablo* (2008). He has also made televised documentaries for Channel 7 and *Canal Encuentro* (Argentina), PBS (United States) and Channel 4 (Great Britain), among others. He founded BAFICI, the Buenos Aires Festival of Independent Cinema, which he directed for its first two years (1999-2000). Since 2002, he has directed the Princeton Documentary Festival at Princeton University, where he has also taught.

The university recently published a book about his work, *Conversación en Princeton. Andrés Di Tella: cine documental y archivo personal*, edited by Paul Firbas and Pedro Meira Monteiro. *Cine Documental en América Latina*, a reference book edited by Pablo Antonio Paranagua, lists him among the 15 most important documentary filmmakers on the continent. He has the distinction of having been awarded a Guggenheim Fellowship. His essays have been published in the volumes *El guión cinematográfico, Historia de la vida privada en la Argentina, City of Coop, O cinema do real* and *Telling Ruins in Latin America*.

Mauricio Durán Castro (Colombia) holds graduate degrees from the Universidad de los Andes and the Pontificia Universidad Javeriana, and has completed advanced coursework in Urban Studies at the Polytechnic Institute of Cataluña and the CCC in Barcelona. He is the author of the book *La máquina cinematográfica y el arte moderno* and articles included in the volumes *El medio es el diseño audiovisual*; *Conversaciones con Bogotá, 1945-2005*; *Movimientos y Renovación en el cine*; *Memoria Impresa, antología del Magazín Dominical del Espectador* (Vol. 3); he also contributed to the Norma thematic enciclopedia with the chapter, *El Cine (dedicado a Colombia)*. He has been an invited speaker at international conferences in Buenos Aires, Lima and Caracas. He has collaborated on both local and international periodicals focused on the arts, cinema, and audiovisual production. He is the director of the film club of the Department of Humanities at the Central University and the editor of its journal, *Cuadernos del Cineclub*. He is a full-time professor in the Department of Visual Arts at the Pontificia Universidad Javeriana in Bogotá, which he directed for a time, and a lecturer at the National University and the Universidad de los Andes.

Paz Encina (Paraguay) began her film career in 1996 at the Universidad de Cine, the institution from which she received her degree in 2004 after returning to her home country for a time in 2001. She has made a number of shorts on film and video, including *La siesta*, *Hamaca paraguaya* and *Supe que estabas triste*, which have won numerous awards. In 2006 she completed work on her first feature, also called *Hamaca Paraguaya*, winner of various prizes, including a Fipresci Award at Cannes, an award for best picture at the Film Festival of Belgium, a Critics' Award at the Sao Paulo festival in Brazil, a Viewer's Choice Award at the Goteborg Film Festival, the prize for best Latin American film at the FICCO Festival in Mexico, and a Critics' Award from the festival in Lima, Peru.

Daniela Goggi (Argentina) graduated from the Universidad del Cine in 2001. She has made a number of short films and has worked as an Assistant Director on various projects. Her first feature film, *Vísperas* (2006), was shown at festivals and screenings in Spain, Cuba, Brazil, Uruguay, Bolivia, Mexico and Argentina. She directed the television series *Mi señora es una espía* (2007), written by and starring Andrea Garrote and aired on the channel Ciudad Abierta, or Open City. She contributed the audiovisual aspect of the theater pieces *Nadar perrito* (2006), also by Garrote, and *La Paranoia* (2007) by R. Spregelburd. Since 2000, she has been a contributor to the film journal *Kilómetro 111*, and participated in the book *De los que aman: el cine de Isabel Coixet* (2007). She is currently a professor of filmmaking at the Universidad del Cine, the CIC and the National University of Tucumán.

Carmen Guarini (Argentina) holds a bachelor's degree in Anthropology from the University of Buenos Aires (UBA) and a PhD in Anthropology with a focus on cinema from the Sorbonne and Nanterre, under the direction of Jean Rouch. She has been a researcher at CONICET since 1992. She created the program in Visual Anthropology at the Institute for Anthropology at UBA, where she is also a lecturer. She is a professor of documentary cinema at multiple institutions, including the Fundación Universidad del Cine, TEA Photojournalism, EICTV at San Antonio de los Baños, Cuba, the Universities at Santiago de Compostela and Barcelona, among others. She has been a Visiting Professor at the Ecole des Hautes Etudes in Paris. In 1988 she founded, and continues to co-direct, the documentary production company Cine Ojo. She has directed and co-directed numerous feature-length documentaries, including: *Hospital Borda, un llamado a la razón* (1985), *Jaime de Nevares, último viaje* (1995), *Tinta Roja* (1998), *H.I.J.O.S. el alma en dos* (2002) and *Meykinof* (2005). Her most recent film is the documentary *Gorri* (2010).

Jorge La Ferla (Argentina) holds a Master of Arts from the University of Pittsburgh and a Licence d´enseignement from the Université Paris VIII, Vincennes. He is a professor of undergraduate and graduate courses at UBA, the Universidad del Cine and the Universidad de Los Andes (Bogota), among other institutions. He founded and directed the EuroAmerican festival of Film, Video and Digital Art (1995/2007). He has edited 30 volumes published between 1999 and 2007, and has published more than 50 articles in Argentina, Germany, Brazil, Chile, Colombia, Spain, France, Switzerland and the United States. He is also a jurist and curator of the Rockefeller grants from New Media (New York, 2006), the Festival of the Moving Image (Geneva, 2005), the International Short Film Festival at Belo Horizonte (2004), L.A. Freeways (Los Angeles, 1995), among others. He has organized seminars on film, video, television and new media with Robert Atkins, Roy Ascott, Lucas Bambozzi, Carlota Alvarez Basso, Xavier Berenguer, Chista Blümlinger, Pierre Bongiovanni, Raymond Bellour, Robert Cahen, Michel Chion, Wendy Chung, Jean-Louis Comolli,

Philippe Dubois, Diana Domingues, Anne-Marie Duguet, Oliver Grau, Jean-Paul Fargier, Alain Fleischer, Claudia Giannetti, Sandra Kogut, Sandra Lischi, Arlindo Machado, Lev Manovich, Christine Melo, Antonio Muntadas, Marcel Odenbach, Lourdes Portillo, Francisco Ruiz de Infante, Eder Santos, Valentina Valentini, Edín Vélez, Siegfried Zielinski and Peter Weibel, among others. His most recent book is *Cine/Digital. Aproximaciones a posibles convergencias entre el cinematógrafo y la computadora* (2009).

Marcos Loayza (Bolivia) was born in the city of La Paz, where he lives to this day. He graduated from a Salesian preparatory school for the priesthood, then entered a program in Architecture at the Universidad Mayor de San Andrés, where he remained for more than five years. After that, he signed up for any film workshop that crossed his path, among which those of Jean-Claude Carriere, José Sanchís Siniestra and Alfredo Bryce Echenique stand out. He finally enrolled in the EICTV, the international film school at San Antonio de los Baños, Cuba. He worked for several years as a screenwriter and director on various audiovisual projects in different formats and with different aims. To date, he has made four feature films: *Cuestión de fe* (1995), *Escrito en el agua* (1998), *El corazón de Jesús* (2004), and *El estado de las cosas* (2004), which was screened at more than a hundred festivals and received several dozen awards and distinctions. When he is not working on a film, he dedicates himself to teaching in higher education, drawing, and writing for a variety of publications.

Gustavo Montiel Pagés (México) is a producer, screenwriter, and director who has dedicated much of his life to developing programs in film studies. He has served as the director of the Centro de Capacitación Cinematográfica and also as Presidentas the president of CILECT, the global association of film schools. He was the Founding President of the Federación de escuelas de la imagen y sonido de América Latina (FEISAL) and participates in numerous local and international workshops as an evaluator of projects in development. He was once a film critic, and wrote the chapter on the history of film production in Mexico for the Ibero-American Encyclopedia of Film, published by the Universidad Complutense de Madrid. His first feature film, *Entre paréntesis* (1982), was nominated for the Mexican Academy of Film's award for best first picture. In 2006, he made *Limbo*, an experiment in digital cinema. He has also made narrative shorts and documentaries for film and television. He has produced more than 20 feature films, many of these through Ibero-American collaborations, and nearly 500 short films, including *El último fin de año*, by Javier Bourges, which won the Academy Awards' Student Film Contest in 1993. He produced and directed a script he wrote himself, the feature *Marea de arena* (2009), a co-production between Mexico, Argentina and Spain filmed on the coast of Patagonia in Argentina.

David Oubiña (Argentina) holds a PhD in Cinema and Literature and teaches at the University of Buenos Aires and at the Universidad del Cine. He is a researcher at CONICET and was a visiting scholar at the University of London and a visiting professor at the University of Bergen and at New York University. He is a member of the editorial advisory board of the journal *Las ranas (artes, ensayo y traducción)* and *Cahiers du cinema*, España. His most recent books include *Filmología. Ensayos con el cine* (2000, awarded the Premio de ensayo by the Fondo Nacional de las Artes); *El cine de Hugo Santiago* (2002), *Jean-Luc Godard: el pensamiento del cine* (2003); *Estudio crítico sobre La ciénaga, de Lucrecia Martel* (2007), *Una juguetería filosófica: Cine, cronofotografía y arte digital* (2009), and *El silencio y sus* *bordes. Discursos extremos en la literatura y el cine argentino* (forthcoming).

Paulo Pécora (Argentina) is a journalist and filmmaker. Having graduated with a degree in Journalism from the Universidad del Salvador, he is currently completing a degree in film direction at the Film School of Buenos Aires (FUC). He has written, directed, and produced about twenty short films and music videos, including *Una forma estúpida de decir adiós, Siemprenunca* and *8cho*, which were screened at BAFICI in 2007 as part of a retrospective of his work. *El sueño del perro* (2008) was his first feature film. As a journalist, he works at the Télam news agency and at the publications *Haciendo Cine* and *Babia*, where he writes on film and photography. He has been a member of the Argentine branch of Fipresci, the international federation of film critics, since 2005.

Jorge Ruffinelli (Uruguay) has been a critic and scholar of literature and film at Stanford University since 1986. He currently directs the Department of Iberian and Latin American Cultures. He has also taught at the University of Buenos Aires (1973) and Veracruz University (Mexico, 1973-86), where he directed the Center for the Study of Literature and Linguistics, and was in charge of the literary section of *Marcha* in Uruguay and currently runs *Nuevo Texto Crítico*. His books include *Palabras en orden* (1974), *José Revueltas, ficción, política y verdad* (1977), *El otro México. B. Traven, D.H. Lawrence y Malcolm Lowry* (1978), *Crítica en Marcha* (1979 and 1982), *La viuda de Montiel* (1979), *El lugar de Rulfo* (1980), *Las infamias de la inteligencia burguesa* (1981), *Literatura e ideología: el primer Mariano Azuela* (1982, Premio Nacional de Ensayo), *John Reed en México: Villa y la Revolución Mexicana* (1983), *Poesía y descolonización. Nicolás Guillén* (1985), *La escritura invisible* (1986), *La sonrisa de Gardel* (2004), *Patricio Guzmán* (2001/2008),

Víctor Gaviria: los márgenes al centro (2005/2009), *Sueños de realidad*. Fernando Pérez (2005), *El cine nómada de Cristián Sánchez* (2007), *El cine de Patricio Guzmán* (2008), and *América Latina en 130 películas* (2010). He is currently working on a book about Fernando Solanas. In 1993, he made the documentary *Augusto Monterroso: a short story*.

Eduardo A. Russo (Argentina) is a critic, lecturer, and researcher of cinema and the audiovisual arts, and holds a Doctorate in Social Psychology. He directs the PhD program in the Arts at the National University at La Plata, and is a professor of the theory, analysis, and criticism of the audiovisual arts in both undergradate and graduate programs. He has been an invited lecturer at graduate programs throughout Latin America, and has served on the jury of various film festivals and international screenings. He is the director of the UNLP's publication *Arkadin —Estudios sobre cine y artes audiovisuales*. He writes for the journals *El Amante-Cine* (Buenos Aires), *Ventana indiscreta* (Lima), and *La tempestad* (Mexico). He is the author of *Diccionario de Cine* (1998) and the editor of and a contributor to *Interrogaciones sobre Hitchcock* (2001), *Cine Ojo: un punto de vista en el territorio de lo real* (2007), and *El cine clásico: Itinerarios, Variaciones y replanteos de una idea* (2008). He has published more than 180 articles in different academic and specialist publications in Argentina and around the world.

Foreword

Thirty years ago, the region's cinema was limited in its distribution and only circulated outside its country of origin in a few isolated cases. Video, for its part, was beginning to assert itself as an innovative medium and an alternative to film, and digital technology hinted at the imminent technological and conceptual transformations that could favor productions with limited resources.

Cultural institutions were also making an effort to adapt to the changes that would come at the end of the century. Attention was paid once more to film schools, and it was understood that without the help of public and private funding, it would be impossible to finance films that were less stereotypical than what was being produced in the international commercial market. Video camera in hand, these directors saw that it was possible – perhaps for the first time – to develop their own projects; they also realized that without a professional system of production they would not be able to forge an effective cultural alternative.

In a number of countries in the Northern Hemisphere, these changes included reception by, and the experienced support of, institutions that promoted the production of alternative content and forms, with the essential aim of airing them on public television. The Rockefeller Foundation was one such institution; by subsidizing independent and intercultural productions and creating a vehicle for their dissemination, it made itself part of the transformation. In an innovative move, the Antorchas, Vitae and Andes foundations (of Argentina, Brazil and Chile, respectively) joined forces with the organization in the North and, together, offered the filmmakers of those countries an indispensable hand. Some of the cultural objects to which this book refers are products of this strategic alliance. New laws for the promotion of audiovisual media were established in different countries in the nineties, and toward the end of the century the fruits of these efforts – both private and public – were beginning to be seen.

Of course, these changes did not come about without resistance or debate. It is not unusual for a 'concerned citizen' of any Latin American city to ask us: Why should my taxes or individual contributions go to an inexperienced director to make a film? What makes an artist so special, as compared to someone in another profession, that justifies using my money to satisfy his need for self-expression? Why doesn't he just follow the rules of the marketplace and of supply and demand like any other purveyor of goods and services? The reader may already have an answer to these questions, as we all know what supply and demand looks like in the context of cinema: Hollywood productions and their imitations. The films that will be discussed in the following chapters present a clear artistic project that, in many cases, anticipates any hypothetical demand. Unlike other less risky professions, in order for a director to gain experience he needs to actually direct films; yes, these are large sums and there is a good deal of risk that goes into the investment that must be attended to.

In a number of countries in Latin America, the State plays an important role in this process through the allotment of subsidies; a system that, questionable as parts of it can be, has meant a notable step forward in the facilitation of new productions. In other cases, non-profits not only provide funding but can also put directors in touch with producers who might be interested in combining their investments with public resources or other private funds. The situation here described, which may seem to be balanced, is far from enjoying such equilibrium. The imbalances are constant and, in some cases, even compromise the possibility of making these films. Nor is there any consensus with regard to the importance of forging on despite the challenges. The criticisms, levied by those unable to comprehend that a society without artistic production is no more than a producer of meaningless services, are persistent and occasionally predominant.

A cultural good has the capacity to reveal shared identitarian or symbolic values, rendering the work of art a relevant object that is made complete through its consumption by the public. It is able to illuminate a value that may have gone unrecognized until it was manifested artistically. No one asks for what they do not know (how could one have asked for a Buñuel film before his films were known?) These cultural goods, as compared to simply commercial ones created to satisfy a specific or imagined demand, suffer from a malady known to economists as *cost disease* and which can, in brief, be described as a sustained and cumulative rise in costs above and beyond a country's normal rate of inflation, which is not reduced by technological innovation or the reduction in price of non-cultural goods. Furthermore, it is impossible for ticket sales to meet these rising costs, due to space limitations, access to pirated copies of the films, oligopolist policies and inequitable access to the sale of goods. This means that the market will not be able to make up for this economic imbalance. Consequently, if the funds available for cultural production do not increase at a rate greater than inflation, it will inevitably provoke a withdrawal in the quantity and quality of that production. Studies conducted on theater productions reveal that a piece performed during the Elizabethan era needed two weeks to recuperate its financing; after the First World War, four weeks were needed; in the thirties, it took 5.5 to 8 weeks if 60% of the performances were sold out. Today, a quality work of musical theater takes at least a year to break even.

In the case of film, it could be said that access to digital recording and editing has saved a certain number of man-hours; a claim that would be impossible to make for chamber music, on the other hand. A quartet by Haydn that lasted thirty minutes in 1796 still requires the same elements – two musician-hours divided among four instruments – while the rest of the economy enjoys a 2% reduction in the labor that goes into every product due to technological advancement. Nonetheless, this reduction in the cost of cinematic production is absorbed by increasing production standards, which imply additional costs and are indispensable to a public grown accustomed to high visual and sound quality. In this way, the so-called golden age of Argentine cinema in the fifties required far fewer weeks in theaters to break even, in absolute terms, on a production that was less sophisticated technically than those we see today.

These days, Hollywood productions make up 80% of the titles playing in Argentina's movie theaters (with four times as many prints as national films); Argentine cinema is seen by about 12% of all filmgoers and that of the rest of Latin America is seen by no more than 0.5% – less than European cinema or that of any other continent. The situation throughout the rest of the region is no better; on the contrary, the figures tend to be equally grim. The figures above confirm a phenomenon that has been observed around the world: the danger, in the name of global trade, of the monopolization of image and sound and, consequently, the suppression of original cultural content from different parts of the world, which finds itself without any means of reaching the public. In recent decades, the capitalist economy has found a new form of supranational ownership in copyright law, to which it applies the experience it has amassed in the acquisition and accumulation of wealth. A good sign has come, however, from a surprising majority of nations in 2006, in the form of the UNESCO Convention for the defense of cultural diversity.

We understand the challenges and opportunities that face the cinema of the region. As such, with objectives that are both modest and clear, at the Fundación TyPA we propose to facilitate access to alternative sources of funding for Latin American filmmakers and assure that the most diverse public possible, along with producers from other parts of the world, get the chance to see the new works of these artists. Unlike non-cultural products, cultural goods acquire a collective, patrimonial, public value once created, which differentiates them from the goods and services of the individual or private sphere. Cinema can count its ability to be incorporated into collective memory, both on an individual emotional level and as an anonymous experience shared by thousands, among its indices of effectiveness as a form. Above and beyond their unit value, films attain the status of intangible and non-transferable patrimony, clearly different from goods whose market behavior is easily comprehended by those 'concerned citizens.'

We wish to express our sincere gratitude to the essayists who contributed objectively and passionately to the debate surrounding this complex reality, as well as our recognition of the work of Eduardo Russo, who managed to bring into the spotlight a series of reflections that will allow us to better understand our field of battle.

Fundación TyPA

Américo Castilla, President

Ilse Hughan, Vice President

1. National Perspectives, Regional Projections

Our audiovisual universe is growing ever more complex. Global and corporate forces challenge traditional modes of filmmaking. Routine actions and perspectives that were once effective are, these days, increasingly difficult to sustain. Most evident in this situation is the crisis of models that once were central to production. Other surprising phenomena have begun to appear, as well, at such a rate that it is difficult to reflect upon them. Much is happening in Latin American cinema and audiovisual arts: the problem lies in defining the characteristics and structure of it all. What does it mean to make films in Latin America today? What possibilities are open to us: what do we have to work with, and what are we lacking? And, a question no less important, what do we need to invent?

A mere inventory of what is new in Latin American cinema and in the audiovisual arts of the continent would take a great many pages. It would be more difficult still to establish the dynamics of this landscape, which is a challenge simply to identify or comprehend, even with the appropriate conceptual tools. We are witnessing an explosion of new films, of new directors, and renewed forms of audiovisual production within the framework of a profound mutation. This change affects not only production in the audiovisual arts, but also their circulation in society and their means of reaching the viewers for whom they were created. This collection explores different perspectives on production and directing, incorporating texts from a variety of authors of diverse national and cultural backgrounds, with perspectives that are just as varied. These directors, producers, historians, critics, scholars, and specialists in audiovisual creation come from a dozen Latin American countries and from different generations. Together they constitute a tapestry of interlacing threads that form complex and evolving shapes. Recurring themes that exist beyond the distinction between one situation or place in Latin America and another evoke the image of communicating vessels.

This section covers different points on the continent. Points that represent particularities, yet which are joined to the others. A geographic perspective that is more peripatetic than adherent to a political map guides this leg of the journey. Following the established framework of national cinema, but well aware of a context that has, for some time now, acknowledged post-national identities, the authors of these articles do not forget the former category as a point of departure in a landscape with an increasing propensity for crossing and hybridization.

We begin our journey with a text that inscribes the local within a regional framework, carefully outlining a few fundamental concepts. David Oubiña traces the historical and critical trajectory of cinema in Latin America under the sign of the "new" and the "independent," elucidating, in a panorama that is both far-reaching and acute in its perception of detail, several issues that attend those contemporary audiovisual projects that take aesthetic risks and play with the limits of the system.

Then we head just south of the Rio Grande with Gustavo Montiel Pagés, who reflects, as a producer, on a Mexican cinema that has largely existed in a succession of crises – a situation that, from where we sit, has come to seem like the normal state of affairs – and considers areas of opportunity within the country. María Lourdes Cortés, for her part, delves into one of the regions of the continent least known for its cinema, Central America, and the unexpected events brought to the area by the turn of a new century. Her study demonstrates the power of a cinema that, despite complications with continuity and circulation, is growing with a pioneering spirit.

Luciano Castillo's article examines Cuban cinema in context, both addressing the films and the cultural ground to which they belong and describing how the cinema of the Caribbean island has interacted with that of the continent, placing emphasis on the space of encounter that is the Havana Film Festival, cinematheque culture, the Cuban Institute of Cinema (ICAIC) and, in the last quarter of acentury, the inescapable referent in audiovisual education that is the School of San Antonio de los Baños.

Addressing a cinema as rich and varied as Brazil's in just one article creates challenges in terms of proportion. José Carlos Avellar has chosen the analysis of specific works as a means to propose a reading not only of the imaginaries of Brazilian cinema but also, by extension, one of certain significant points of contact with neighboring cinematic productions, which repeat certain images that touch upon the act of searching in a world of blurred borders and a growing sense of orphanhood, common to the region at large.

For his part, in an article on Peruvian cinema, Ricardo Bedoya frames the rise of so-called New Cinema in his country within the context of specific moments of political and socio-cultural strife, from which a new space for film emerged, not only in terms of the possibility of making films, but also with regard to new avenues of circulation and vital forms of existence, as is the case in certain regional movements within the country itself. In a piece that emphasizes the critical dimension of filmmaking and the struggle at the margins, particularly meaningful coming from a director of his stature, Marcos Loayza examines the current state of Bolivian cinema from a perspective that is as lucid as it is passionate, in search of possible means of continued creation as a form of resistance.

Bringing the journey of this section to a close, Jorge La Ferla and Andrés Di Tella focus their analysis on a concept always open to debate: that of "New Argentine Cinema." Their approaches are different but complementary. The former examines the paradoxical field of audiovisual production, establishing a tension between creativity and market, creator and instrument, and looking at the overdeterminations or confusions that tend to lurk within the buzzword "new." The latter opts for a singular perspective: a series of reflections in the first person that combine analysis, aesthetic judgment, and the testimony of a protagonist in the events. Both contributions discuss an object that is difficult to pin down but that nonetheless asserts itself as an ever-changing and vital presence at the very heart of a polemic, as well as the perennial misunderstandings that seem to accompany it.

Building at the Margins: Trajectories of New Independent Cinema in Latin America

David Oubiña

The origins of independent cinema

One of the passkeys to cinematic modernity was the formulation, by young critics associated with the magazine *Cahiers du cinéma* (François Truffaut, Jean-Luc Godard, Eric Rohmer, Claude Chabrol, Jacques Rivette), of a theory of the "auteur." At its inception in the 50s, auteur theory meant the recovery of a number of directors who had been disregarded for working under the restrictions of the industry: in response to the solemn and pretentious films of the so-called "tradition of quality" in French cinema (the *qualité française*), these new critics – who would go on to become directors – found in certain 'minor' filmmakers the signs of a unique and nontransferable audiovisual corpus.

This debate was of little importance in the traditional arts because the assignment of authorship had always been obvious. In a collective discourse like cinema, however, this differentiation relies on the director's control and his ability to make creative decisions. The conceptual framework of the auteur radically transformed modes of cinematic practice just as it transformed the history, theory, and criticism of film. As Godard asserted, "We won the day when we imposed the principle that a film by Hitchcock, for example, is as important as a book by Aragon. Film *auteurs*, thanks to us, have finally entered into the history of art."

Curiously enough, the invention of a cinematic canon on par with the other arts allowed for the emergence of a group of cineastes that made films very different from those of their creative influences. If, by the end of the 50s, auteur theory represented a frontal attack on the establishment of French cinema, it would end up setting the terms in a broader sense for the turbulent (though also productive) relationship the new cinema of the 60s and 70s maintained with the industry. In response to openly industrial traditional cinema, modern cinema would be based on the revitalization of language and would organize itself around the figure of the director as a creative force.

In Latin America, the program of independent cinema was often associated with the assertion of national identity, on the one hand, and an aesthetic of rupture and alternative modes of production on the other. Due to its base-level industrial requirements, cinema tends to spread first through more economically developed societies. For this reason, the emergence of national cinema in Latin America meant the beginning of a process that should have led to a new system of movie production and circulation. This process, however, varied from country to country. Compared to Cuba or Brazil, where new cinema had an almost foundational character (these were countries without a clearly established industry), in Argentina the emergence of alternative cinema coincided with the disappearance of the film industry and involved, therefore, a strong opposition to large-scale studio productions.

In Brazil, the idea of independent film was not only a question of style, as it tends to be in developed countries; rather, it bore the marks of a quest for sovereignty. Individual expression challenged the mandate of imitation (which had come to colonize aesthetics), to the extent that films were expected to present a political dimension in the struggle for sovereignty. In other words, aesthetic renewal was combined with the definition of a national project. The modernism of *Cinema Novo* was the result of a singular cross between the aesthetic avant-garde of new European cinema and the debate over cultural identity. Nelson Pereira Dos Santos, Glauber Rocha, Leon Hirszman, Carlos Diegues, Joaquim Pedro de Andrade and Ruy Guerra were united in their rejection of commercial Brazilian film (both the lowbrow *chanchadas* and the "serious" cinema of the Vera Cruz production company, which combined the Hollywood studio system with a European sensibility) and the colonization of the market by North American distributors. In this sense, being modern and experimenting with visual language was, above all, a means of breaking down inherited models of representation and an attempt to establish a national inflection for cinema.

Cinema Novo coincided with the *Generación del 60*. In fact, between the late 50s and early 60s a number of new independent directors, actors, technicians, screenwriters, critics and producers came onto the scene in Argentina. Educated by film clubs and short films, this new generation appeared as a response to, and a revitalizing force within, a nearly paralyzed industry that had declined precipitously after long dominating the Latin American market. Their modern, intellectual films were accused of being "foreignizing" and "Europeanized" because they challenged a model of cinema deeply rooted in popular tradition. Influenced – like the Brazilians – by new trends in European cinema, young Argentinean directors (Leopoldo Torre Nilsson, David Kohon, Manuel Antín, José Martínez Suárez, Rodolfo Kuhn, Lautaro Murúa) questioned the style of studio film: the contrived language, the artificial sets, the *star system*. A "cinema of expression" to challenge the "cinema of spectacle." Their films were narratively experimental, cosmopolitan, conceived for the cultured middle class of Buenos Aires, and shot in the streets of the capital city with unknown actors and low budgets.

Political cinema, experimental cinema, professional cinema

In Brazil, as in Argentina and the rest of Latin America, this new cinema went hand in hand with modern art and literature. It meant a rupture with the parameters of the industry, which was a prisoner to the market and to a language that had come to be seen as an externally imposed mode of representation. Nonetheless, in each of these cases the moment of renewal brought on by the new cinema was short-lived. A brief period of time brought significant change to the socio-political context and, with it, the reaction of the filmmakers. If, up to the mid-60s, these films could still consider themselves to be a renewal in dialogue with traditional cinema, by the 70s the cinematic landscape was fragmented beyond repair. From different fronts, both political and experimental cinema proposed alternatives that did not follow the channels of the film industry or the revitalizing channels of new cinema, but rather established a new space in open conflict with them.

The disparity between political and experimental, as opposed to commercial, cinema can be summed up by the fact that whereas the first offered *a different mission for cinema*, the second presented itself as *a different cinema*. Political cinema (*La hora de los hornos*, Fernando Solanas, 1968; *La batalla de Chile*, Patricio Guzmán, 1977; *La sangre del cóndor*, Jorge Sanjinés, 1969; *El chacal de Nahueltoro*, Miguel Littín, 1969; *Memorias del subdesarrollo*, Tomás Gutiérrez Alea, 1968) generated new collective forms of production and exhibition at the margins of the commercial circuit that nonetheless threatened to steal a segment of its audience. In Europe, Godard had broken not only with the film industry but also with the *Nouvelle vague*, and had founded the cinema collective Dziga Vertov, comprised of militants from various Maoist organizations. The objective of the group was to make films that would provoke critical interventions and challenge the social, cultural and political apparatus. Their actions were directed against the bourgeoisie and revisionism, on the one hand, and conventional cinematic form on the other. The concept of *Tercer cine*, or Third Cinema, coined by Solanas and Gerino, demonstrates this position: neither the film industry, which copies the model of Hollywood, nor auteur cinema, which courts an independent bourgeois model (and whose renewal, as in the case of the *Generación del 60*, remains within the system), but a third option instead: a cinema of aesthetic and ideological decolonization.[1]

Experimental cinema, on the other hand, in its most aestheticist Argentinean version (*Film-Gaudí*, Claudio Caldini, 1975; *Come Out*, Narcisa Hirsch, 1972; *Mimetismo*, Marie Louise Alemann, 1977; *Quién es esa loca*, Horacio Vallereggio, 1975; *Point Blank*, Silvestre Byrón), as well as the mystic poetic version of the Chilean director Alejandro Jodorowsky (*El topo*, 1970; *La montaña sagrada*, 1973) and the more violently countercultural version of the Brazilian *udigrúdi* (*O Bandido da Luz Vermelha*, Rogério Sganzerla, 1968; *O Anjo Nasceu* and *Matou a Família e Foi ao Cinema*, Júlio Bressane, 1969; *Bang Bang*, Andrea Tonacci, 1970), turned its back on all types of conventional cinema, as though they were incompatible activities that had nothing in common but their medium. The pursuits of experimental cinema did not point toward a new type of representation, but rather called into question the very foundations upon which the mechanism of cinema, in a narrative sense, had been built. The term *Cuarto*, or Fourth, Cinema even came

---

[1] Fernando Solanas and Octavio Getino, "Hacia un tercer cine: apuntes y experiencias para el desarrollo de un cine de liberación en el tercer mundo" in *Cine, cultura y descolonización*. Buenos Aires: Siglo XXI, 1973.

to be used to describe experimental film as an autonomous space and to differentiate it from the alternative proposed by political cinema. In contrast to the *oppositional*, which confronted mainstream cinema, the *optional*, which suggested pure alterity. Adapting categories established by Noël Burch, the filmmaker Silvestre Byrón once wrote: "The Optional Mode of Representation [MRO] gives rise to a fourth cinema. This category consists of experimentalism, video art, porno, and student films; the *underground* both as an unconditioned space – the optional as opposed to the conventional and an aversion to the image – in which freedom is the condition of all conditions. Or in which the image falls into a trance, without a predetermined end, being in itself the object of interest. Released to its non-necessity, the MRO values the "is" of the image above the "should be" of the MRI [Institutional Mode of Representation]".[2]

This tense and conflict-filled dialogue between radicalism and the aesthetic avant-garde in the context of national cinema was interrupted by the military dictatorships of the 70s. During the years of the dictatorships, the last vestiges of the industry were dismantled, films were censored, and filmmakers were persecuted, exiled, and even murdered. It was no longer a question of a break with the mechanisms of the industry (as in auteur cinema) or an attack on the conventions of film in favor of "a different cinema" (as in political cinema), but rather the wholesale dissolution of any possibility of making film.

At the end of this dark time, during the re-democratization process of the 80s, Latin American cinema showed itself to be dominated by the idea of specialization. Though

---

[2] Silvestre Byrón, "MRO", in *EAF (Extensión Archivo Filmoteca)*, www.geocities.com/eaf_underground, 1998. On the concept of the MRI, upon which Byrón based his approach, see Nöel Burch, *El tragaluz del infinito (Contribución a la genealogía del lenguaje cinematográfico)*, Madrid, Cátedra, Madrid, 1987.

there is no industry, there are professionals who got their start in commercials. The cinema of the 80s tends to distance itself from the modernist agenda in order to establish itself along more professional lines: rather than a creator who employs artistic techniques, the filmmaker becomes an expert with a trade who employs strategies of communication. These are years of academism and the abandonment of the combativeness that characterized the avant-garde of the 60s and 70s.

New independent cinema

The change came in the mid-90s. In Argentina, for example, the establishment of several film schools and the appearance of a new generation of critics provided a different context for the development of young filmmakers. Over and against films that were expensive to produce and had to recuperate the capital invested in them, leaving little room for innovation, an independent – nearly always low budget – cinema emerged, offering new ideas and taking formal risks. Without question, the support of alternative funding sources and the upsurge in spaces for experimentation were major factors in the consolidation of this exciting process of cinematic renewal. Many (probably most) of the new films of the 90s received subsidies from various foundations and institutions: the Centro de Capacitación Cinematográfica (Mexico), the Göteburg Film Festival Fund (Sweden), the Hubert Bals and Jan Vrijman Funds (Holland), Fond Sud (France), the Rockefeller and MacArthur Foundations (United States), Programa Ibermedia (Spain), Cinergia, Fondo de fomento al audiovisual de Centroamérica y Cuba (Costa Rica), Fundación Vitae (Brazil), Fundación Antorchas and Fundación TyPA (Argentina), among others.

In recent years, I have had the opportunity to advise the Fundación Antorchas and Fundación TyPA on the selection of audiovisual projects to receive funding, whether in the form of production subsidies, awards to attend international residencies, or even grants to participate in feature-length film workshops. It is clear that an independent foundation can aspire to goals different from the ones producers or state agencies tend to pursue. While producers need to achieve at least somewhat profitable results and state agencies look for works that embody a given idiosyncrasy (however one might define such a vague term), an independent foundation can offer support more freely to projects engaged in and with experimentation. Based on my experience, the mandate of both Antorchas and TyPA has been to promote original and provocative projects dedicated to exploring new audiovisual possibilities. This implies some risk, given that experiments do not always lead to interesting results; but, in any case, this mandate sees the exploration of untested alternatives as a necessary precondition of getting to the new, the audacious, the transformative.

Although the final product is always a primary concern when taking on a film project (or when deciding to support one), what makes an independent foundation so unique is that it allows for experimentation in its purest state. Even if that experimentation leads to a dead end, it always represents an experience in the aesthetic sense. Perhaps this, here, is the noblest and most useful goal: unlike investments that come with the strings of capital recovery attached, subsidies and grants can permit errors as long as they are learning experiences. Under these conditions, what selection criteria can be used to determine which projects to promote? Beyond the intrinsic qualities of each script, which should be offered support, and why? What determines the appeal of future films? One might answer: those projects that take aesthetic risks, that explore new avenues, that are based on radical premises or are conceived on a grand scale.

A review of the titles selected by the Workshops for Emerging Filmmakers organized by TyPA in recent years allows us to identify certain parameters that have remained constant, even across a variety of styles and heterogeneous aesthetic proposals. From the bold, comic strip poetics of *Las mariposas de Sadourni* (Darío Nardi, Argentina) to the calm, classic narrative of *Los suicidas* (Juan Villegas, Argentina); from the reflective and contemplative images of *Hamaca paraguaya* (Paz Encina, Paraguay) to the grotesque in *Dios los junta y ellos se separan* (Harold Trompetero, Colombia); from the experimentalism of *Virginal* (Eduardo Baca, Argentina) to the tragicomic drama of *La perrera* (Manuel Nieto, Uruguay); from the science fiction of *Deserto azul* (Eder Santos, Brasil) to the extreme naturalism of *Los muertos* (Lisandro Alonso, Argentina); from the psychological explorations of *El circuito de Román* (Sebastián Brahm, Chile) to the perverse *costumbrismo* of *Aguas verdes* (Mariano de Rosa, Argentina).[3]

Almost invariably, these are films about young people. If the films of the 90s were innovative, it was largely due to their choice of strictly contemporary subject matter that had not been fully appreciated in earlier cinema, as well as to the fact that the filmmakers approached their characters, who were of the same age and had the same problems, with a gaze that was neither condescending nor paternalistic. Although politics seems to be noticeably absent from these projects (which is not the case at other moments), in another sense one would have to say that it is omnipresent: it has disappeared as a subject because it permeates every

---

[3] A complete list of recent participants in the "Talleres de análisis de proyectos cinematográficos" or "Workshops for Emerging Filmmakers" can be found on the Fundación TyPA website (www.typa.org.ar).

human bond. The conflicts between characters do not aspire to function as allegories of a reality that transcends personal history; yet perhaps, precisely because of this lack of pretension, the films manage to express, obliquely, a complex and volatile socio-cultural context. Narrative structure, for its part, tends to be more erratic and more fluid than in the overly scripted movies of past decades; but even so, the production (often austere and verging on a documentary style) holds its shape.

With aesthetic strategies derived from short film and utilizing alternative modes of production, it is possible to identify in these new films the challenges, proposals, and risks of any project of renewal. This is not an attempt to classify these tendencies. The panorama is not only inevitably partial and incomplete, but also open, dynamic and heterogeneous. But, in any case, it may prove useful to record how certain recent films have aligned themselves with the trajectory of independent film in Latin America: what they have inherited, what they have incorporated and, most importantly, what they have been able to bring to this tradition.

The Cinema of the Future and the Future of Cinema

The modernist cliché of the death of cinema has been widespread over the past few decades. And it is true that an entire cinematic universe (together with the critical tradition that began with André Bazin and ended with Serge Daney) is in decline. In this universe, popular cinema remained separate from alternative cinema, though they circulated along the same channels. For this reason, certain films and certain filmmakers were able not to draw obvious lines within the dominant tradition and still occupy a central place in the cinematic landscape. Today, the circuits of production, distribution and screening increasingly tend to validate what Daney himself termed "post-cinema"; these are lazy movies that no longer know anything of what cinema once knew.[4]

Nonetheless, this does not necessarily mean the death of cinema, but rather a radical reconfiguration of the space occupied by these films and the relations of power among them. In the constellation of the contemporary cinematic imaginary there is no longer room for certain works if not at the periphery and, even there, they are only included as an outside presence. The margin left for films that are not part of the *mainstream* has narrowed in comparison to the space open to them 40 years ago. If modern cinema could only be understood in terms of its tension with the industry (in that "hidden dialectic" that, in the words of Andreas Huyssen, establishes a connection with precisely that which it seems to reject), in the present moment the industry seems to have expanded to such a point that there is nothing left outside it.[5] There is no longer, as there was for modernism, an opposition to or contestation of mainstream film; the latter has dismantled the possibility of dissent to such a degree that it is now in a position to turn its back on any new alternative. It is not, then, that cinema is disappearing, but rather that its conditions of possibility have changed drastically. Daney wrote at the end of an era, when cinema still made an effort to function as a sovereign territory run through by internal, albeit homogeneous, tensions. The work of a critic at that time could consist of understanding the world through film. This, precisely, is is the definition of cinephilia: not so much a relation to the cinema, but rather a relation to the world through

---

[4] Serge Daney. *Perseverancia: Reflexiones sobre el cine.* Buenos Aires: El Amante, 1998.
[5] Huyssen, Andreas. *After the Great Divide. Modernism, Mass Culture, Postmodernism.* Bloomington, IN: Indiana University Press, 1986.

the cinema. In the contemporary landscape, on the other hand, it has become necessary to construct a world *for* film.

The circuits of production, distribution and screening tend increasingly toward standardization, toward reinforcing a model that, broadly speaking, was established by North American cinema. There exist, more and more, two disproportionate spaces: on the one hand, the forms of an omnipresent spectacle governed by a strict set of rules and, on the other, diverse and more or less artisanal forms of oppositional or alternative expression. If mainstream cinema adopted technology as a sensationalist measure that nonetheless manages to preserve traditional modes of perception and ends up confining film to the realm of entertainment, this other, marginal cinema makes critical use of technology and maintains a productive tension with it. How do contemporary works position themselves in relation to aesthetic tradition; also, what unassimilated use can these movies find for this new technology? The answer lies in the distinction, as established by Theodor Adorno, between *technique* and *technology*, which, in these new media, tend to be loosely aligned: whereas the first refers to the mechanics of composition, the second alludes to the medium of (re)production.[6] Obviously, the challenge to any contemporary aesthetic proposal is to be able not only to take advantage of this new technology but also to convert it into compositional techniques. That is, to work from a critical juncture (not one that reinforces conventional perception) between technique, materials, and content in the face of a widespread fetishization of technology.

"I am making the cinema of the future," Glauber Rocha declared around the time of *A idade da Terra* (1980). Twenty-five years later, what does film stand to learn from

---

[6] See, for example, Miriam Hansen's "Introduction to Adorno, *Transparencies on Film* (1966)." *New German Critique* 24-25. Fall – Winter 1981/82.

this trajectory in independent cinema? What elements are still present in the long-awaited and much celebrated cinematic renewal that has been taking place since the mid-90s? In at least one sense, the experience of alternative cinema from generations past is still desperately topical: there is a model there of a passionate and restless cinema whose value lies in its perpetual willingness to gamble all the proceeds of the previous film, to risk losing it all on the next one. As Glauber Rocha himself said in Godard's famous *Vent d'Est* (1970), "The path of new cinema is as dangerous as it is marvelous." While some films still insist on answering old questions, new cinema is always a cinema that poses new ones.

Modern art is hypertelic; as such, its borders should not be seen as a last frontier, but rather as a new point of departure. Paul Klee once posited that "art does not reproduce the visible, it *makes visible.*" As a complement to this faculty for illumination, a number of movies and recent projects have continued to expand art's potential for disturbance. If the filmmaker represents modern art *par excellence* at the periphery of its mainstream industrial applications, it is because he seems to operate under the sign of these critical and transformative elements. Rather than the cliché of the death of cinema, one can think in terms of the dawning of a new age for the image. As Godard has stated, "We live in a time in which film and – in a broader sense – art have gone missing; they no longer exist, and need to be reinvented." It is a matter of constructing a periphery in which these new films, whether independent or experimental, can survive and make themselves known.

Cinematic Production in Mexico Under the Sign of Crisis

Gustavo Montiel Pagés

> *I look to genre in order to define it. I examine its intestines, in the furthest reaches of its strange being. Is it backwater comedy? A whorehouse drama? A melodrama of the community? Is it a film about wrestlers? If I had to find a genre to describe it in the inventory of its delirium, would Mexican cinema present a term that would completely comprehend and reveal it? Is it burlesque, grotesque, farcical, a caricature? Does it denounce, explore, experiment, invent? Is it dependent, independent, authorial, commercial, transcendent? Is it banal?*
>
> *Disconcerting, perhaps, might be the best word for it. It disconcerts.*

I.

In the first decade of the century, discourses collide. They are haunted by an old ghost: the ghost of the crisis. Mexican cinema is also in crisis; this is a declaration that has been carried over from the middle of last century. It has been said that fifty films are made every year, that Mexican directors are having enormous success at Cannes, in Hollywood, in England; they compete with each other for Goya awards, Golden Globes and Oscars, and the films win at all sorts of festivals. The documentary is in the middle of one of its finest moments and a wealth of short films is being produced. It is a cinema with its own rich and famous.

Crisis? What crisis? Yet this is all happening in a country prone to the institutionalization of mistruths.

They say "fifty cinematic productions" in the same way one would assert a hundred, or prove twenty-five. In any case, the annual volume of productions in Mexico depends on the terms established for the census, and these are becoming more and more varied. Given that the cinematic implies the audiovisual – and no, I am not falling into the trap of pleonasm – a film can be anything created digitally or on film, able to be reproduced in any conducive environment: from the big screen to a laptop, in screening rooms, in the country, in bedrooms, elevators, offices, airports, public plazas, on the internet or over the phone. In this context, we could speak of thousands of productions; it is pointless to distinguish the feature from the mid-length or short film, and it would be equally pointless to turn one's back on the undefined yet critical significance of this phenomenon – which is no longer a matter of communication, but of expression – in society today.

The interaction between the individual and audiovisual production is a new mainstream phenomenon that is widespread and all encompassing: a remaking of the spectacle. Although the difference between an audiovisual message and what we understand as a film seems obvious in principle, one cannot disregard what bit of cinema this message might have in it, or what cinema might become by following the paths opened to it by these alternative technologies.

It is the industrial apparatus that produces and gives shape to that which we know as film, that establishes difference, imposes criteria, allots privileges; among other things, it is what situates the *professionals* above the *amateurs*, determining whose films are distributed and shown on the big screen, and whose occupy an alternative, non-cinematic space. But the term professional – which ties production to the industry and its relationship to the market – is a label from which all would like to free themselves. When the creative impulse is decoupled from market imperatives, these differences begin to break down and the only thing left to discuss is the quality of the films and, perhaps, their craft.

I am not familiar with the percentage of the world population that goes to the movies, but it seems that only 1% has internet service. And although this number is in the millions, there is nothing popular or 'mass' about it. Expression – art – has been forced to search for spaces outside the industry and, because of this, would feel an affinity with any counter-industrial manifestation and would try to reinforce it with its presence. Internet and telephone communication and the spaces created within these new dimensions seem like an alternative, but their dynamic is not unlike the one they left behind; the hegemonic control of the film and television industries in a few centralized hands. The illusion, created by sites like *YouTube*, of the spontaneous circulation of any sort of audiovisual text without the intervention of specialists, is interesting and fun, but we know that deep down, presence is not the same as existence, a visit is not feedback and the question of access implies a lack of equality in terms of exhibition. Perhaps the technological conditions that will have the greatest effect on what we know as the film industry will lead to the creation of alternative channels, the invention of screens. But one can sense an unavoidable phenomenon: a space has been pre-established, assigned, dedicated to a segment of the world population that, multitudinous as it may seem, is far from the majority. The worst of it is that film, the superior mode of audiovisual expression, is slowly losing its space. And it is cinema, in its most elevated form, which must be protected and saved.

II.

The traditional Mexican film industry is, has been, and certainly will always be in a perennial state of crisis. Nothing can save it, just as nothing can save practically any of the cinemas faced with the reality of a market dominated by the major studios of the United States. The land of corn now imports its corn; this element, which is the essence not only of our sustenance, but of a complex cultural make-up, has been snatched from us, its price has been raised, and it has been turned into a speculated commodity. This epitomizes the tenor of state policy in all aspects of the national economy. The sacrifice of identity, the abandonment of cultural values, in exchange for a sinister and ineffective dream of commercial success. This is why I see an error in the call for Mexican cinema to become more competitive in the marketplace both locally and globally. The crisis has reduced the terms of this discussion to the commercial, and there has been a superhuman effort (and a futile one, I think) to modify the behavior of the market. It is an error tied to a real necessity: that cinema reach the public. This change will be difficult to bring about, simply because the market does not require it, and because the 180 million tickets sold in Mexico's box offices satisfy – with programming that consists mostly of Hollywood movies – the taste of a public comprised of the mid- and upper classes (4 of the 120 million that live in Mexico) that is not interested in anything else, and because the media are not interested in circulating other types of material, preferring instead to remain in the service of those who control the spectacle and to enjoy the government's approval. It is a formidable business: Mexico is one of the five largest markets in the world. Films from anywhere other than Hollywood do not make sense here; even if sixty Mexican films were made every year, only 70% of them would ever be screened, and these would last only a week or two in the theaters, with abysmal attendance figures.

III.

Mexico began making films just one year after the first projection by the Lumière brothers. The cinema quickly became a part of cultural life, as both an instrument of expression and a witness to the development of a country that was about to experience its great revolution of 1910. It has been a presence, a gaze, an identity. I hate the term for its sclerosis, but it has also been a *tradition*. The face that Mexico, that multifaceted being, shows the world is in fact invented by film: a festive tequila-soaked appearance perpetuated by its own clichés; a personality completely like or unlike the eclectic original that inspired it. The gun-slinging, drunken Mexican wrings his fame from the world, oozing melancholy euphoria between shrieks and gunshots, far beyond his joys, beliefs and truths. These are idyllic universes, even when they are afflicted by the sordid or the incestuous. Mexico has a strong cinematic dimension, an identity; perhaps its greatest challenge will be, if not to conquer, at least to renew some of its archetypes. If not to change, then to redefine its essence; if not to convince otherwise, then at least to stop putting that distorted face forward.

They say that Mexican cinema is in a state of transition, thanks to the excellence of its artists. I draw a distinction between local cinema and the film industry, not only for the emphasis of the first on the auteur, but because it implies a cultural reality that is not questioned over weak performance in the marketplace. Good Mexican films do exist; diverse, multifaceted, pluralistic, even contradictory works, but they are quashed by the tendency to set them alongside the superannuated tradition of commercial cinema.

It is true that quality cinema is produced slowly, receives little support and means even less to the industry. When one talks about the number of films made in a year, emphasis should not be placed on breaking records or fabricating optimistic statistics. This is very dangerous; it is also confusing. The volume of production, no matter how ambitious or excessive it may be, is of no interest if what is being produced is base. What must be defended is this so-called quality cinema, whether it has commercial aspirations or not, and not a numerical substitute imposed when, looking at the year's production, the greatest percentage of films are not "bad" (films turn out better or worse, regardless of one's intentions), but base ones. The State should also examine, instead of boasting about statistics, what films it has supported and what films have not been made due to a lack of support; what films are being made and what films could be made. In this way, it would be forced to confront the contradictory nature of the spirit that determines its policies and its support.

It is not easy to explain the reality of a cinema that has been built atop the rubble of an industry that boasts generations of good old days. It is hard to understand the phenomenon of Mexican cinema when its roots, now dried out and infertile, want to impress upon us a nostalgia for another time, a time of genre film and archetypes etched into the hearts of viewers across Latin America, or for a time when there was a film Reserve that emptied its coffers for producers favored by the State's erratic policies. It is an old story composed of two types of nostalgia: a longing for consistency and a longing for the capacity for abuse; both are elements of an eternal paradox.

It is a polemic that arises from the opposition of two concepts that are, to me, essential to the rescue of local cinema: the industry as the mythical image of a dead tradition, and the fight for a vigorous, developed form of expression that flies the banner of art and can be summed up with the term *national cinema*. The former demands, imposes the capacity for abuse. The latter searches, increasingly in vain, for consistency.

These two concepts cannot be reconciled, and as long as there is nostalgia for the great industry that never was, the possibility of national cinema will continue to be obstructed, though it has been demonstrated that the real strength of Mexican cinema is not the result of the sustained activity of its film industry (if it ever had been), but rather of the sporadic but rich manifestation of individual talent not necessarily grounded in serial production. The key would seem to be the production of a significant number of films outside the influence of the industry. Yet it is difficult to think about production outside the general structure of business, nor would this improve the relationship between local films and the country's movie theaters. This structure corresponds to the relationship between Hollywood films and national theater chains that has, since the nineties, established ideal market conditions. Today, without any sort of protection (there are no longer screening quotas), local films are cast into the unequal competition of a savage marketplace. This arrangement suits theater owners very well; it is also a paradise for the major studios, which been given a formative role in the definition of the norms of their sphere of activity and enjoy exceptional financial privileges, among other perks. They have even gone so far as to present themselves as the real producers of Mexican cinema; as such, however, they believe that only the films they decide to produce, according to their preferred genres and subject matter, should exist.

On top of all this, the image that the foreigner expects from Mexican cinema is looked down upon within the country; it would seem that quality cinema is also quite far from the public's taste. Such has been the case of a number of the best films of our time, close in spirit to what we know as independent, auteur, or quality cinema, that is, to the kind of work that establishes a national cinema. The lack of communication is one of the fundamental elements of the crisis; it is due in large part to the gradual impoverishment of taste, combined with the speed of electronic media and the degradation of our customs, as well as the ascendency of bad taste, clearly visible in the actions of political leaders, media figures and representatives of authority.

IV.

The lack of definition caused by the apparent failure of these two groups to reconcile or coexist affects the financing of local cinema; it is for this reason the discussion is relevant. You can spend ages contemplating certain issues, debating them again and again in sport without ever really trying to find a solution. The subject of quality versus commercial film is a perfect topic of conversation for gatherings; in this case, however, it is also fundamental to unraveling this tangle we are in. An historical element emerges that, though it must be viewed without nostalgia, is a milestone that continues to influence Mexican cinema, for better or for worse: state involvement in film production, and the question of whether this is industrial or cultural policy.

The milestone came during the period between 1970 and 1976, in which film production was essentially nationalized, marginalizing the superannuated private interests without appropriating their power. It is a unique moment in Western history: the State as film producer was a phenomenon limited to socialist countries, and it proved a very strange figure in its time. Nonetheless, it seemed to breathe new life into the dinosaur, shaking it from its slumber and presenting it with new horizons. In this period, given the impossibility of moving the old structures of Mexican cinema in a better direction, the State (for a thousand reasons, most of which have to do with the populist opportunism of President Luis Echeverría) took on the production of so-called "New Mexican Cinema." This shift was accompanied by the emergence of a number of very interesting directors who were, in some way, freed from the sentence imposed upon them by unions and trustees in a vote of confidence (almost a vote of faith) in their creativity and their capacity for innovation.

One speaks of new cinema when one imagines that a new form of production has been invented. These forms have generally been tied to changes in the government's systems of support for such productions. It is more a point of political pride than a real aesthetic tendency or the sudden appearance of new artists and original productions. Because the films we are making are not all that different from those we have made in the past. Perhaps this is the biggest problem: the lack of evolution.

The generation of the seventies, the first new cinema, lived the dream of a seemingly ideal patronage. More than just an illusion, and the most recent cause for nostalgia, it is a paradise lost: films subsidized at a rate of nearly one hundred percent that appear to have been made with total freedom. The decades that followed experienced only reduced variations of that incredible support, under the authority of vaguely defined policies.

It is indisputable: as part of a concept of national cinema, it is impossible to avoid State intervention. In Mexico this intervention, which is a responsibility, an obligation, a policy, becomes a rare sense of entitlement. The State loves to play the producer, instead of limiting itself to creating a cohesive system of support, subsidies, credits, and so forth. The National Cinema Reserve existed until 1983, when it was dismantled. In principle, it was an ideal instrument, but it became an institution of power and a corrupt organization. It was a vehicle for politics. From the trenches, in the seventies, the State feigned a battle to the death with the old system. In reality, it was an attempt to justify a general misdirection; the appearance of democratic freedoms that the regime of Luis Echeverría (who has been charged with criminal acts and is responsible for the student massacre of '68) tried to create in order to improve its image. That is how it was; like all games, it had its moments of improvisation and success, as well as its consequences. Most importantly, I believe, it established the need – in opposition to the tendency of independent film – for an alternate form of cinema.

By never actually changing this structure, State participation established itself as a government policy limited to the circumstances and whims of its functionaries and business alliances. It remains a significant paradox that independent cinema gained its greatest momentum when it set itself in opposition to State cinema. This is paradoxical because the latter strengthened and gave life to auteur cinema. In this generation, the careers of important filmmakers like Arturo Ripstein, Felipe Cazals, and Jorge Fons took root.

Nonetheless, there was something there in the belly of the beast, a fundamental contradiction that called for dissent. Yet the struggle between official and independent cinema was a struggle fought on cultural terrain, in the field of expression, not in the realm of the industrial. The common enemy, the old private sector – studios that produced absolute trash – let this fight go on and, with the change in the government, came out of hiding and started producing their garbage again. To add another layer of paradox to the situation, they called themselves independent producers, given that – in the strictest sense – they were, since they were making film without state support and could thus consider themselves to be marginal. An absolute joke because, in reality, they still controlled the industry and all the major business. They no longer had the Film Reserve to shelter their questionable business practices, but they controlled distribution and held tremendous power over exhibition as well.

V.

There is no more aberrant image than that of the State as filmmaker. There is no possibility worse than the functionary who is also a producer. The State should not produce, it should create the conditions that support production and, in any event, regulate them.

Over the past two decades, Mexican cinema has been the victim of confused State intervention in its development. This has much to do with the influence of neoliberalism, that dismal ideology that sows failure wherever it goes. The Mexican neoliberal State, consolidated during the administration of President Salinas, expanded by Zedillo, bastardized by Fox and now verging on the ridiculous under President Calderón, was developed with the intent of understanding the nation as an anonymous society. 18 years of exertion to turn the country into a profitable business. The damage is done.

During this period the State began to approach its obligations, with respect to artistic and cultural development, in a particularly contradictory way. In its very structure, it gradually abandoned the things that strengthened these practices and relegated the matter to government decision-making, that is, to time and circumstance instead of keeping them apart from the structure of the state. This was more pronounced in cinema than in any other case, as the commercial aspect was assigned, with no restrictions, to the interests of large companies with ties to Hollywood while production and, above all, the mechanisms that existed or could exist to generate resources were left out in the cold, outside this structure and subject to the changeable and circumstantial will of the government, with no promises or laws to guarantee their continuance. What is worse, they sanitized two fundamental elements: subsidies and the need to retain the resources generated by the film industry, and particularly box office receipts, for future productions.

After nationalization came the privatization of the entire state structure related to film. And this privatization followed the model of neoliberal governments that devastated the productive infrastructures of a number of Latin American countries. Cinema is one example, but this occurred in all fields, and the threat remains in the insistence on privatizing electricity and oil. The passion for disaster, so much to the taste of these sons of Santana (the general to whom the sale of Texas – or, if you prefer, the loss of half the nation – in the 19th century is credited), is the ghost that haunts us today.

VI.

Throughout the eighties and nineties and now, in the first decade of the century, the government facilitated support through financial instruments fueled by the profits coming from the films, but these slowly lost their legal backing and ended up being subject to strictly budgetary decisions. This budgetary dependence was extremely delicate; for this reason, a ticket receipts clause was introduced into the laws governing film production, so that the activity of the industry might underwrite the production of new films. The distributors and theater owners, backed by articles established by NAFTA, sought protection and fought to prevent the law from being passed. They did this with the support of certain branches of the government itself, such as the Secretary of Revenue and the courts.

Through this strange interaction of private and public interest, an alternative system was proposed that would redirect up to ten percent of the taxes to be paid in any given year, to be invested in film production. Article 226 of income tax law has become the panacea. The maximum investment per contributor, 20 million pesos (just under 2 million dollars), cannot represent more than 80% of the total cost of the film. This is a good way to attract private investment though – to reaffirm an old tradition – the money is rarely destined for the production of quality films.

In this context, producers find themselves in a very difficult position. In fact, the independent producer is an endangered species. The nebulous interpretations of what their role should be doom them to failure from the moment they take on a new project. I am speaking particularly of independent producers, those who try to find impossible financing, those who don't work for representatives of the major studios and keep their production companies right on the barely discernable line between decadence and collapse.

These producers confront at least three sizeable challenges to their existence. The first of these is the lack of sources of funding, credits, or subsidies that allow them to retain control of the product. They depend on official support that usually proves insufficient and lack the tools to integrate possible marketplace strategies. The elimination of production subsidies has meant that support is, in reality, an investment. The Funds are partners in the films. On the other hand, there is no such thing as an advance on distribution, or advance sales of television rights; in Mexico it would be suicide to work on the basis of bank loans, since interest is so high and tends to go up with unseemly consistency. Furthermore, Mexican currency is not stable and its relationship to the dollar condemns this option outright in a country that permanently faces the threat of devaluation.

The second reason is the untenable cost-recovery figures that Mexican films face. The costs of production are extremely high and the recuperation of funds, as has already been indicated, is practically impossible. The percentage of box office receipts that goes to the producers, who do not get the benefit of anticipated sales, is criminal: 17% of box office receipts a year and a half after making the initial investment. The costs of production are the strange result of customs that have been carried over from a film industry that has lost everything but its most expensive habits. Although with the advent of digital technology the possibility of making films outside these schema exists, these alternatives face significant challenges in finding a space within the channels of exhibition. In this sense, it is important to recognize that the market has become homogenized to the point that there are no longer alternative channels of exhibition for Mexican films, nor is there any means of finding viewers other than in giant screening complexes. To place a film within this system means entering into a perverse game with big movies that do not necessarily correspond to the type of product at hand, which is certainly not capable of competing with major premiers that are, on top of everything, accorded special privileges. In a word, there is no market for Mexican cinema.

What is more, a misguided position on the part of the government has recently become more acute: its offices of cultural support do not want to work with producers. They prefer to make it obvious that their support is directed at the artists, that is, the directors. Because of this, there is no way for a producer to develop more than one project at once, which is the worst way for him to work. It is impossible to establish a practice that combines, for example, production with the development of new projects and, simultaneously, the management of funding. In this way, it has become impossible for a production company to get any traction. This also impedes the founding of consistent systems of production, special deals with vendors and services, and the advantages of regular production. The fact is that the inconsistency of cultural policy must be considered alongside the lack of what could be called policies of industrial growth, which have become fundamental at this point, given that – in this world full of paradoxes – the notion of industry is still being kept alive. Article 226, unless individual arrangements are stipulated, does no more than add owners to a film conceived, developed and realized by a producer under the guise of a simple employee, but one charged with all responsibility for the project. In short, the art has been abandoned and the industry stands in ruin.

VII.

The public face of this reality, however, is different. The success of Mexican directors who make their films outside the country and according to models in which protection, business, and funding are one and the same popularizes the idea of natural talent and render the failure of films made according to our internal model inexplicable. Their success has led to talk of great potential and the need to protect local cinema at the same it molds and delimits this cinema, idealizes its modes of production. The media has no reason to share information (this is no longer its purpose), and it exploits these successes. It treats the films like soccer games; winning or losing an Oscar becomes a series of penalty kicks, success or failure is a matter of national pride or shame. The films are few, but they have deservedly large repercussions. They are films made by Mexicans, and I see no reason not to include them in a general notion of our culture of cinema. They are Mexican films, but they are not part of local production. On an industrial level, they are foreign.

There is a second category of films that form part of local cinema: those that are made one way or the other by individual talents, usually with State support, which are condemned to commercial failure but enjoy success at international festivals. It is the world of the good movie, and also that of lost capital. In this terrain one can find both productions of a more industrial nature and the majority of independent films, many of which are very independent, indeed. There, names like Juan Carlos Rulfo, Luis Estrada, Arturo Ripstein and Felipe Cazals, Carlos Reygadas, Francisco Vargas, Amat Escalante, Gerardo Naranjo and Jicolás Pereda appear; all directors who make personal films that are recognized outside the country and with profoundly varied styles. Some closer to, some further away from industrial or commercial models, but all recognized for the value of what they offer. Young directors working in digital formats, along with international co-productions and so forth, are situated in this field.

A third category is a sort of hybrid between the artistic filmmaker and the filmmaker-for-hire. He produces, with private capital and public funding, films of a clearly industrial nature, to mixed results: good films that find success with the public (the minority); bad films that find success with the public (several), and bad films that find no success with the public. These compete in complex and apparently unfavorable territories. The idea of employing recognized craftsmen (many of whom are famous for their advertising work) in order to make quality commercial films emerged as a tendency at the end of the nineties, particularly with the rise of new companies associated with the entertainment industry (Altavista Films, Televicine, Lemon Films, etc.) or the North American majors that, in their eagerness to produce films in Spanish for their typical audience (situated between the upper-middle and upper classes), have developed productions with uneven results. This model pursues the dream of building a Mexican Hollywood. They are doing a poor job of it.

In Mexico – so they say – it is only a small group of 2 to 4 million viewers that accounts for all annual ticket sales (180 million every year). This group is set apart by two circumstances: its acquisitive power and its lifestyle. A number of intellectuals and artists lurk among the members of this group, but it is mostly made up of youths. The vast majority of the population does not go to the movies; they rarely even go to the malls in which the multiplexes hold pride of place. They content themselves with watching television or by renting videos, or with piracy, which arouses suspicion because the industry's coverage is so great that it seems illogical that a business should exist outside the purview of those at the head of the table. And yet this is how the masses view these films. For this reason, the spectacle dedicates itself to the mall's *chosen few*, those who pay four dollars and change for a ticket and prefer to watch movies in English.

There is, for some reason, a desire to offer this population good commercial cinema in Spanish, understood as genre films that produce celebrities and are sound enough, technically, to be competitive. These requirements may be met without the film's ever achieving success. This is topped off by Hollywood's consecration of the "Three Musketeers" of Mexican cinema, Alfonso Cuarón, Alejandro González Iñarritu and Guillermo del Toro, who have attracted the attention of that same public with fascinating genre films like *El laberinto del fauno*; these are Mexican in terms of their directors, but not in terms of the manner in which they were made. Average films in other markets, exceptional in ours, that by means of their quality, structure and format have been able to find an audience; to put it lightly, they are very *E! Entertainment Television.*

One cannot say that these movies cause the box office failure of auteur films. They simply demonstrate that, even in following the models of the major studios in Spanish in a market cultivated for that specific purpose, these films can still fail (like one that was a massive fiscal failure despite selling 850 thousand tickets); alternative or experimental cinema, or whatever one chooses to call it, is simply powerless in these spaces. The challenge is to create these spaces and guarantee a healthy relationship between quality cinema and its popularization, both in terms of the cost of production and their promotion among the public. This challenge, this phrase, is repeated over and over, in a number of different ways. It is a challenge, a question without an answer, that has by now become something of a cliché; the abiding expression of the crisis.

As in all things, I believe that what we need is a revolution, or at least the reinvention of Mexican cinema from the ground up.

The Unexpected Rise of Central American Cinema

María Lourdes Cortés

Is there such a thing as Central American cinema? Central America has long been one of the least visible producers of film in the world. Its forays into cinematic production must not only negotiate issues common throughout Latin America, but also those that have turned the isthmus into a region subjected to the geopolitical interests of major global powers, to extreme violence, and to the lack of a culture industry of its own.

We Central Americans try to reproduce our identity through images, but we do so without a sense of continuity or memory. Though no one – not even our audiovisual artists – may remember it, nearly all the countries of the region were familiar with the cinematograph by the first decade of the twentieth century,[7] when projectors were set up throughout the isthmus to screen shorts accompanied by marimbas and film local landscapes and customs. From the first three decades of the last century, feature films were being made in Guatemala, El Salvador, and Costa Rica. Panama followed with its own productions in the

---

[7] A reference to *El agente N° 13*, by Alberto de la Riva, of Guatemala, of which there are no remaining copies. Cfr. *Cronología General de la Producción de Cine en Guatemala*, CUET, (unpublished), cited by Magda Aragón and Edgar Barillas in "Guatemala: café, capitalismo dependiente y cine silente." *Revista Estudios*, Guatemala, IIHAA, Escuela de Historia, Universidad de San Carlos, Guatemala. (Vol. 3-9, 1996).

mid-twentieth century, and Honduras and Nicaragua followed suit in the sixties and seventies, respectively.

Four dominant tendencies emerged in cinematic production during the first 70 years of the twentieth century. The first, and most widespread, was official cinema – short documentaries or newsreels that presidents or dictators would commission as reports on ongoing projects or inaugural ceremonies. The image of their countries and themselves that these officials wanted to portray is of particular interest, from the Minervalias – festivals dedicated to the goddess of knowledge[8] – that Manuel Estrada Cabrera (known as "Señor Presidente" in a novel by Miguel Ángel Asturias) organized in an illiterate country, to Anastasio Somoza Debayle's final newsreel, "Nicaragua en marcha," made two months before his fall from power in 1979.[9] A number of tourist documentaries have also been preserved, which depict an idealized image of each country and were made by local or foreign directors like Leo Aníbal Rubens, a native of Argentina living in Mexico who shot in Honduras, Nicaragua and Costa Rica.

A second tendency is that of artisanal – as opposed to commercial – cinema, often marked by the influence of *costumbrismo* and produced with the intent to reflect local traditions. The earliest narrative films of each country, such as *Águilas civilizadas* (1927) by Virgilio Crisonino, E. Bianchi and Alfredo Massi in Salvador, *Al calor de mi bohío* (1946) by Carlos Luis Nieto in Panama, *El sombrerón* (1950) by Guillermo Andreu in Guatemala, and *Milagro en el bosque* (1972) by Felipe Hernández in Nicaragua, fall into this category, as do more recent films like *La Negrita* (1985)

---

[8] Aragón, Magda and Edgar Barillas. "Guatemala: café, capitalismo dependiente y cine silente." *Revista Estudios*, Guatemala, IIHAA, Escuela de Historia, Universidad de San Carlos, Guatemala. (Vol. 3-9, 1996). p. 67.

[9] Interview with Felipe Hernández. Managua, July 3, 2001.

by Richard Yñiguez and Roxana Bonilla, and *Los secretos de Isolina* (1986) by Miguel Salguero in Costa Rica. Each of these stories is grounded in an idyllic rural past and depicts customs, legends and traditions.

A third tendency that emerged, particularly in Guatemala and Costa Rica, was the attempt to make commercial films with the aid of producers; Oscar Castillo's *La segua* (1984) and *Asesinato en El Meneo* (2001), for example, in Costa Rica, and Rafael Lanuza in Guatemala, whose numerous co-productions with Mexico include *El Cristo de los Milagros* (1972), *La mansión de las siete momias* (1973), *Terremoto en Guatemala* (1976), *Candelaria* (1977) and *Judas* (1986). These attempts were ultimately not viable due to economic limitations, the absence of cinematic tradition and a film industry, and the fact that some of these local productions were actually just cheap copies of films made in more developed countries.

Yet the most interesting tendency of the period leading up to the seventies was the attempt to make auteur cinema, almost always under the influence of artistic (surrealism), philosophical (existentialism) or cinematic (neo-realism and New Wave) movements. This was true of José David Calderón, Alejandro Cotto and Baltazar Polío in El Salvador, and Sami Kafati in Honduras. Their films are the product of tremendous bursts of individual energy. As a whole, this period had little to no effect on the public, the market, or the festival circuit, and the cinema it produced remains a secret.

The isthmus ablaze: film and revolution

Nationalism, anti-imperialism, and the stirrings of revolution were constant throughout the seventies and eighties. From the struggle to regain the Panama Canal to the Sandinista revolution in Nicaragua, the civil war in El

Salvador, and the guerillas in Guatemala, the isthmus was marked by political and military tumult.

This period saw the consolidation of a significant percentage of regional productions, which had almost always been fostered by the State in the interest of developing a popular, nationalist cinema. In overt dialogue with trends across the continent, and for the first time in its history, Central America systematically began to produce genuine expressions of its individual nature.

The quest for a local and regional cinema of our own, one with a unique audiovisual language, arose at the same time as the military conflict. Central American liberation meant establishing a cinema to be used as a weapon of criticism, propaganda, and political indoctrination. This was the case in countries at war like Guatemala, El Salvador and Nicaragua, as well as in Panama, whose production was forged alongside the nationalist recovery of the Canal, and even in 'peaceful' Costa Rica, which produced its most important films during this period.

In Panama, the support of General Omar Torrijos and the direction of the writer Pedro Rivera helped found the Grupo Experimental de Cine Universitario (GECU). Between 1972 and 1977, the GECU made more than 30 documentaries about national sovereignty and the conflict with the United States on 16mm film. These filmic texts affirm a Panamanian identity from a nationalist perspective, and document the Torrijos-Carter treaty negotiations and the restoration of the Canal. Their focus is more on content than on the search for a cinematic language.

Although its cinema was born on the field of battle, the majority of Nicaraguan films were made thanks to the success of the revolution and the creation of the Instituto Nicaragüense de Cine (INCINE), one of the first institutions founded by the Sandinista government. Its productions include 50 short documentaries (newsreels, as they are called in the Cuban school), 16 documentaries, four mid-length narrative films and three co-produced feature films. Prizes awarded to these films culminated in an Oscar nomination for best foreign film, which went to *Alsino y el cóndor*, by the Chilean Miguel Littín.

The discourse of Sandinista films, while official, was that of an optimistic cinema that aligns itself with the construction of a new society. INCINE was also more diverse than GECU, bringing professionals from all social classes and cultural milieux together – some of whom even had experience. This led to a diverse range of aesthetic ideas and approaches. Despite the time that has passed from the moment they were conceived, these films retain their relevance and universal meaning. The literacy campaign filmed by María José Alvarez – the first female filmmaker in the region – spread a sense of enthusiasm and joy at satisfying a basic human need.

As the conflict grew more bitter, INCINE made a foray into narrative film in order to defend the government's accomplishments and denounce the counter-revolution. Nonetheless, directors like Fernando Somarriba made critical films: the documentary *Los hijos del río*, for example, which addressed the conflict between the miskito community and the Sandinista government.

"If Nicaragua could do it, El Salvador will, too" was the slogan – very popular at the time – that brought on the development of Salvadoran cinema. The Instituto Cinematográfico de El Salvador Revolucionario (ICSR) and Sistema Radio Venceremos (or 'we will prevail'), gained a foothold in areas liberated by guerilla fighters and bore witness to the triumphs of the insurrection in films like *El Salvador, el pueblo vencerá* and *La decisión de vencer (Los primeros frutos)*. These optimistic films, made in 1981 on the premise of an imminent victory, sought to contribute to the construction of a utopia that would eclipse the war.

The cases of Guatemala and Honduras were different. Violence and repression did not allow widespread documentary production in the former. Although underground films about the guerilla fighters were made, the filmmakers were often murdered or exiled; even today it is difficult to access the footage. In Honduras, the State spearheaded a department of film that made only four ethnographic documentaries.

Cinema in Costa Rica is also an exceptional case. As the only democracy in the region until the 1980's, the State founded the Department of Film under the control of the Ministry of Culture – now the Centro Costarricense de Producción Cinematográfica – and made documentaries that were critical of the state of the nation, such as *Las cuarenta* by Víctor Vega, about prostitution, *La cultura del guaro* and *Desnutrición* by Carlos Freer, *Los presos* by Víctor Ramírez, about the penal system, and *Costa Rica, Banana Republic* by Ingo Niehaus, about the inequities of international commerce.

This documentary cinema, inspired by New Latin American Cinema and its slogan of giving 'a voice to those who do not have one,' created the paradox of a State critical of its own policies. The model fell into crisis at the end of the decade. Its major directors abandoned state institutions and founded private enterprises that, at least at first, allowed them to continue producing the combative cinema they made before.

The production company Istmo Film was the most important of these. Two of the founders of its Department of Film, Antonio Yglesias and Víctor Vega, directed one of the first documentaries about the anti-Somocista insurrections, *Patria libre o morir*. It also co-produced seminal films like *La insurreción* (1980) by Peter Lilienthal, from Germany, *El Salvador, el pueblo vencerá* (1981) by Diego de la Texera, from Puerto Rico, and *Alsino y el cóndor* (1982) by Miguel Littín, among other films on regional subjects. The cinema of Nicaragua and El Salvador was developed in Costa Rica, and a permanent dialogue was established with GECU, Cuban cinema, and the politically committed artists of the continent.

Nonetheless, the late eighties were marked by political polarization and a shift to the right, a return to nationalistic myths, and a withdrawal from regional connections. Ingo Niehaus made *Senda ignorada* (1983), the first and only feature film produced by the Centro de Cine, about the origins of Costa Rican democracy. Also released were Antonio Yglesias' *La segua* (1984), about a popular legend, *La negrita* (1985) by Richard Yñiguez and Roxana Bonilla, about an important religious tradition, Miguel Salguero's *costumbrista* work, *Los secretos de Isolina* (1986), and Oscar Castillo's *Eulalia* (1987), a parody of the *telenovela* and one of the greatest successes of the nation's cinema.

The arrival of video

The majority of audiovisual production from the mid-eighties on was funded through international cooperation. Though the projects are not contentious, as they might have been in the seventies and eighties, they offer varied critical perspectives on a complex reality engendered by the post-traumatic stress of civil war, by underdevelopment, and by growing domestic instability and violence.

Beginning in the 1990's, a generation of 'video-filmmakers' began to appear in Central America; the popularization of video allowed its widespread use as a tool of the trade and a means of self-expression. *El silencio de Neto* (1994) by the Guatemalan Luis Argueta, which was awarded multiple honors at international film festivals, was the only narrative feature film made that decade.

During that time, audiovisual production in Central America was undergoing a period of transition that would culminate in 2001. Cultural distribution and consumption were transformed; traditional screening rooms disappeared and were replaced by multiplexes attached to malls.

Narrative returns to the region

Panama waited 60 years to produce another narrative feature. *Chance* (2010), by Abner Benaim, had greater box office earnings than the Hollywood mega-production *Avatar* in the nation's theaters. Benaim's comedy tells the story of two domestic workers who kidnap their employers, who are supposedly wealthy but who have actually gone into debt to their servants in their attempt to keep up appearances. The women are mistreated, and take matters into their own hands. The film is a portrait of a social stratum typical of our societies, in which appearances are more important than the values of family and solidarity.

The feature-length documentary *Los puños de una nación* (2005), about the boxer Roberto "Fists of Stone" Durán, five-time winner of the world title in five different categories, also stands out. "Fists of Stone" was iconic in the country for his struggle for independence from the United States. As such, the film interweaves the boxer's life with the history of Panama.

Honduras did not make a single feature during the entire twentieth century, but in 2003, it released three: *Almas de la media noche*, by Juan Carlos Fanconi; *Anita, la cazadora de insectos* by Hispano Durón and *No hay tierra sin dueño*, by the mythic Sami Kafati. It took the director 17 years to make; he died during the process and the film was completed by a team of Chileans at the request of the family. As a result, it was shown posthumously both at Cannes and the Tribeca Film Festival. It is an epic, a traditional Latin American story in which young peasants struggle against landowners. A story typical of the literature of the first half of the twentieth century, if you will, but one that is still lamentably topical in our region.

Almas de la medianoche is a horror movie that combines legends of the Lenca people with zombie storylines. The film, the first to be shown in the country, was made on a budget of less than $40,000 and ran in theaters for three months, recuperating its investment and becoming a cult phenomenon among young viewers. *Anita, la cazadora de insectos* is about consumerism and appearances, as well; in this case, in the middle class. It is an adaptation of a story by Roberto Castillo. Six years later, in 2009, *Amor y frijoles* by Mathew Kodath and Hernán Pereira appears in theaters. It is a *costumbrista* situation comedy about love and small town gossip.

Nicaragua "knocked out" a number of Hollywood super-productions with *La Yuma* (2009) by Florence Yaugey. It had been 21 years since Ramiro Lacayo, director of the mythic Instituto Nicaragüense de Cine (INCINE), made his feature *El espectro de la guerra* (1988). With the fall of the Sandinistas, cinema lost the support of the state; it took until 2009 to make and screen a film that, as we mentioned, surpassed *Ironman* and other big-budget movies, in addition to winning eleven international prizes in its earliest screenings. *La Yuma* is the story of a girl surrounded by domestic and social violence who manages to escape her world of misery through boxing. She decides to save herself and rescue her brothers; after a number of incidents, she escapes the destiny of poverty, aggression and abuse to which she seemed to have been born. *La Yuma*, in addition to depicting different social strata in Nicaragua, presents a light at the end of the tunnel that has allowed it to reach a broad public.

El Salvador did not make feature films during the seventies, either. In 2008, Roberto Dávila relived the recent civil war in *Sobreviviendo Guazapa*. It was a polemical film, as many survivors of the conflict thought that it aligned itself with the political right. Nonetheless, viewers flocked to the theaters, fostering a real dialogue about the film. More importantly, it was an excuse to reflect on the recent civil war.

Luis Argueta, the director of *El silencio de Neto* (1994), returned to the cinema in a radically different way. In his *Collect call* (2002), he depicts the difficult economic situation and limited opportunities he faced when making his second film. The protagonist of *El silencio de Neto*, a peasant at the time, would play Neto eight years later. The young man, having experienced the 'glamorous' world of film, wants to be an actor again. He turns to Luis Argueta, supposedly a famous director in the United States. He starts out seeking the American dream, but together with Argueta and his wife (who play leading roles), ends up washing dishes and hustling tourists. The film was made with meager resources: shot on digital with Argueta's family as actors, in the present day, with no costumes to speak of. It breaks down the borders between narrative and documentary filmmaking, and in doing so, fans out a range of possibilities for cinema.

One year later, a more traditional film was made in Guatemala: *Donde acaban los caminos*, by Carlos García Agraz, is the adaptation of a novel of the same name by Mario Monteforte Toledo. Another literary adaptation was also released that year: *Lo que soñó Sebastián*, adapted and directed by the book's very own author, Rodrigo Rey Rosa. Both have strong aesthetic qualities. The first treats the subject of a forbidden love between a Ladino and an indigenous woman. The second, more contemporary, film takes the region of El Petén and the issues of poaching, logging and forest fires as its protagonists.

Casa Comal began producing a number of films, most of them exposés. La *casa de enfrente* (2003) and *VIP, la otra casa* (2007), by Elías Jiménez, presents the country's political corruption, the world of drugs and the sex trade, whereas *Las cruces, poblado próximo* (2005), by Rafael Rosal, is about the recent civil war and how indigenous communities were devastated by the military. 2009 saw the release of Ray Figueroa's *La bodega*, a story about the revenge two citizens exact on a member of a gang. *Un día de sol* (2010), a film by Rafa Trejos about a woman who surrounds herself with things having to do with soccer, also appeared in theaters. Movies like Alejo Crisóstomo's *Fe* and *Las marimbas del infierno*, will open soon, as well.

Gasolina, by Julio Hernández, is an auteur film with an aesthetic all its own. It presents a post-war Guatemala where violence is no longer relegated to the mountains, but occurs in the streets. A group of adolescents bands together to steal gasoline and travel around without a set destination. It is a country without hope that has turned its back on its roots – they run over an indigenous man and one of the boys sets him on fire – and one which has no future to look toward. The film has won a number of international awards, including the "Horizontes Latinos" prize for best picture at the San Sebastián Film Festival.

Film production in Costa Rica

Cinema is advancing at an unprecedented rate in Costa Rica, as well; audiovisual production has become a part of everyday life. Over the course of the twentieth century, nine feature films were made. In just the first decade of the twenty-first, 18 – double the amount of the previous century – have already been completed. This is evidence of the fact that national and regional cinema is on the rise and that there is a wave of young directors eager to tell their stories in images.

From *Asesinato en El Meneo* (2001) by Oscar Castillo, which exposes corruption in politics and business through comic interludes and half-naked girls, to *Mujeres apasionadas* (2003), by Maureen Jiménez, about a professional seducer and his many lovers, to the more recent *Donde duerme el horror*, also produced by Castillo; the list gets longer year after year.

Donde duerme el horror, like *El psicópata* (a "B" movie made by Luis Mena in 2008) and, to a certain extent, *La región perdida* (2009) by Andrés Heidenreich, makes inroads into the horror genre. The latter film is about the murder of a national figure, the doctor Ricardo Moreno Cañas. The act is presented from a number of different perspectives, combining narrative and documentary styles.

Mauricio Mendiola's 2003 film *Marasmo* tackles a foreign subject: guerilla fighters in Colombia. The film, which was painstakingly made, was criticized for traveling outside the nation and using local actors with a Colombian accent. Esteban Ramírez, on the other hand, had two successes with *Caribe* (2005) and *Gestación* (2009). The first is a more ambitious film, with foreign actors and a plot that combines romance with ecological concerns, and in which the tropical landscape becomes a character in itself. *Gestación* is a simpler, more direct, more conservative work; it was really able to reach the public and, thus far, it has had the greatest box-office success of any film released in the first decade of the twenty-first century.

The plot of *Gestación* is a fairly typical one: an upper middle class boy falls in love with a poor girl, they make love, she gets pregnant and has trouble at school. The boy does not know what to do, as she refuses to get an abortion. In the end, he offers to marry her but she decides to stay on her own with the baby, as opposed to what happens in the *telenovela*. In a happy ending, the young father supports the mother and embraces his responsibility.

Hilda Hidalgo's *Del amor y otros demonios* (2009), adapted from a novel of the same name by Gabriel García Márquez, was also released in this period. With its careful, painstaking aesthetic, Hidalgo does not fall into the stereotypes of magical realism. The film, rather, is more intimist in nature. It focuses on a girl who has been bitten by a rabid dog and, later, her infatuation with the priest who tries to save her. The film has been criticized for its pace, which – like that of *El camino* (2008) by Ishtar Yasin – is slow. But this is an aesthetic choice, rather than an accident. The problem is that we are used to the action of Hollywood. Yasin's film, *El camino*, presents the issue of Nicaraguan immigration into Costa Rica from the perspective of a little girl. It is the film that has won the most international awards to date.

Agua fría de mar (2009) by Paz Fábrega, which had its premier on the international festival circuit and won one of the most important prizes in the industry, the Tiger Award from the Rotterdam Film Festival, is also an intimist work. An encounter between an adolescent from the upper middle class and a child of little means changes the lives of both girls, especially the bourgeois one.

Tercer mundo (2009) by César Caro also premiered at a festival, and combines three stories that take place in Chile, Bolivia and Costa Rica. Under the pretext of the search for extraterrestrials, the film examines the problem of personal and collective identity in both the characters and their surroundings.

Another intimist film, *A ojos cerrados* (2010), by Hernán Jiménez, tells the story of a successful young executive who lives with her grandparents. Her grandmother dies and she finds herself having to choose between accompanying her grandfather to spread her ashes in the Caribbean and keeping a million-dollar project afloat. It is grounded in the construction of characters, in the paths that open up and the decisions we have to make, and how love and family are values that have not lost their meaning. Jiménez is already filming *El regreso* (2010).

El último comandante (2010), directed by Isabel Martínez y Vicente Ferraz and starring the great Mexican actor Damián Alcazar, takes the Sandinista revolution as its starting point as it paints a portrait of a human being, his dreams, in a round trip journey between Nicaragua and Costa Rica. Ultimately, the story becomes an internal and universal drama.

For his part, Miguel Gómez has become a "film phenomenon." His first work, *El cielo rojo* (2008), which was not publicized and was shown on only one screen, was on the marquee for ten weeks and touches on fundamental themes like youth and the moment of choosing one's course of study, love, and the future of the country. Ultimately a comedy with well-constructed dialogues, the film is also a criticism of certain events within the country. Gómez has finished shooting a horror film, *El sanatorio* (2010), and is currently working on *El fin* (2010), which parodies the idea of the end of the world. Ramírez, too, has announced preparations on two additional films, as have Gustavo Fallas, César Delgado, Ishtar Yasin, Laura Astorga, and others.

Aside from these narrative features, all the countries mentioned also regularly produce short films, documentaries and television series with subject matter that deals with a variety of contemporary concerns: the pacification of the region, ecology, gender relations, domestic violence, popular culture, immigration, historical memory, etc.

A region finds itself

A combination of factors can help explain the development of our cinema. In 1998, Guatemala founded a film festival for the region, the Icaro, which has been growing little by little and will soon be in its twelfth year. The Muestra de Cine y Video, running in Costa Rica since 1992, screens the year's crop of short films, documentaries and animation. 2003 saw the founding of 240, a festival that shows the work of young or inexperienced directors, or those just getting started, in any format. The 240 was opened to artists throughout Central America in 2008.

The academy also recognized the importance of the audiovisual. Most directors, up to that point, had been self-taught. Starting in the nineties, many were graduating from different schools in Europe, the Soviet Bloc and, above all, from the Escuela Internacional de Cine y Televisión (EICTV) in San Antonio de los Baños, Cuba.

The University of Costa Rica created a major in audiovisual production as part of their Communications program; in 2009, they established a masters degree in filmmaking. Veritas University established tracks in film, television and digital animation in Costa Rica that have already graduated a dozen students. In Guatemala, the production company Casa Comal – together with EICTV – opened a technical program in audiovisual production, and what began in El Salvador as an audiovisual workshop at the Escuela Mónica Herrera is now a formal diploma.

Film laws were passed in Panama and Nicaragua. Costa Rica and El Salvador have laws in the Legislative Assembly awaiting ratification. There are associations for directors in all these countries that have had an impact on raising awareness about the importance of the audiovisual. Panama, Costa Rica and Guatemala have also joined Ibermedia, the most important project in cinematic co-production in Ibero-America, through which the government of each country pays annual dues of $100,000 USD and the projects that get funding are awarded twice as much as the country originally invested in them.

In the same way, portals for the audiovisual community – like Delefoco and the Portal Centroamericano de Cine, Video y Animación – have been created online. These sites facilitate communication about services and resources in the region: its producers, major works, etc. New technology and its reduced costs, together with other conditions, have made the growth of our cinema possible, with Guatemala and Costa Rica taking the lead.

If the region manages to come together in an organic way, it is possible to imagine the organized, stable, and sustainable development of an audiovisual industry. Central America has a potential viewership of nearly 40 million; it would be foolish to continue to think in terms of small, isolated countries. Although the steps recently taken give us hope, the real work of audiovisual production in Central America has yet to begin. Central America is again at war: this time it is a war of images and stories. Little by little, we are piecing the mirror of our images back together.

Cuban Cinema Beyond Strawberries and Chocolate

Luciano Castillo

On the fifteenth of January 1897, the Frenchman Gabriel Veyre arrived in Havana, via Mexico, to install the Lumière cinematograph at 126 calle Prado. Many of those who watched the doors of the spectacle open for the first time on January 24 were, though tempted by curiosity, unable to pay for a ticket. They could not imagine that 62 years later, on January 1, 1959, the Cuban people would go from being frustrated spectators to being the protagonists of an epic: the triumph of the Revolution.

Just three months later, Law 169 – the new government's first within the cultural sphere – was passed on March 24, creating the Cuban Film Institute (ICAIC). An organization without precedent in the country, the ICAIC was determined to start from zero, despite the fact that there had been numerous quixotic attempts to make film on the island during the previous administration. One of the first principles established by this seminal law indicates that the seventh art "represents, by virtue of its nature, an instrument of opinion and the formation of both individual and collective consciousness, and can be used to deepen and illuminate the revolutionary spirit and maintain its creative vigor." Another insisted that "cinema – like any art that is nobly conceived – should represent an appeal to the conscience and should help abolish ignorance, elucidate problems, propose solutions and present, in a dramatic and contemporary way, the great conflicts of man and of humanity."[10]

From its first documentary, Julio García-Espinosa's *Sexto aniversario*, and the premiere of its first feature length narrative film, *Historias de la Revolución* by Tomás Gutiérrez Alea (1928-1996), authenticity was a distinguishing feature of this new kind of filmmaking.

Panorama in a major key

At the height of the sixties, the Argentinean Fernando Solanas and Octavio Getino, anchored in the principles of "Third Cinema," secretly screened their provocative *La hora de los hornos* (1966-67), the structure of which demanded that the audience contribute their own conclusion through testimonies and experiences with the military; Glauber Rocha triumphed at Cannes before the letter Z had even been added to the alphabet of cinema with another detonation: *Tierra en trance* (1967). The political chaos that reigned in this imaginary land identified itself with that of any other point in the geography of Latin America.

With his camera drawn like a gun, in *Yawar Mallku* (1969) the Bolivian Jorge Sanjinés denounced the covert atrocities committed in the highlands by the *gringos* during Operation Condor. In Chile, Raúl Ruiz filmed his claustrophobic *Tres tristes tigres* (1969); that same year, his compatriot Miguel Littín recreated events ripped from the headlines in his *El chacal de Nahueltoro*: a multiple murder committed by José del Carmen Valenzuela Torres, an illiterate peasant. In Colombia, Marta Rodríguez and Jorge Silva observe, as active witnesses, the exploitation of

---

[10] All quotations from the text of the law have been taken from *Cronología del cine cubano*, by Arturo Agramonte (Havana: Ediciones ICAIC, 1966). 116-120.

the working class, which they would later shape into their *Chircales* (1972). They were no strangers to the sense of political commitment that spread like a breath of fresh air over the continent, bringing its directors and their continual search for identity together as part of a movement that would come to be known as New Latin American Cinema.

As the arrival of mobile cinema brought the art of the moving image to the furthest corners of Cuba for the very first time, Santiago Álvares (1919-1998) contributed works that were classics from the moment they were first screened: *Now!* (1965), *Hanoi, martes 13* (1967) y *L.B.J.* (1968), the astonishing genesis of what would come to be called the "Documentary School of Cuba." With its imaginative and thematic opulence, the documentary on the biggest island of the Antilles was immediately and enormously influential for its union of the political and the popular.

The volatile year of 1968 brought with it two of the most significant and unrepeatable works of Cuban cinema, which nourished the cultural patrimony of Latin America: Tomás Gutiérrez Alea's *Memorias del subdesarrollo* and *Lucía* by Humberto Solás were free of stereotypes, stylistic contrivances, and scenarios that imitated cinema "à la Nouvelle Vague" or the pronounced neorealist influence of the early years. The Cuban Revolution and the entire cultural movement that it generated became the obligatory point of reference for any analysis of Latin American reality in the decade between 1960 and 1970.

During this "prodigious decade," Cuban cinema laid the foundations of "a cinema with profound political content and high aesthetic standards",[11] according to Ugo Ulive (Uruguay). The organic incorporation of documentary elements within fiction, which blurs the borders of both,

---

[11] Ulive, Ugo. "Crónica del cine cubano" in *Cine al día* vol. 12. Caracas, 1971.

is one of the distinctive traits of a cinema that emerged as an industry alongside the Revolution. Characterized by improvisation and the way its directors learned as they went in an atmosphere of feverish activity that many still look back on with fondness, the ICAIC was the wall against which 'social realism' – which wreaked such havoc on artistic forms like theater and the visual arts – collided.

The Cuban Cinematheque, founded on February 6, 1960, extended its reach to all the major centers of the interior and other socio-economically significant populations, expanding to a total of 28 screening rooms. The institution started a "revolution" of its own by breaking with the traditional and limited canon of conventional film libraries, which centered on a specific nucleus of the population, nearly always confined to its major cities. The work of this itinerant museum contributed to the metamorphosis of public taste.

As the sixties came to a close, Julio Garia-Espinosa, whose iconoclastic calling was to explode the genres established by "Made in Hollywood" cinema as evidenced by his *Aventuras de Juan Quinquín* (1967) and, later, *Son... o no son* (1980), wrote the provocative and aggressive text: "Por un cine imperfecto." Among the imperatives presented in an inflammatory and polemical spirit was that of showing a problem as a process, putting it on trial without passing sentence; this can be seen as a response to the demands made by certain critics, as well as the public, who expects for cinema to provide answers and solutions.

The seventies – particularly the latter half of the decade – brought the consolidation of Cuban cinema as a powerful artistic movement, persevering in its intention of fostering an ever more genuine art form and of creating a qualitatively superior viewing public. During these years, Tomás Gutiérrez Alea ("Titón") put out two masterworks: *La última cena* (1976) and *Los sobrevivientes* (1978). It was also Titón that facilitated the first and only feature film of Sara Gómez (1943 – 1974), whose piercing gaze would leave a profound mark on the documentary form. After giving free reign to an unprecedented sense of imagination, freshness, and originality in his approach to history in *La primera carga al machete* (1969), Manuel Octavio Gómez (1934-1988) surprised audiences once again with *Los días del agua* (1971), a film whose solidity he was never able to surpass in his later work. One principle he shared with Titón was the idea that "when Cuban cinema talks about current events, it is actually talking about the future."[12] For his part, Pastor Vega (1940-2005) addressed the perennial theme of the woman and her role in the new society with *Retrato de Teresa* (1978).

A new generation of directors, predominantly trained in documentary cinema and the newsreel tradition of the *Noticiero ICAIC Latinoamericano*, were given the chance to take their first steps toward narrative film in the 1980s. This infusion of talent examined themes that dealt directly with the constantly changing reality of their time with a critical eye, which had been unheard of before. While Solás, in *Cecilia* (1982), *Amada* (1983), and *Un hombre de éxito* (1986) looked to history for resonances with the present, with *Clandestinos* (1987), Fernando Pérez approached heroic figures without the use of stereotype. Juan Carlos Tabío launched a measured attack on generational prejudices and conflicts in *Plaff o Demasiado miedo a la vida* (1988), while Orlando Rojas examined the corruption behind the scenes of a theater in *Papeles secundarios* (1989), the most important film in the country in the nineties, according to national reviews.

---

[12] The author's transcription of an interview with Titón from the documentary *Memorias del cine cubano* (Venezuela-France, 1987) by Atahualpa Lichy.

Somewhere along its uneven path, Latin American cinema left the adjective "new" behind it in favor of stories and subject matter that, despite developing specifically within the context of the countries south of the Rio Bravo, took on universal dimensions. In the final decade of *Lumière's Century*, Cuban cinema was not immune to the economic restrictions imposed upon the country by the so-called "Special Period." The Democratic Republic of Germany (DDR), a long time underwriter of untested cinema, crumbled as quickly as its wall, taking with it the entire socialist bloc in a series of events unimaginable up to that point.

The fall of socialism meant the coup de grâce for the *Noticiero ICAIC Latinoamericano*, an effective medium of communication; the reduction in the number of documentary films – which declined from 51 in 1980 to 13 in 1990 and six years later, to 7 (three of which were made on video). Added to this were the disappearance of the magazine *Cine cubano*, the only specialized publication on the continent with such a long run, and the dissolution of the so-called Creative Groups formed in 1988 as a means of decentralizing production.[13]

The "art of our time" requires substantial resources; above all, that of international distribution, which amortizes costs and contributes to self-financing. Co-production with a few key European countries became, for Cuba – as for the rest of Latin America – unavoidable: to co-produce or not to produce, that is the un-Shakespearian dichotomy our directors must consider in these globalized times. The

---

[13] I am, obviously, not addressing the case of other centers of production, such as the Television Film Studios, Educational Cinematography, and those of MINFAR (now Trimagen), which also make up Cuban cinema, though in general when an evaluation or comparison is made, it tends to adhere to the production of the ICAIC. My colleague Juan Antonio García Borrero has called this "*icai*centrism."

services offered by competent ICAIC professionals, known for their effectiveness in conveying what they imagine, and not simply as resources, are exploited as inexpensive labor for the "directors" of the First World. Washed-up European actors earn higher salaries in these films than the hallowed figures that have only barely been able to make their way into national cinema and are relegated to secondary roles. Being able to shoot for practically nothing compared to the international average has turned Cuban locations into a perennial temptation for foreign producers, while at the same time allowing the fees collected to be reinvested in national cinema.

Narrative film production in Cuba in 1996 is comparable to that of 1970, at the height of the "Ten Million Ton Harvest," a time during which only two short narrative films made up the entire production of the ICAIC. Only two mid-length films made by graduates of the International School of Film and Television, Manuel Rodríguez's *El sardine* and Fernando Timossi's *Blue Moon*, represented Cuba in the Havana Festival (1996). Yet the Caribbean island is among the few Latin American countries with its own film industry – and the only one financed by the State. Cuban cinema survives, despite the unique combination of events presented by the 90s; instability did not cast a shadow over the cinematic horizon.

Neither the period nor the circumstances are the same as those that generated the splendor of New Latin American Cinema, which – like any movement or trend – has developed in a plethora of directions and "artistic, cultural and political successes and frustrations," according to Alfredo Guevara, who promotes the movement from the international festival over which he presides. "It is not about bringing back past conditions, or of ignoring them. It is about finding an answer to the questions that afflict us today. Not as a dictionary, but as the source of a new kind of suffering, of different challenges. We are, essentially, at a crossroads, but not one of paths or practical considerations. It is an intellectual crossroads of ethics and aesthetics."[14]

Cuban filmmakers inhabit this crossroads without abandoning the principles of "talent, intellectual rigor and self-discipline" as they embrace as their own the standards expressed by Costa-Gavras, who stated that "an artist cannot but think about the society in which he lives, he cannot live in a society without trying to understand it and communicate its problems." The Cuban songwriter Pablo Milanés, in one of his works, admits that he does not live in a "perfect society"; Tomás Gutiérrez Alea, on more than one occasion, has commented on the importance of critical interventions in the development of one's own society. "It is very important to look critically at reality but, at the same time, we must not forget that we are surrounded by enemies and that, as such, we also must affirm our reality," he explained, in an interview filmed by Atahualpa Lichy for the documentary *Memorias del cine cubano* (1983).

He had not yet enjoyed the taste of tolerance that came with *Fresa y chocolate* (1993), a work that was especially timely in the way it brought a taboo subject to the screen. The unmistakable critique present in the confrontation between a young communist militant and a homosexual, along with the theme of freedom of choice, led to its being (mis)understood outside the country as "a film that got past Castro's government," ignoring the fact that Cuban cinema receives state funding. The circulation of *Fresa y chocolate*, which brought with it an Oscar nomination for best foreign film, made it, in the eyes of many, the most important work in Cuban cinema, even though it did not

---

[14] Guevara, Alfredo. "Las revoluciones no son paseos de Riviera" an interview with Wilfredo Cancio Isla for *La Gaceta de Cuba*, December 1992, in *Revolución es lucidez*. Havana: Ediciones ICAIC, 1998. 98.

attain the notoriety of other works in Gutiérrez Alea's own filmography. How many other works did the master leave unfinished due to a lack of funding or approval![15]

Caustic humor, used as a means of confronting conflict and contradiction, from which the present reality in Cuba is not exempt, was one of the defining characteristics of many of the works in his brilliant filmography. Bringing it to a close with *Guatanamera* (1995), he once again took on, three decades later, the obstacles presented by the inefficacy of certain functionaries and their practices, the persistence of which makes *La muerte de un burócrata* (1966) seem as though it were filmed yesterday. Four years earlier, as he was finishing up his first comedy, *Las doce sillas* (1962), Titón wrote: "Humor and satire are resources that we have nearly forgotten beneath the weight of an exaggerated sense of responsibility. It would be an error to fall into that abyss."[16]

For his friend and collaborator Juan Carlos Tabío, the co-director of *Fresa y chocolate*, humor with metaphorical connotations – that "belled whip," in the words of José Martí – serves to punish behaviors no longer compatible with a socialist country, either in an isolated place where we witness the evolution of cinema and its transformative relationship with the inhabitants of an imagined community (*El elefante y la bicicleta*, 1994), or a bus station on an equally isolated corner of the island, at which people find themselves hopelessly trapped (*Lista de espera*, 2000). The buñelian *exterminating angel* flies again, a quarter of a century

---

[15] It enjoyed an international distribution and reception that one of his most important films did not – *La última cena* (1976), underappreciated for having appeared among the "negro-metrajes" of Sergio Giral (thus baptized by Creole humor), which treated the question of slavery ad nauseam.

[16] Gutiérrez Alea, Tomás. "Doce notas para Las doce sillas" in *Alea: una retrospectiva crítica*. Havana: Editorial Letras Cubanas, 1987. 55.

after alighting on the mansion in which Titón confined his *sobrevivientes*, giving birth to the irrational universe of Orlando Rojas' comedy *Las noches de Constantinopla* (2001).

For a long time, Cuban cinema was criticized because, despite being a country characterized by the good-natured mockery of the "*choteo*" – which took no prisoners, even at the most significant historical moments – comedy was something of a *rara avis* in its creative production, which was dominated by "historicist" film. Paradoxically, in the 90s many complained that the treatment of the many issues and facets of the situation at the time was through techniques belonging to comedy, which is by no means synonymous with superficiality. These films multiplied by the dozens, beginning with the absurd virulence unleashed in Daniel Díaz Torres's *Alicia en el pueblo de Maravillas* (1990), with its satirical questioning and critical interpretation of aspects of Cuba worthy of censure today, no matter how chimerical the setting of the work.

The fact that reality can often be quite a bit stranger than the most feverish of fictions was demonstrated not long after the film's fleeting premiere, when an extremist functionary, an ideologue who was part of an unprecedented and slanderous campaign to pull it from theaters, was brought down by deals made behind closed doors. Just like the inhabitants of Wonderland in the censored film, no time was lost in sending him to work at a distant outpost. The film would be vindicated but, twenty years later, the public would still not have a chance to view it. Díaz Torres is perhaps the director who has used the genre like a scalpel to the greatest extent, opening fissures in society with well-received films like *Kleines Tropikana* (1997) and *Hacerse el sueco* (2000).

Humberto Solás, in bringing *El siglo de las luces* (1992) to the screen, returned to his literary refuge and allowed himself to be carried away by what Carpentier would call a "river of words," translating it into a hurricane of baroque imagery, immersing himself in the eighteenth century in order to gain insight into its central preoccupations. Nearly a decade went by before, with *Miel para Oshún* (2001), he would address a situation barely alluded to in Cuban cinema: that of the division of a family brought about by exile. In the film, he examines the personal history of a young boy who, in his infancy, was brought to the United States by force.

Jesús Díaz (1941-2002) had already addressed the subject superficially in *Lejanía* (1985). Ana Rodríguez (1952-2005), who made her debut in the brief *Laura*, the fifth short that made up the collective feature *Mujer transparente* (1985), was much more daring in her approach to the sisterly bond between two friends of opposing political views, and to the fear that torments the one who decided to stay on the island when faced with a possible reunion after many years. The Brazilian critic and scholar Paolo Antonio Paranaguá once wrote: "the tensions created by the tourist sector, the bureaucratization of the elite, the lost hopes, the squandering of energies, the rejection of the demonization of those who left the country and, furthermore, the need to rekindle the dialogue that had been interrupted are a few of the things that Laura reveals over the course of a brief wait, a walk around, and an internal monologue."[17]

The multifaceted subject of the woman – the most repeated in the evolution of Cuban cinema – is an axis that allows for reflection on the contradictions of society through the active and liberating role assigned to her; endures from the widest range of perspectives.

---

[17] Paranaguá, Paulo Antonio. "Nuevos desafíos del cine cubano" in *Encuadre* vol. 7 Caracas, 1991. 27.

A filmmaker like Fernando Pérez, who was chosen by national critics as the most prominent of the 90s, who would make reference to the recent past in *Clandestinos* and *Hello, Hemingway* (1990), opted for the mundane for his mid-length *Madagascar* (1994). A generational conflict offers him a pretext to set his gaze upon the times in which we live. Before the classic that is *Suite Habana* (2003), there was a mature work full of allegory: *La vida es silbar* (1998). The unusual point of view is that of a female narrator who, from a point in the future, observes the intersection of the lives of a cast of characters that have settled in a mutant social reality that is neither sentimentalized nor free of imperfections. The cinema is an exceptional witness, and Fernando prefers to avoid the communicative devices of the comedy of manners, or any other tone, in order to grapple with the here and now as though it were a matter of tomorrow and always. For this artist, "the Cuban cinema of the past few years is a cinema that presents complexities; it is not a cinema that is free of contradictions. And I think that the Cuban reality of today, in its complexity, remains a singular, unique, and revolutionary reality."[18]

Reina y Rey (1994) is a sensitive account of a person fighting to survive under the increasingly adverse conditions of the Cuban shortages of the nineties. With this heart-wrenching and hopeful tribute dedicated to the memory of Cesare Zavattini, the father of Italian neorealism, Julio García Espinosa was trying to repay a debt of gratitude to this unquestionable influence on the Cuban cinema of the sixties. An old woman struggles with the anguish of trying to feed her dog, her only companion, and the suggestion of her former employers that she travel "up north" to take on work as a maid. When García-Espinosa was asked, in an

---

[18] Ricciarelli, Cecilia. "Conversaciones con los realizadores cubanos" in *Kinetoscopio* vol. 58 Medellín, 2001. 40.

interview given in Mexico in 1997, about the motivations behind *Reina y Rey* and whether Cuban cinema had entered a period in which its directors were working with subjects of intense social relevance, he responded that "There are not enough testimonies of the drama Cuba is living through today; bringing this to the cinema, underscoring the human element, seems a vital necessity to me."[19]

At the dawn of the new millennium and in the absence – with some notable exceptions – of a documentary movement in Cuban cinema that would take social themes as its object, narrative film filled this role, perhaps involuntarily, by generating works rooted in current events, without concern for the reaction of the critics. We owe one of the most honest and beautiful reflections on the stifled Cuban cinema of the nineties, a time of formal and thematic undernourishment, to Fernando Pérez, who, with his perennial lucidity and objectivity, has said:

> It is not easy to make films. It has never been easy to make films. Least of all for us, the poor of the Earth. The harsh reality of the last decade of the century has also imposed restrictions on recent Cuban cinema. In some cases, painful restrictions. [ ] For those Cuban filmmakers who are able to film – it does not matter where or when – the most important thing is knowing that each new film, in its very existence, could contribute to the idea of a "culture of resistance" promoted by Lezama and the "Orígenes" group.[20]

The International Festival of New Latin American Cinema proves that the Cuban public – which is, according to many filmmakers, indescribable – simply let itself be conquered by cinema, never offering the least bit of resistance. It was 28 years since the inception, in 1979, of

---

[19] García-Espinosa, Julio. "Llevar al cine el drama de Cuba, necesidad visceral" in *La Jornada*, Mexico, September 2, 1997. 27.
[20] Unpublished text, read on January 24, 1997 at the commemoration of the centenary of the cinema's arrival in Cuba.

a competition that would revive the spirit of the festivals at Viña del Mar, Mérida, and Caracas. In that first gathering, it defined its principal objectives: "to promote regular encounters between Latin American filmmakers who enrich the artistic culture of our countries with their work [...] and to contribute to the diffusion and international circulation of the most important examples of our cinema." Every year, the first fortnight of December turns into an anticipated popular event; many plan their vacations around it, letting themselves be swept up in the cinematic whirlwind; personalities from all over the world create a space of solidarity where they work together with great intensity to strengthen the cinema of the continent, that land of rebels and creators whose history demands to be told by its filmmakers.

The refrain: independence vs. subsistence

The digital revolution, and the reduced production costs it implies, landed on Cuban shores with *Miel para Oshún*, directed by Humberto Solás, one of its greatest advocates as a means of resistance and a driving force behind the Festival Internacional de Cine Pobre – a rather unfortunate title, far less fitting than its English translation, *The International Non-Budget Film Festival*. Years later, Solás would return to the medium for *Barrio Cuba*, a collaboration in which he visits places never before captured by a camera, distant from the idyllic Old Havana, restored or with its foundations showing through, and without a glimpse toward the infamous *malecón* along the sea. Fernando Pérez would not have been able to achieve such a sense of intimacy with his subjects-turned-characters of his unclassifiable *Suite Habana* without the smaller crew that the use of digital implies; he repeated this experience in *Madrigal* (2006), another co-production with Spain (Wanda Visión).

It fell to Juan Carlos Cremata, a graduate of the first class of the School of San Antonio de los Baños, to be a pioneer in using this alternative format to make the first Cuban film independent of the ICAIC, though the filmmaker himself prefers to say that it is "an alternative, at least, to the model our 'industry' follows."[21] *Viva Cuba* (2004) – co-produced by a team from Cuban television and a company with the highly evocative name of *El Ingenio* (for 'ingenuity'), created specifically for this project and its opulent dynamism – is about the flight of two boys across the island in their attempt to prevent one of them from being forced to leave the country. *Viva Cuba* would achieve such powers of conviction and communication that, from the moment of its discovery in the festival at Cannes, it would corner the market on awards in festivals at all latitudes.

In his student works (*Diana, Oscuros rinocerontes enjaulados...*), Cremata established himself as a genuine creator in his own right, endowed with a restless talent and a notable stylistic drive, impossible to categorize – except under the rubric of auteur cinema – which allowed him to reinvent himself from one film to the next, whether it be a documentary, a narrative feature, or a delirious mise en scène. A nonconformist by nature, he prefers the search rather than the discovery. While he was waiting for the funding to complete the trilogy begun with *Nada +* (2001) and, later, *Nunca y Nadie*, he did a *casting* for another project: an adaptation of Carlos Montenegro's novel *Hombres sin mujer* and shot – in digital – two other adaptations, this time from the stage, of Héctor Quintero's classic Cuban play *El premio flaco* and *Chamaco*, by the young playwright Abel González Melo.

---

[21] There is a widespread notion that the first independent film was Manuel Herrera's *Zafiros, locura azul* (1997), but this is a co-production with HMC Productions from the United States and Cuba's RTV, as well as the ICAIC.

Humberto Padrón, who made his debut with the important mid-length film *Vídeo de familia* (2001), his qualifying project at the school of Audiovisual Communications of the Instituto Superior de Arte, got the funding together to make his first feature film, *Frutas en el café* (2005) through channels outside the ICAIC. Others would not delay in following suit: Ismael Perdomo – with his substantial documentary filmography – tackles his first narrative feature, *Mata, que Dios perdona* (2004), a stylistic exercise in genre film that blurs the edges of its sociopolitical context; Carolina Nicola writes, produces, and directs *Así de simple* (2006). After its world premiere at the Islantilla Film Festival, it was entered in competitions at Biarritz and Trieste. The plot centers on the existential crisis experienced by a Cuban youth who lives with his mother and is faced with the decision of staying with her or emigrating to the United States, where his father lives. The famous Cuban editor Nelson Rodríguez, always attentive to the emergence of a new sensibility, stands out among the technical team of this directorial debut.

Perhaps one of the most provocative and polemical films offered by contemporary Cuban cinema is another debut work, *Mañana* (2006) by Alejandro Moya, who had extensive experience in television. He signed the pseudonym Iskánder to a considerable portion of the credits of the film, which – despite its numerous pretenses – offers an interesting script that paints an acute portrait of a certain sector of Cuban society. It recounts 24 hours in the life of a young man whose daily routine and idle way of life, devoid of all responsibility, are interrupted by a violent twist of fate. The financial contributions of prestigious visual artists and musicians made this production possible, though the ICAIC later claimed it as its own.

A "dolly back" on narrative film production in Cuba in 2006 reveals that it is unquestionably a year that signals the recuperation of the rhythm so sorely missed in the national cinema: five feature films were released, three on 35mm and two shot in digital. The most important thing about this creative crop is its diversity of subject matter and style: each of these films offers its own proposal, a characteristic we should keep in mind.

The ICAIC embraced the digital alternative and all its benefits, contributing to the production of a number of films. The first of these to be produced entirely on a national level was *La pared* (2006), the first attempt at feature film from another Cuban filmmaker, Alejandro Gil, who also had more experience in documentary and television. The chance to film a script that he had already written, using just one location, a few actors, and without the need of a big budget, was all the impetus he required. In the story, a man haunted by his past and unable to understand humankind decides to isolate himself from reality. The combination of images, music, and art direction, with the balanced, collective efforts of the cast suggests that we are in the presence of a talented director, and need only to wait for him to put that talent to work in the service of a story of greater transcendence.

Other titles worth mentioning are: *La noche de los inocentes* by Arturo Sotto; *Kangamba*, a military drama by Rogelio París; *Los dioses rotos*, the first film of Ernesto Daranas, whose background had been mostly in television, and *La anunciación*, for which the veteran Enrique Pineda Barnet got behind the digital camera of Cuban cinema nearly two decades after the raucous success of *La bella del Alhambra* (1989). The body governing audiovisual production in Cuba allowed Tomás Piard, with his extremely personal style, to translate the universe of writer José Lezama Lima into images using a 'high definition' camera in *El viajero inmóvil* (2008), inspired by passages of the novel *Paradiso*.

In the meantime, Leornardo Pérez, known for his work with the renewed Animation Studies of the ICAIC, completed his ambitious first attempt at feature film, *H2O*, which was shot in 2005. Alfredo Ureta, the winner of numerous awards for his documentaries and *'video clips'* ventured into narrative film at the end of 2006 with *La ausencia*. It is the story of a man who, after living outside Cuba for fifteen years, returns and faces the encounter with his roots. *La ausencia* is a *'road movie'* that presents subjects like displacement, emigration and familiar alienation up close.

Favorable winds now encourage the productions of the ICAIC, which is regaining its pulse after years of uncertainty and a drop in pressure due to the events of the Special Period.

Parenthesis for reed flute and *tumbadora*: the Gabo School comes of age[22]

Nearly a quarter of a century has passed since that afternoon on which, amid the scent of fresh paint and recently planted vegetation on the grounds of San Tranquilino, just a few kilometers from San Antonio de los Baños in the southeast of Havana province, the participants in the eighth International Festival of New Latin American Cinema would attend the opening ceremony of the International School of Film and Television (EICTV); Commander in Chief Fidel Castro, presiding. In his opening remarks – "Trabajadores de la luz" – Fernando Birri read the birth certificate of the School, signed by the Latin American Filmmakers Committee, the New Latin American Cinema Foundation (created one year earlier in the din of the Festival), along with all the members

---

[22] TN: The *tumbadora* is a drum played in Cuba, similar to the Conga; "Gabo" is a commonly used nickname for the Colombian author Gabriel García Márquez.

of a teaching center, through which Havana's competition took on the quality of a Festival-classroom.

This annual gathering of filmmakers from all over Latin America had, for years, served as a series of meetings that would create that "space for the production of a global audiovisual image" designed to turn out "telefilmmakers." As always, the ICAIC opened its doors to any Latin American director who came with his reels on his back to edit works that would have been impossible to make in his home country; others found, in the eaves of the film library, the possibility of preserving unforgettable images that any dictatorship would have been proud to have made disappear. The hand held out in solidarity by Cuban cinema made possible, to a great extent, the utopia of Latin American cinema. That old dream of having a school for the professionals of New Latin American Cinema that would allow them not to have to enroll in European or North American academies finally became a tangential reality.

One definitive spark was the phone call by which Julio García-Espinosa, the director of the ICAIC and of the Festival at the time, would awaken Birri one morning in Rome, the same city in which years earlier they and Titón, intoxicated by the influence of the Neo-realists, had studied in the Center of Experimental Cinema. At the seventh Festival of New Latin American Cinema, Fidel Castro had been receptive to the idea of creating the School; the decisive first step was taken immediately: the Cuban government donated the land, the fittings and the basic equipment to lay the foundations of the dream shared by so many filmmakers across the continent. It appeared, in the words of Birri, the School's first Director, on the internationalist horizon of the audiovisual collective at Tres Mundos.[23]

---

[23] TN: "Tres Mundos" is another name for the Escuela Internacional de Cine y Televisión (EICTV) at San Antonio de Los Baños.

"This School is made with prefabricated blocks of cement, but not with prefabricated ideas. This School is a school of artistic development: in the Arts, freedom comes first," he stipulated at the opening ceremony of the institution established with the non-academic as the cornerstone of its labors.

The teaching aspect of the New Latin American Cinema Foundation, presided over by Gabriel García Márquez, came to life as a non-governmental organization. As Julio García-Espinosa, its founder and sixth director, would state on one occasion, "It is not only an educational project, it is also a life project. Here, we study while we learn about ourselves. It is not a school that marginalizes the technical, but it is not a technocratic school; it is a school that fosters the development of talent, which sees itself as a factory of creative energy."

From the classrooms of this "flagship of magical realism", as it was described by a Spanish journalist who, in 1999, set it alongside the University of Southern California, New York University, and the mythical FEMIS in Paris as one of the most important film schools in the world – have emerged several generations of "telefilmmakers" from the continent.[24] Among these, or in any of the hallways of the buildings in which all kinds of projects are being developed, can be counted a diverse group of working filmmakers so prestigious that mentioning only a few of their names would

---

[24] From its inception to September 2005, the total number of students to graduate from the standard course has risen to 540, 441 of whom are from Latin America and the Caribbean. The statistics are as follows: Argentina (25); Barbados (1); Belize (1); Bolivia (21); Brazil (56); Chile (25); Colombia (44); Costa Rica (15); Cuba (66); Ecuador (15); El Salvador (6); Guatemala (5); Haiti (3); Honduras (13); Jamaica (2); Mexico (23); Nicaragua (5); Panama (14); Paraguay (7); Peru (22); Puerto Rico (15); The Dominican Republic (11); Trinidad and Tobago (1); Uruguay (12); Venezuela (33). There was no graduating class in 2006 because the program was extended to three years.

be an injustice to the rest, who make a special place in their calendar every year to live with the students in San Antonio de los Baños, one of the most filmed towns in the world.

Many of its graduates have enjoyed impressive careers as the directors of acclaimed feature films or narrative shorts, editors, directors of photography, sound operators or screenwriters, to name just a few of the specializations offered at the School, which will be entering its third year of increasingly integrated training. Some have been recognized with awards in the Festival, which – year after year – welcomes them into its classrooms; others are invited to sit on the juries while new students submit their work to the competition in a perpetual cycle.

After two decades of the existence of the "Gabo School," the product of a collective gestation that was long overdue in the years of the ICAIC and the Havana Festival, García-Espinosa, in his innate role as a founder, wrote: "When we started the EICTV, Gabo said to us: 'You could end up being the most expensive unemployed people in the world.' We have tried to make sure that his words do not come true.[25]

That afternoon in 1986, wearing the blue overalls that were the uniform of the students from "the school," Birri said that they were all in the presence of "the result of necessity, experience, and the critical – as well as self-critical – reflections of thirty years of New Latin American Cinema." This unusual school, the "productive center of creative energy for audiovisual image. (A factory of the eye and ear, a laboratory of the eye and ear, a theme park for the eye and ear)" continues in its inexhaustible efforts to train Latin American filmmakers, even when its contributions extend to Asia, Africa, and Europe. Faced with the unstable panorama of cinema in their respective countries, some

---

[25] García-Espinosa, Julio. "La Escuela del Gabo" in *Cine Cubano* vol. 162 (Oct-Dec 2006). 2-4.

tend to insert themselves within other, more developed traditions, such as that of Spain, where professionals forged in the – mythical, for many – School of San Antonio de los Baños are so highly regarded that it is not unusual to find their names both in the credits of important films and as recipients of awards like the Academy of Cinematic Arts and Sciences' Goya.

Coda, to a bongo rhythm

Getting a sense of which films from the period between 1959 and 2008 were the most significant in the trajectory of Cuban cinema and providing an overview of its most important moments were the aims of a rigorous effort to select the best films of Cuban cinema announced recently by the Cuban Association of Film Journalists (an offshoot of FIPRESCI, the International Federation of Film Critics). The first ten titles to be chosen were: *Memorias del subdesarrollo* (1968), by Tomás Gutiérrez Alea; *Lucía* (1968), by Humberto Solás; *Fresa y chocolate* (1993), by Gutiérrez Alea and Juan Carlos Tabío; *Madagascar* (1994), by Fernando Pérez; *Papeles secundarios* (1989), by Orlando Rojas; *La muerte de un burócrata* (1966), by Gutiérrez Alea; *La primera carta al machete* (1969), by Manuel Octavio Gómez; *Retrato de Teresa* (1979), by Pastor Vega; *La bella del Alhambra* (1985), by Enrique Pineda Barnet and *La última cena* (1976), also directed by 'Titón.'

Now! (1965) by Santiago Álvarez takes first place in the documentary category, followed by *Por primera vez* (1967), by Octavio Cortázar; *Suite Habana* (2003), by Fernando Pérez; *Coffea Arábiga* (1968), by Nicolás Guillén Landrián; *L.B.J.* (1968), by Santiago Álvarez; *Vaqueros del Cauto* (1965), by Oscar Valdés; *Ociel del Toa* (1965), by Guillén Landrián; *Ciclón* (1963), by Santiago Álvarez; *Nosotros, la música*

(1964), by Rogelio París and *Hanoi, martes 13* (1967), another classic by Santiago Álvarez.

Juan Padrón's *Vampiros en La Habana* (1985), holds first place in the animation category, followed by his first feature, *Elpidio Valdés* (1978); the adult humor of *Filminutos* (various contributors); *Elpidio Valdés contra dólar y cañón* (1983), also by Padrón, whose shorts, starring the Mambi guerilla of Elpidio Valdés, were included as well, particularly the one in which he faces off against the New York City police force (1976); the short ¡*Viva papi!* (1982), and the series *Quinoscopios* (1986-87), about the drawings of the Argentinean artist Joaquín Lavado (Quino). *El bohío* (1984), by Mario Rivas and *El paso del Yabebirí* (1987), created by Tulio Raggi, round out the selection.

Memorias del subdesarrollo, which just led off the selection of the best Ibero-American films presented by the website Notecine.com, earlier held 88th place in *The History of Cinema in 150 Films*, sponsored by the International Federation of Film Societies in 1976, and was at the head of the selection of *The Best Films of the Third World 1968-1978*, in which *Lucía* occupied fourth place, according to the Canadian journal *Take One*. Both titles are part of *The Ten Best Films of Ibero-American Cinema*, according to a widespread vote during the seventh Huelva Festival (1991). The anthology of Latin American cinema proposed by the XXXVI International Film Week at Valladolid (1991) also included these distinguished works by Gutiérrez Alea and Humberto Solás, to which Sara Gómez also contributed, with her *De cierta manera*.

Between the years of 1959 and 2009, Cuban filmmakers produced a total of 243 narrative films,[26] 1,191 documentaries, and 725 animations; added to these are 41 filmic works of a didactic nature produced by the Department of Popular

---

[26] This figure includes shorts, mid-length films and co-productions.

Science (1962-1972), 32 episodes of the series *Popular Encyclopedia* (1961-1963) with entries on different topics, 1,490 installations of the *Noticiero ICAIC Latinoamericano* (1960-1990), from which a series of 14 episodes conceived as monographs (1990-1991) would be derived.

In the artistic landscape, the filmography of Cuban cinema produced by the ICAIC represents a rich visual testimony, a valuable source of information about a history that is constructed day by day, and a prominent element of Cuban cultural patrimony. As Alfredo Guevara, one of its founders, has said, "the work of the artists that make up this – not organization, but Cinematic Artistic Movement – will remain, as they have been, on par with their (our) Revolution."

Half a century separates us from that seminal date of March 24, 1959, when the ICAIC was created by a law that proclaimed in its first article that "Cinema is an art." From *Memorias del subdesarrollo* (Gutiérrez Alea, 1968) to *La edad de la peseta* (2006), artistic transcendence aside, much rain has fallen on Cuban cinema – even more, perhaps, than on García Márquez's Macondo. Different times, stormy and adverse, are stirring and imposing their own rhythms while a promising new generation steps in to relieve the last, bringing fresh blood to the veins of what some have ventured to call New Cuban Cinema, yet the dedication to their utopia remains unchanged.

Father, Country

José Carlos Avellar

I.

"It's okay, Mom, forget about it," São Paulo, March 1990, a cramped apartment next to the *Minhocão*.[27] Paco tries to convince his mother that it is best to forget.

He carries a book back and forth, spends the entire day in his room with that book. She is worried: classes have started and her son has not gone to college yet; she asks permission to come in, softly, says that she doesn't want to disturb, "this book is always with you, isn't it?" She wants to see what book it is, "not Physics, is it?" The answer, "it's something else....I won't tell you now....But, if everything goes well, my life is going to change completely." The partial answer increases the worries of his mother: "Are you going to leave the house? And what about our plans? San Sebastián? Did you forget?" Paco has not forgotten, but he thinks that his mother should forget. "It's okay Mom, forget about San Sebastián, at least for now." A dressmaker alone with her son, Manuela plans to return to her native land. She has sold two more dresses, the money in the savings account is already enough to pay for her and Paco's ticket in thirty-six installments with very low interest, as advertised in the newspaper. "Pay attention, mother," the son insists as the television shows President Fernando Collor assuming

---

[27] TN: An elevated road in the city of São Paulo.

office, "We have no means of getting to Spain now." Manuela in the tone of one who knows that her son is right, says in a small voice that he doesn't understand. It is not a whim. She knows it is not possible, but she wants to go back, he simply cannot keep saying, "forget San Sebastián."

"Forget it, it was stupid." Alex acts distant and cold when she gets rid of Paco in the yard of the Cabo Espinchel to catch the bus back to Lisbon.

"I am not your mother! Yesterday night...." – she says – "That's it, it's over! It was stupid! Away from home, away from everything, alone, Paco doesn't know what to do. He wakes up. Alex is not there, he calls for her without any answer. He searches in the emptiness, walks in the yard in no particular direction, sees Alex far away, runs, grabs her arm firmly, he asks angrily, "Where are you going? You are going to leave me here!" he protests, and, even angrier, commands: "Do not run away!" She moves away with an angry face that says there is nothing to be done, she is going back to Lisbon. He screams aggressively "Who are you? Who the hell do you think you are?" Paco, disoriented, thinks that Alex is his only chance of getting the money that they promised to deliver in Lisbon, in order to continue the trip to San Sebastián. Alex, frightened, thinks that Paco is involved in what happened to Miguel and tries to get rid of him. Strangers to each other, they neither know one another nor the situation in which they find themselves; they are two foreigners in a foreign land, exiled Brazilians in Portugal.[28]

---

[28] On exile, Walter Salles and Daniela Thomas comment that it is "Not the political exile from the time of the dictatorship, but a new one, economic, that is transforming the Brazil of the 90's into a country of immigration for the first time in five hundred years. Here appears the image of the foreign land as an idealized solution, the absence of perspective, self image, identity." The directors continue: "The geography of this exile in *Terra estrangeira* is Portugal. It is no longer the nearby, complacent,

The spectator follows the tense argument and the exaggerated gestures of the two youngsters guided by a different tension than that which the characters experience. What really matters, in this scene and in the movie as a whole, is not exactly the action in the picture, but the picture as an action.

The tone of the image, a black and white with dense blacks, and the framing, the angle and the movement of the camera, make *Terra Estrangeira* (1996), by Walter Salles and Daniela Thomas something like a fable, a pretended passion, to use the words of a character that passes fleetingly across the screen, at the margin of the protagonists' adventure: the actress that in theater recites one of Hamlet's speeches. The truth is that this character is not only at the edge of the story told in the movie, she is equally at the edge of the image in which she (hardly) appears; the camera is located next to Paco, who has just entered the theater through the service door, and sees the stage from the point where he is located. He sees the stage from the aisle, next to the machine operator and lighting technician, between ropes, large screens and wooden frames that support the scenery. While showing the materials that, behind the scenes and out of the reach of the public's eyes, help to support the scene of the theater, the movie reveals part of the dramatic materials that (though not hidden, they are at least not evident in the image) support the cinematographic scene. Onstage, while talking about the actor's work, the character in fact discusses the work of the film, but the meaning of

---

possible father/country, but a land in a crisis of identity, crisis like ours, that refuses its children, Brazilians, Angolans, Mozambicans, Cape Verdeans – mirroring the way the Portuguese themselves are treated by the rest of Europe." In *"Desejo de cinema"* the text presented at the opening of the film in 1995 and included in the book *Terra estrangeira* with photographic reproductions of stills from the film. Rio de Janeiro: Editora Relume Dumará, 1997.

the latter (or the former?) will only become clear at the end of the projection, when very probably, the spectator will not remember any of what the actress had said. After having forgotten what he had heard, he truly understands what he has heard to be forgotten:

"Isn't it monstrous that this actor, for a fable, a pretended passion, can force the soul to feel what he wants, in a way that his face turns pale? He has tears in his eyes, anguish in his expression, his voice trembles, and all his looks adjust themselves to what he intends."

The film, in a way, does the same. The same and simultaneously the opposite, because in it the soul feels the things it doesn't want to feel – the oppressive day to day that provokes a tear in the eye, anguish in the expression, a paleness in the face and a tremor in the voice – and forces everything that one really feels to become a fable, a pretended passion.

What becomes apparent as Paco runs after Alex in the convent yard is not Paco, or Alex, or even the yard; it is not the characters that run or the scenery through which they move. What one really sees is the design, almost an abstract of the image, the way the camera reveals first a cross in a picture marked by two diagonal lines, one to the right, the other to the left – straight , wide, dark lines, in search of a point of escape in a distant, twisted, unbalanced horizon.

At first we experience the place in which we are located – we, the spectators and they, the characters – as a foreign land. This place (the yard and the projection room, the physical space of the setting and the magical space of the cinema), this one here and all the other visible places in the screen, everything else that the sight reaches, appear as a land that transforms people into nobodies – the cinema is the ideal place for the spectator to lose himself in a amusing game in which one pretends to be nobody, moves into the other reality of the film. On the screen, the transformation into nobody is a condition imposed upon the characters by the aridity of the dramatic space: the dark street under an elevated road in São Paulo, the subway in Lisbon, the building crushed by the big advertisement stuck to its façade, Pedro's bookstore, Igor's antique store, the Hotel dos Viajantes in Lisbon and Manuela's apartment in São Paulo, the open space in Cabo Espichel; all these spaces crush and reduce the characters to nothing. Paco does not understand why Alex left him alone: "Who are you? Who the hell do you think you are?" But before Alex answers, even before Paco phrases the question, it is answered by the image of him running toward her: she is a small scribble with no precise shape that moves wandering in a large dimension geometric order. She is nothing. She is nobody running away from some other nobody. A nobody that suffers because of the death of a third nobody. When she finally screams the answer, when she commands Paco to forget, to vanish, disappear, go back to Brazil, Alex repeats what the image expressed before: "I am nobody. And you, even less! And the other nobody was killed three days ago."

Terra estrangeira tells the story of a specific time: it happens in the two weeks between Collor assuming office, on March 15, 1990, and the first of April in the same year, the anniversary of the military coup in 1964 and All Fools' day. It tells of "Brazilians lost in themselves" as absolute foreigners, not just going more and more toward nowhere, but also coming more and more from nowhere, observes José Miguel Wisnik, who created the sound track of the film, in the press release. "We wanted, consciously, to tell a story that started from the documentary, the chaos caused by the Collor plan, ending up in a fiction," Walter and Daniela explain. "Maybe because we were overly threatened by the capacity of the television to control and define the recent past of Brazil, we exempted ourselves from dealing with contemporary reality in the cinema. But there is something fascinating about the possibility of making an urgent film that discussed something that changed the country's entire life."[29]

The film on the screen, this process of construction that jumps from a fact that really happened to fiction, makes the spectator follow the reverse path which starts in fiction and ends in a documentary. On the screen, what really counts is the spectacle: what the picture says, what the image makes one feel. It doesn't matter that Alex's revolver doesn't have

---

[29] José Miguel Wisnik in the press materials for *Terra estrangeira*, September 1995: "It has already been said in several ways that in Brazil one lives the chronic lack of the father figure to set a limit to pleasure and provide names for the subjects. Along these lines, the Italian psychoanalyst Contardo Calligaris says, for example, that the colonizer, who came to enjoy America without assuming the weight of their intervention is a predator that exploits the land and at the same time disqualifies it. The immigrant settler, comes in search of a name and a dignity that the colonizer doesn't give him, making him evoke the native land as a nostalgic and irreversible good. Curiously, *Terra estrangeira* takes place in this intersection: a son without parents suffers, or inherits, the mortal struggle between the predator colonizer in his ultimate form (Collor) and the unrealized desire of the Basque immigrant mother of feeling again *in loco* the scent of the native land." This observation made by Walter Salles and Daniela Thomas in *"Desejo de cinema."* It was made at the opening of the movie in 1995, and included in the book *Terra estrangeira*, Relume Dumará. In a statement to the magazines *Cinemais*, (vol.9, January/February 1998), Walter Salles also says that "It was one of the first films after we took the country back, and we had the desire to make cinema again in a way that was possible in that moment. It would be as though you, after not being able to speak your language, got permission to talk again, four years latter. Then, every syllable, every phrase, every word, acquires - you know? - a very special sensation. And the film (...) about the search for identity, the film about the crisis and the search for (and with) identity" a kind of flirtation with the idea of new cinema: get a camera in your hand and point it at something, make cinema in a state of emergency."

bullets, it is the gesture of suicide that counts: the revolver to the head, the finger on the trigger, the dry noise of the shot. Image is fiction, it doesn't document, it doesn't portray, it doesn't mirror: it builds a critical representation, it thinks of exile, a life lost in a foreign land, as a suicide.

The immediately visible is what counts: the revolver to the head, the fork against the neck, the diamonds at the violinist's foot, the Hope panties under the Mash underwear, the car at the border gate, the couple in the stranded ship on the beach, the visual verse that incorporates the lyrics of *Vapor barato* sang later: "Yes, I am so tired but not to tell you that I am leaving. I am going to catch that old ship."[30] The image counts, the purely cinematic action: Manuela's desperate face in front of Minister Zélia Cardoso de Mello's distorted face in the television as she announces the confiscation of savings accounts. Manuela dead on the sofa and the television still on without an image, a smoking gun after the shot. What leaps out at the eye counts: the minister, from inside the television, got her hands on Manuela's savings account, as Nhinhinha from *A terceira imagem do rio*, by Nelson Pereira dos Santos (1993), put her hand into the television and grabbed candies from a chocolate advertisement to give as a gift to her grandmother sitting next to her on the living room sofa. The immediately visible counts: the minister from the television robbed and killed Manuela, transformed the country into a nowhere, transformed the Brazilians into nobodies. This is how the country, in the middle of March 1990, appears to the characters and to the spectators of *Terra estrangeira*, as a nowhere. With fiction held up to the eye like a magnifying glass, like contact lenses, the spectator can then return to reality with a critical filter in order to better decipher the pressure that tried to transform him into nobody or even less.

---

[30] *Vapor barato*, by Luis Melodia, performed in the film by Gal Costa.

Nobody and Even Less are sitting at the edge of Europe. "You have no idea where you are, do you?" asks Nobody, only to answer: "This here is the end!" The shot starts with the sea. The camera moves back to show both their backs: Nobody, Alex, and Even Less, Paco. "Courage, isn't it? Crossing this sea 500 years ago," continues Nobody, "that's because they thought that paradise was there." She points to the horizon, commenting sadly under her breath, "Poor Portuguese, that ended up discovering Brazil..." Paco laughs, Alex cuts his laughter short: "What are you laughing at?"

Nobody feels a cold sensation in her spine when she thinks about going back to Brazil. She wants to go away to some other land. The more time passes, the more she finds herself a foreigner. In her search for money to get away, she decides to sell her passport, but the buyer says, "*a Brazilian passport isn't worth anything these days.*"

Even Less, who does not even have the money to pay for his mother's burial ("That much? Can't be!") doesn't understand anything anymore, feels himself a foreigner in his own land ("The entire country went crazy!"), and lets himself to be pushed into an adventure in another foreign land, "The ideal place to lose somebody or to lose yourself," as Pedro, the bookseller to whom he goes for information about Miguel, another Nobody "killed three days ago," observes.

With no land to call their own, Alex and Paco live out the verse of Carlos Drummond de Andrade in *Hino Nacional* as a tragedy: *"There is no Brazil. We need to forget Brazil."*[31]

---

[31] Drummond de Andrade, Carlos. "Hino Nacional." *Brejo das almas*, published in Belo Horizonte in 1934.

II.

"These damned photographs should not exist, so people wouldn't have to remember." Dora walks with Josué in Vila do João, in Walter Salles' *Central do Brasil* (1998). The camera walks with them, sometimes a little behind, other times a little ahead. Almost at the end of the trip, near the house where she expects to meet Josué's father, Dora asks if the boy will be able to recognize his father when he meets him. "Your mother had a picture of your father?" Yes, he says, "She did!" She wants to know if Josué can remember his father's face. He doesn't know. "There are times that I remember (*alembro*), then it dissolves in my head." Dora, who sometimes also forgot her father's face, says that photography should not exist so people would not have to remember, "They could let us forget," and says that she left home when she was 16 years old and never got to see her father again. Years later, "I froze," when she ran into her father in the street; "So, I had the guts and went to talk to him: do you recognize me? Do you remember? Do you remember me?" She saw in his face that he did not, "he did not remember his own daughter!" He talked to her as though she were anybody: "Girl! Come here! How could I forget a cute young lady like you…" She cut off the conversation and left. "I told the dirty old man that I had the wrong person and left." Silence. And then Dora dryly concludes, in half a voice: "I learned that he died soon after." A longer silence. She interrupts the walk, gives Josué a friendly slap on the arm, changes her tone and asks: "Do you understand?" He did not, did not understand, "What did I do?" so Dora explains, "In a while you will forget me too." He denies it, "I don't want to forget you," but she says that there is no way, "It won't work." She moves offscreen, leaving Josué alone in the picture and proclaims "You are going to forget me!"

In the cinema, while a film is on the screen, the spectator is half Dora and half Josué, half Paco and half Alex: he is in the ideal place and condition to forget himself; but since he has the photography, he doesn't forget completely.

Through the photography, without taking his eyes off the story of Alex and Paco, the spectator also sees the viewpoint from which the story of *Terra estrangeira* is told. He perceives only one because simultaneously he perceives the other: he sees the film as though he were next to Nobody and Even Less, sitting at the edge of an abyss, in front of the sea that the Portuguese threw themselves into one day, in search of paradise. The spectator sees Nobody. He sees Even Less. He sees a piece of the sea and this nowhere land and perceives Brazil exactly how it was in 1990, in the first days of Collor's government; a land of nobodies.

In the photography, in particular that in which Dora and Josué are together, one finds an image of the generative impulse of *Central Station*. The film walks at the same time with Dora and with Josué. With her, who moves through the will to forget, and with him, who moves through the will to remember (*alembrar*), to prevent his memories from dissolving in his head. The scene – Dora and Josué, she in the bus, he in Vila do João, both looking at the little picture of them together – the scene, not only for its meaning inside the story in which it exists, but mainly because, apart from its first and fundamental sense, it is a possible representation of the process of the construction of the film. The scene tells us that what is really important is the photography.

The picture in the monocle confirms a shift in the sensitivity of the letter writer. Dora, when she left the Vila do João, confesses to Josué that it has been a long time since she has sent a letter to anyone at all. "Now I am sending this letter to you." She says that he was right, that his father was going to reappear and he would be certainly everything that Josué said he was. She remembers her father "taking me in the locomotive that he rode. He let me, a little girl, blow the whistle of the train during the entire trip." She says that she misses her father, that she misses everything, that she is afraid that one day Josué will forget her. "When you want to remember me, take a look at the little picture that we took together," she writes, happy that photography exists for us to remember.

Although at first glance it seems as if the photography is only interested in following what the characters are doing, attentively but discreetly, like someone who doesn't want to be noticed, it also suggests that we see *Central Station* as a picture – a picture not so different from the one of Dora and Josué in the Bom Jesus do Norte market. A picture not to forget. A picture to remember a forgotten country, the country "that people do not even want to see, that people sweep under the rug."[32]

Pictures: it is not only the picture that makes Josué remember his father, or the picture on the wall at his brothers' home, or even the picture that Josué and Dora took at the market. There are also the "pictures" of people who dictate the letters to Dora, since all these anonymous characters appear in images that forget everything else in order to concentrate the picture of their faces. And there are pictures of landscapes discovered along the trip. The camera, which saw the city with a myopia identical to Dora's, in pictures without any depth, closed in the first shot of the scene; the camera, when leaving Rio de Janeiro, opens its eyes with a curiosity identical to Josué's. Little by little the shots become more open, and more colorful, clear and

---

[32] Salles, Walter. "O documentário como socorro nobre da ficção," interview with *Cinemais* (vol.9, January/ February 1998). 15.

deep. Pictures: photography as the memory of the father and of the country.[33]

The image in *Central do Brasil* may bring the spectator to understand better what is being photographed in addition to the photography itself. In *Terra Estrangeira*, on the other hand, it is more the "photographic impulse," more the photography than the photographed. The camera "is the one that demonstrates the state of the characters." Handheld, the camera "transmits the crisis at the beginning of the 90s." In the apartment where Paco lives with his mother, on a street narrowed by buildings, posters and elevated roads, in the confusion of the bar and the piles of objects in the antique store, what one sees is that one cannot see any space; the image doesn't portray a fragment of the photographed reality - that precise piece of São Paulo- but rather the sensation of the country as wall, ceiling, shadow without door or window, without a horizon. Wall, shadow, prison, nowhere, the will to run away; "that the magic cloak be mine and carry me to foreign lands." Paco, in the essay, borrows his words from Goethe's Faust.

Following *Central do Brasil*, in *Abril despedaçado* (2001) the photography again participates as an active character. What in *Terra estrangeira* was in black and white, a handheld camera and unsteady picture, in *Abril despedaçado* is in color, a steady and tense picture; less action and more reflection. Photography lives another tragedy, parallel to the one lived in the photographed scene. That's how it is

---

[33] "The places where the possibility of migration is very present rouse the need for pictorial capture of the departed. If you go into a home in the northeast of Brazil, you will find an impressive number of pictures and images that allow the remembrance of the ones that left. The image is not decorative, as it often is for us. It is part of memory, of a need almost as intrinsic as that of survival. A way of resisting is to remember the person who is gone." Salles, Walter. "O documentário como socorro nobre da ficção," interview with *Cinemais* (vol. 9, January/ February 1998). 23 - 24.

in the cinema: every image is plural, exists in fusion with another, or with others, is inseparable from them, moves constantly from one to the other of its poles. And because it essentially fuses and multiplies the image of the search for the father, this story is also the search for the country and the search for the self. March 1990 is also April 1500. And soon, we will notice, April is also nowhere, the fragmented, the divided, the foreign, the dry, the place without photography, the place of forgetting.

III.

"Well, better forget it, anyway!"

From the kitchen the mother observes the younger boy that doesn't let go of the book that he got as a gift, and complains, "Boy! Will you ever put that thing down?" No, he doesn't put it down. He does not know how to read the words, but reads the figures, the story in images of the mermaid that came out of the sea and went inland. The mother doesn't like to see the son with the book in his lap, talking to himself. "Don't you know it is bad for your sight?" But he is not seeing. He wants to remember the imagined story, but sometimes he forgets. The mother concludes with an order: to forget about it anyway.

Throughout *Abril despedaçado* the spectator naturally forgets that the story is told by a boy without a name. He won a name as gift but has not gotten used to it yet, and he decided to tell his own story: his and his older brother, Tonho's, because he has forgotten the story of the mermaid. The film, it seems, also forgets the story teller that knew to read images. Only near the end it returns to its starting point, at the same time it goes to an image previous to the one described here, a beginning before the beginning. Tonho, standing in front of the sea, is almost the Manuel after the final race through the backlands in *Deus e o diabo na terra do sol* ("The backlands will turn into sea, the sea is going to turn into backlands"). The images have different designs, which, paradoxically, is why one makes reference to the other: what makes them similar also highlights the differences between them. Instead of Manuel's nervous race in Glauber's film, Tonho is seen in the lower part of a picture that is dominated by a big wave. An allusion - maybe this is not the exact word - evokes something of a forgotten thing that all of a sudden is sparked in the memory. It doesn't seem to be a quotation, reference or reverence of Glauber's film, but of an image that Walter incorporates in his film because it is part of our cinematic vocabulary. What *Abril despedaçado* says then (after saying what has to be said and concluding the story that it narrates), is that it is at the same time both a whole as a part and a part as a whole. It cites a point of departure (in the style of the image) in *Terra estrangeira* (the definition of landscape). A point of departure in (the human, geographic, politic landscape of) Nelson's *Vidas secas*. A point of departure (in the feeling that, when divided badly, the world goes wrong) in *Deus e o diabo na terra do sol* by Glauber. It says that it starts with the feeling of a common tragic situation as the reason for the relocation of Manuel and Rosa, of Fabiano and of Vitória with the two boys, of Paco and Alex, of Tonho and Pacu, of Josué and Dora. It starts with the sensation that one common tragic condition expels, transforms into the foreign, pushes towards the dry riverbed, obliges one to run from the backlands to the sea, from his place to that other one where the *Hino Nacional* announces: there is no country.

"A movie never exists by itself," insists Walter. Every film "brings with it the memory of cinema,"[34] and with

---

[34] Walter Salles, statements after the prize for *Central do Brasil* in Berlin, reproduced in *Cinemais* (vol.9, January/ February 1998). 39. Among other references to the cinematic memory that composes *Abril despedaçado*

it, in the landscape created by the set of films that are part of that cinema, it happens that this and every film invents itself freely. In this way, the landscape of *Abril despedaçado* is almost the same of *Vidas secas*. We are at the border of emptiness. Near the house, what was once a river- the Riacho das Almas, perhaps a once-prosperous *Brejo das Almas*, with perhaps a third bank like that one that Drummond sang in his *Hino national*. In *Terra estrangeira* we know precisely where and when we are: São Paulo and Lisbon, end of March 1990. In *Abril*, time is shattered: we know where we are, but not exactly when. "This story could have happened in the beginning of the century in the Brazilian backlands, but also at other times and other latitudes," Walter says of his movie, but the observation applies equally to Nelson's *Vidas secas*.[35] The two families are almost the same, father, mother, the older and younger boys. The children of a land burned by the sun in Nelson's film, dream of things from the sea – so, too, the dog that follows the immigrants in their flight from the drought is called Baleia. Walter's children of a shattered land without water also dream of things from the sea, of a mermaid that brings the gift of a book filled with fish. The parents do not dream anymore.

---

we can mention, besides the example of Glauber Rocha and Nelson Pereira da Silva, Humberto Mauro (who, like Salustino, used to say that he was "born dead") and Mario Peixoto (whose full name was Mário Breves Peixoto; Breves, like Tonho and Pacu's father. Of Mario Peixoto, Walter mentions the dialogue between the old blind and Tonho, what was said about the hands of the watch showing the minutes as a kind of announcement of the little time he had left to live, that the arms kept repeating: "one less, one less, one less").

[35] Walter Salles, presentation booklet of *Abril despedaçado*, September of 2001. In truth, *Abril* and *Vidas Secas* bring an indication of date in small inscription in the bottom of the image: Nelson locates Fabiano's family around 1940; Walter places the Breves in 1910.

The father speaks little – if one day he found a river full of water, the father of *Abril despedaçado* could as well do what the father of Nelson Pereira dos Santos's *A Terceira margem do rio* (1994) does: he gets in the river in a canoe and never says a word anymore, never stepping on the ground anymore. The father speaks little. Talking a lot can lead to the fate of Gabriel's father in *O amuleto de Ogum* (Nelson Pereira dos Santos, 1976): murdered, his death ordered by a landowner, even before getting in the story. The mother has just as little to say. The boys talk, yes, – but to each other. There is no conversation between them and the father or with the mother. Meanwhile, the children don't even have names. In *Vidas secas* (in Graciliano Ramos's text and in Nelson's images) they are called "boys" by their parents, the older, old enough to continue the tradition and collect on a debt of blood, has a given name, Tonho. The younger continues to be called "boy" by the parents. He gets a name as a gift from the itinerant artists that pass by searching for a town. He got the name of a fish, because he likes things from the sea that he has never seen: Pacu. The name is a gift from others, not from his parents. The speech, the talk, belongs to others. The little communication in the family is done by gestures and looks. Words, for the mother and for the father, are only useful to indicate tasks that need to be done: "Bring the sugar cane," "Do your chores," "Ask for a truce," "Fix the roof," "Don't talk to strangers." Although very different from each other, the father of *Abril despedaçado* and the father of *Vidas secas* only speak when they don't need words, when they growl a sound to command the ox. Words get in the way.

The younger boy in *Abril despedaçado* gets a book that's filled with sea creatures rather than words. Fish that look like the dog Baleia in Graciliano and Nelson. That look like the fish-dog of Manuel de Barros (*um peixe esquisito pra cachorro* from the book of pre-things).³⁶ As the sea creatures awake, so does the will to use words, the father pulls out the book from the son's hands. Words are hell.

The older boy of *Vidas secas* sees the folk healer sending everyone to hell and asks: "What is hell?" He looks for the father, looks for the mother, asks again; he wants to know if the mother was there to know how it was. As an answer, a punch in the head by the mother. He holds on to Baleia in the thin shade of a tree that is not entirely a tree, repeating the unknown word: hell, hell, hell. The older boy of *Abril despedaçado* tries to say something about the hellish life they're living, but the father screams a prohibition beginning with the words: "Shut up!" The mother sadly obeys, even before hearing to the order. Hers is a silence that cries. The father is a silence that snarls.

The hell that the families in *Abril despedaçado* and *Vidas secas* face is almost the same: in Nelson Pereira dos Santos's film, the father is pressured by the impossibility of articulating a reaction to the unfair order in which he lives: he walks around with the family in a vicious circle, always when the sun particularly strong, in search for a place further south or closer to the sea, in search of a farm that takes him on to work with the cattle. In Walter Salles's film, the father is debilitated by his inability to see that he lives in an unfair order: he walks around with the family without leaving the same place around the *bolandeira*.³⁷ The recently installed plant production reduces the price of

---

36 Manoel de Barros, "The fish-dog" in *Livro de prè-coisas*: "It was very strange for a fish/ but with not enough scaffolding for a dog (...) It was hard to accept this strange thing/ As a fish, even if it swam. As a dog it did not fall within the possible." Originally published in 1985 and republished in the collection of *Gramatica expositiva do chão*, Civilização Brasileira, Rio de Janeiro, 1990.

37 TN: A wheeled mill for processing yucca.

rapadura[38] and forces the small farmers to produce more and sell for less at the warehouse in town. In this near-hell, a remarkable difference: the portrayal of the father's character. The father of *Vidas secas,* when he punishes the boy fallen in the dry river bed with harsh words, "Stand up condemned by the devil," it comes across in a softer way: he growls because he only knows to talk like an animal, growls as somebody who knows that, one way or another, all of them are condemned by the devil – him, the woman, the boys, the dog Baleia. The father, in *Abril,* is the one who condemns, the devil himself.

The father is followed with admiration by the younger boy and with respect by the older boy in *Vidas secas.* The younger tries to walk with a firm step like his. The older takes care of the sheep as the father takes care of the ox. They make the father a hero that dresses in leather armor in order to tame the wild horse that runs galloping into the desert. They want to be like him. In *Abril despedaçado*, the father is everything the children don't want to be. When the father opens the mouth wide, showing his dirty teeth in a happy outburst of laughter, everybody stops laughing. The sad silence of the children in this moment is captured by the comment of the daughter in *A ostra e o vento,* (Walter Lima Jr., 1966): "I have never seen father happy. Never seen father laugh."

Midway between the children of *Vidas secas* and the children of *Abril,* is Josué of *Central do Brasil* (Walter Salles, 1998): the son in search of the father he doesn't know, the son who invented an ideal father, a carpenter who knows how to do everything with wood. Josué, in the search of his father, finds brothers equally abandoned by their father. He is the son who follows the steps of his older brother in order to oppose himself to the brutality that the father's

---

[38] TN: Raw sugar in brick form.

presence announces. Pacu in *Abril despedaçado* is a fish-boy out of water in the creek of souls, the son that no longer recognizes the father's values.

It may be possible to say that in the days of *Vidas secas* the father was closer to Oedipus than to Laio. Closer to the son pulled from the cradle by the father than the father that gets rid of the newly born son. The father, then, was the father-Oedipus, the one who has killed the father-colonizer and married the mother-country. He was the father that was almost the brother of his children. In the space of *Abril despedaçado,* the father is the one who imposes a tragic destiny upon the son, keeping him from walking freely; the one who orders the son to obey the law and die in the desert.

What is told in one movie continues what is told in the other, as a way of composing another possible story, superposed to the one told in the first place. In the central image of Brazil, there is a feeling that we established ourselves, as a country, exactly like Josué/Joseph becoming Jesus' father: the father is the son of his children. And in the fragmented image of April, the feeling that the country, the law, the father expels, arrests the son in a foreign land until he frees himself in a *Hino Nacional:* "There is no father. We need, we need to forget the father."

IV.

Josué does not forget the father that in reality he does not know. The mother says that the father "was the worst thing that ever happened to me," but the boy wondered; he wanted to know the father. Josué's refusal to forget communicated something about the feeling of the cinema in the 1960's. Dora prefers to forget her father. "A drunk, at home he was an animal and in the street a clown." Dora's forgetting translates something from the feeling of the cinema in the 1990's.

Far from Fabiano of *Vidas secas,* far from the father who isolates himself from everything in *A Terceira margem do rio,* far from the father that Josué wants to find in *Central do Brasil,* the carpenter that "works with wood, knows how to make a table, a chair, a door, tabletop, a house – all by himself," very far from all this, the father in *Abril despedaçado* is closer to the one that Josué's mother (in the letter that she dictates to Dora) wants to forget and to the one that Dora had forgotten, the drunk who wrote a letter to her mother, saying "that he was tired of commuting in the bus every day, meaning my mother, and has decided to catch a taxi, meaning another woman," the one whose nickname was Pimbão, "Look, his name, his nickname was Pimbão." Dora shows Josué someone with a father's face and repeats under her breath: "Pimbão hey Pimbão! ...Clown, hey clown." She is sure, knows the type: "Father? Drunk!" she tells Irene. Father, Josué's too, a drunk! Hit his mother "in the face," hit the boy. "Better off without him." Father: "all the same, all drunks."

In the films of the 1960's, the family relationships and the individual traits of the characters appear out of focus in order to be understood as representations of the political and social scene, in order to move the conflict from the particular to the general. In the movies we started to make in the 1990's, the focus appeared to be on the individual and on family relationships, allowing the characters to be felt, while political and social scene is reaffirmed in the individual and in the family: in the father, in the country. In *Abril despedaçado* the parents, at the funeral of the son of one family killed by the son of another family, behave themselves as chiefs of state meeting to discuss peace, or a truce, after losing many soldiers to war.

The question that the two boys of *Vidas secas* have to face is beyond the family nucleus. The problem is not within the house but outside it. The father, the mother, the older son and the younger son are pressured by the power of the government, by the soldier that provokes Fabiano ("Are you disrespecting me, civilian?"), who beats him up and throws him in jail for the night. He is the all-powerful father and that's why, when Fabiano meets the soldier again, this time very small, skinny, lost in the desert, he contains his desire for revenge ("People think such stupid things!") and says to himself: "Government is government."

The conflict of *Abril despedaçado*, as Walter asserts, is precisely within the house, "between the order imposed by the father and the disorder announced by the younger son." The two boys, one almost an adult and the other a very young boy, confront the father, the power, the government, the tradition that forces them to kill the son of the enemy family because of the yellowing blood on a shirt hoisted above the front door as a sign of mourning and as a war flag. The father of *Abril* does not have a name. The same way that the younger child is the boy, he is the father who pushes the son from the table with a slap in the face, in response to his daring to question the law.

The motif of the story, "the tragic collision of a hero forced to commit a crime that he doesn't want to and the destiny that impels him to go ahead," comes from the book of the same title by the Albanian writer Ismail Kadarè. But the film comes from this book as well as from a study of warring families in Brazil[39] and, as suggested by Kadarè,

---

[39] In a letter sent to the collaborators of the film, shortly before shooting began in July of 2000, Walter Salles said that the important information for the narrative of *Abril despedaçado*, to him, Sergio Machado and Karim Ainouz, inspired by Ismael Kadarè's book, came from *Lutas de familia no Brasil*, written by L.A. da Costa Pinto in the 40's. "The book let us understand how the conflicts that we experience in our country approach the ones lived in the Albania of Kadarè, or in the Greece of Aeschylus. Based on the analysis of the confrontation between the Pires and Camargos families, in São Paulo, and between the Feitosa and the Montes in Ceará, *Lutas de familias no Brasil* proves that the revenge, in

from the study of Greek tragedy. In it, one learn that "before the 7th century, no blood crimes committed were judged by the State," but rather by the families involved in the conflict. They "established their own codes for the reparation of the bloodshed". Part of these codes, "the bloody shirts exposed by the families in conflict in Brazil and in Kadarè's romance", are a fundamental tool for "the communication with the ones who were murdered. The stain on the shirt, when it turned yellow, indicated the consent of the deceased to collect on the debt of blood." As the fights for land between families developed in Brazil as well in the State's absence, "one returned then to Brazil through the Greek theater" – more precisely, through the chorus of Greek theater. It is in the tragedy but in the form of the chorus, at once in and out of the tragedy.

There is a certain tragic element that boosts the character of the father in the films made since the 1990's. It is an external, superior, unquestionable pressure that determines what he has to do: the law, honor, obligation, tradition, destiny; these made the parents their own oppressors and victims. Because of the brutality of their presence, or the aggressiveness of their omission or absence, the parents are seen as both oppressors and victims, victims of a stronger oppression that they imitate because they don't know how to oppose to it. Without pointing out the tragedy lived by the father, there is something in the narration (the picture, the light, the color, the texture of the image) that

---

Brazil, happens in the absence of a regulating state. It's something that appears in a natural spontaneous form, and only stops existing when a stronger and more regulatory power shows up." The text, published in *Cinemais* 31, September/October 2001, quotes parts of the book, the documentary of Eduardo Coutinho, *Exu, uma tragedia setaneja*, of around 40 minutes, made in 1979 for television, which deals with the fight between the Alencar and the Sampaio families in the town of Ex' in Pernanbuco, a conflict with characteristics that are not dissimilar to the ones in *Abril despedaçado*.

moves the attention to the tragedy. *Abril despedaçado* for example: the mother and the father become desperate when it seems like it's all over, the camera sees them from afar, almost forgetting them. It follows Tonho, who doesn't cry or shudder like the father and the mother. It follows him all the way to the sea and descends to transform a gigantic wave into a wall bigger than the screen. The camera sees the parents' suffering, but it does not suffer with them, does not see what they see: it carries inside it something of Salustiano's gaze, lonely and distant; something of Clara's gaze, tender and close; in a fusion of these two, shares the solidarity of one and the tenderness of the other, with the older boy and the younger boy. When the camera looks on from the ground, following Tonho's steps while he walks on dry earth and under the strong sun to collect on the blood debt as his father has ordered; when he spins through the air with the mill or on the swing, with Clara's fire balls, or dances on the tightrope; when he freezes in place in order not to get chewed up by the mill, or when he runs alongside Tonho in the dry and thorny underbrush until he loses his breath – in all these cases, the camera doesn't suffer the tragedy of the characters, but another one; one that comes from understanding the story that it makes visible. It acts upon the scene, inscribes a circle, a straight, winding line, an abstract form, a purely cinematic mark stronger and more visible than the live figures inside the picture. What the spectator really experiences is the tragedy/other of the camera. So, as he doesn't suffer the tragedy of the mother, the father, nor that of the older boy or the younger boy, the spectator enters the image as the chorus on the stage of a Greek tragedy: he regrets, he analyses, he perceives the father as one colonized individual that assaults another; he perceives that the father is a creation of the colonizer.

The father in *Dois filhos de Francisco*, by Breno Silveiro (2005), decides the future of the children, imposes it upon them: both will be singers. And he sets about educating them to make them into what he determined they should be. The father in *A ostra e o vento* by Walter Lima Jr. (1996), prohibits the daughter from leaving the island where they live to avoid her becoming contaminated by the city. The father in Andrucha Waddington's *Eu, tu, eles* (2000), who is not even a father, kidnaps the children his wife had with other husbands and goes to the city to register them as his.

These three characters reveal a central characteristic of the father character in recent Brazilian films: the first one shows us a father as the owner of the children, the other two as the owner that doesn't get to control what he owns. The fathers in Walter Lima and Andrucha's films are coincidentally played by the same actor, Lima Duarte, which makes the double personality of each all the more evident. By combining Josè from *A ostra e o vento*, with Osiris from *Eu, tu, eles*, it becomes possible to see in them the continuation of the father-boss of *Os dois filhos de Francisco* and the representation-reproduction of the authoritarian State in the family space. They cannot be reduced to this, but they are the image of the particular authoritarian state of the 1970's and 1990's: the oppressor that presents himself as the protector. A violent oppressor, yes, but an impotent one.

Another characteristic of this special relationship between father and son reveals itself in *Como nascem os anjos*, (Murilo Salles, 1996), a series of conversations started in *Nunca fomos tão felizes* (1983), in which the father, after a long and unexplained absence, returns to pick the son up from a seminary school and, under the pretext of protecting him, says nothing (about his involvement in the fight against the military dictatorship?). He dies before being able to explain himself to his son. The conversation passes to the father in *Faca de dois gumes* (1989), who provokes the kidnapping and death of his son because, although trying to protect him, he reveals only part of the story in which he is involved. And finally it arrives at the parents in *Como nascem os anjos:* the American, who comes to Rio after abandoning his wife and the daughter, and the Brazilians, whom we know only through conversation or the silence of the abandoned children, Japa and Branquinha. Absent parents, hidden in some space far removed from that in which the film takes place. They moved to the city, moved to another country. In the film that Murilo made soon after, *Seja o que Deus quizer!* (2002), they disappear completely: the parents do not want to know about the children. What was once protective and oppressive all of a sudden shifts from dictatorship to neoliberalism.

The violent side of this absence is exposed when the father in *Bicho de sete cabeças,* (Lais Bodanzky, 2001) checks the son into a hospice to get rid of the shame of having a drug-addicted child in the house. The violent side of this presence is seen when the father in *Deserto feliz,* (Paulo Caldas, 2007) rapes his own daughter. Presence and absence provoke a response almost as incoherent as the illegible scribble of the note the son leaves for the father in Lais's final scene or the daughter's final decision to leave the house and prostitute herself after being sexually assaulted by her father in Paulo's film.

The son in *Bicho de sete cabeças* and the daughter in *Deserto feliz* could call themselves the siblings of Andrè in Luiz Fernando Carvalho's *Lavoura arcaica* (2001), and repeat with him: "In my sickness there is a powerful seed of health," or: "Every order carries the seed of disorder; every clarity, a seed of obscurity." The father in Lais's film could repeat what the father in Luiz Fernando's film says, that patience is the greatest virtue, that it is needed to speak clearly and at the appropriate time. The two of them could say nothing and simply laugh with their dirty teeth as the fathers in *Abril despedaçado* and *Deserto feliz* do. With different gestures, all three of them assault their children.

The confused speech of the son as he confronts his father in *Lavoura arcaica* confirms it: he no longer recognizes the values that oppress him. The father says that his heart is crushed when he sees the marks of suffering on his son's face and the confusion that dominates his mind. He says that it is very important to talk. He says that, in order for people to understand each other, it is necessary to set their ideas out in order, word by word. He says that no one should despair, that everything is a matter of patience, that there is no waiting without reward. The son answers that he feels as though his hands were tied and that he will not tie his feet as well by his own initiative. On the screen, Luiz Fernando reproduces the text from chapter 25 of Raduan Nassar's *Lavoura arcaica* that inspired the film, word by word.

One can not expect a prisoner to serve in good will in the jailer's house: in the same way, it would be absurd to expect an affectionate hug from the father whose limbs we have amputated; more absurd still is the villainy of the cripple who, lacking hands, uses his feet to applaud his executioner, acts like someone with the proverbial patience of the ox that, in addition to the weight of the pole, asks that the yoke be tightened around its neck. He becomes uglier, the ugly man who applauds beauty... and the poorest poor man who applauds the rich, the smallest small man who applauds the big, the shortest short man who applauds the tall, and so on. Immature or not, I don't recognize the values that crush me anymore, I find it a sad make-believe existence of a third party, and I don't understand how one sees nobility in mimicking the destitute; the victim that noisily approves his oppressor makes himself double prisoner, unless he debases this pantomime with his cynicism.[40]

---

[40] Raduan Nassar, *Lavoura arcaica*. São Paulo: Companhia das Letras, third edition, 1996.

The same thing, and with a similar or even greater impact, is expressed by Tonho's silence at the end of *Abril despedaçado* when he abandons the house and goes towards the sea (as Paco and Alex set out one day for a ship stuck in the middle of the sea in *Terra estrangeira*). Tonho goes into exile, indifferent to the father's desperation, on a trip that composes itself as the counterpoint to the one realized by Josué, who goes in search of his father.

In this journey to the central question of Brazil, with stop-overs in Albanian literature and Greek theater, in the traveler's hotel and Vila João, the most important thing is to show that, in the search, confrontation, denial or reinvention of the father, they, the children, find themselves. The father (country?) and the mother (homeland?) are the initiators of the stories told in these films, for what they do and what they don't do. But it is not exactly with them that the camera occupies itself. In this sense, *Terra estrangeira*, *Central do Brasil* and *Abril despedaçado* establish a dialogue between themselves, compose a reflection over the construction of identity and a language able to express it as the task of brothers. The truth is, in the search for his father, the son constructs his own identity. In the search for his identity, what really matters is the encounter with the other, with the brother involved in the same search. What is sought is not the destination, but the path: not the result, but the process.

What started with Paco and Miguel continues with Josué, Isaías and Moisès. Josué decides to go deep into Brazil to meet his father, who stopped working and drank, drank and drank before vanishing, leaving a half-empty cachaça bottle behind. Isaias thought, "For my father to leave a cachaça bottle in the middle, something must have been terribly wrong." Once he has taken care of it, "he will come back". Moisès, who inherited his taste for woodwork from his father, thinks that it would be best if he had disappeared for good: "He is never coming back." Josué, who found his brothers in the search for his father, is sure: "One day he will come back." What started with Paco, Alex and Miguel surrounded by different and nearly incompatible ways of speaking the same language (Portuguese from Brazil, Portugal and Angola) passes through Josué, Isaias and Moisès and becomes Tonho and Pacu, who just lost their brother Inácio and turn around the mill, as stuck in the backlands as the ship that Alex and Paco find in the middle of the sea.

The parents are the background, the scenery behind the space in which the story happens: the empty yard that separates Alex from Paco in *Terra estrangeira*, the crowded station in *Central do Brasil*, the dry earth in *Abril despedaçado*. What happens, happens between brothers. The older builds a swing to teach the younger to fly; the younger teaches the older that even where all life has dried out, where there is no longer even the creek that used to be there, it is possible to dream of things from the sea, soar with the ideas, imagine another life where nobody kills, nobody dies. Paco is shot in the back while dreaming of a magic cape that brings him to foreign lands. Pacu is shot in the back while dreaming of the day when the backlands will turn into the sea. They used to dream, they dreamt about what the brothers would dream later, they used to dream where dreams seemed impossible.

The death of the children leaves the parents orphaned. In the time of *Vidas secas*, the parents dreamt. A meager dream, but they dreamt: he, of the day they would stop living like animals; she, of the day when the boys would sleep on a leather bed and learn to write and read like Tomás down at the mill. In *Abril*, the dream is shattered. Nothing is left: no project, passion or dream for the parents. They lose everything. Orphans after the son's death, caught in a tragic destiny, they have forgotten everything.

V.

"Forget it, grandpa, nothing is going to change." In the old man's cell, João disagrees with the old man, who has waited anxiously for the arrival of the New Year. "The nine turns into zero, the other nine, and the other nine also, and the one turn into two. It is the year 2000. It is the year of freedom. It is our turn," the old man insists, even after being denied the promised amnesty: "Everything will turn to zero! Nobody will be left to tell the story, you guards of the devil! Let the nine turn into zero! It will turn!" Forget it, "Shut up, grandpa!" repeats João, "So what! Two thousand, three thousand, fifty thousand, it's all the same shit."

In the police storehouse for weapons, Chico pressures a police officer: he wants money not to tell what already knows, Christmas has already passed and he wants to buy a New Year's present to the family. Locked in the cell, the oldest prisoner, the "old man," the "grandpa," waits anxiously for the first day of the millennium. In a narrow living room of the apartment in Copacabana, Maria, a teacher for deaf, teaches a young man to say "Happy New Year," warning him: "2000? This is silly, the years are all the same." In its way of telling, not exactly the story itself, but in the way it is told, with "a shattered quality" that establishes connections between these characters, *O primeiro dia* locates the conflict in the same context as the stories of Josué, Alex and Miguel, of Josué, Moisès and Isaias, of Tonho and Pacu.

But Pedro goes away, disappears, dies, and Maria falls into desperation as though she had been thrown out by her father (the lover, older, is surprised: "You are so young!") The grandfather disappears, dies, and João is thrown out by the law (by the jailer, by the father and the police) to perform the worst of crimes, kill an old accomplice (a friend, a brother), on the roof of a building in Copacabana. João and Maria are like siblings because they are equally victims of the father: the brutality of his presence or the abandonment of his absence. They meet on the roof of a building in Copacabana a little before midnight on December 31, 1999, with the identical desire to end their lives. João wants to escape from the police that are pursuing him after letting him go in order to him murder a former accomplice. Maria wants to escape pain caused by the disappearance of her lover, who vanished from home suddenly, on the last day of the year, leaving a laconic note written on a type writer and taped to the bathroom mirror: "I am sorry Maria, but if there is one day in life to decide something, that day is today."

O primeiro dia is "in some way, a film that asks to be completed by eyes that see it" says Walter, in part due to the origin of the project, the invitation to make a 60-minute film for the television series *2000 visto por,* which led to a "state of emergency" and in part because one more time the process of realization was shared with Daniela Thomas – the retake of the partnership started in *Terra estrangeira*. "We wanted to make a film that was polyphonic in its realization and also polyphonic in relation to the characters. It was necessary to stop the story of one character and pass quickly to another – all this is very organically connected to what happens in Rio. This form is close to the pulse of the city and also to the pulse of Brazilian society as a whole, today. We wanted a narrative that was a little fragmented in order to incorporate several characters in movement in the afternoon and evening of December 31." In the stories that cross one another in *O primeiro dia*, and in the way of establishing this crossing, what is discussed is "the problem of lack of communication, the problems of the inability to see one another. So, for example, the choice of the corridors. We live in a city where the proximity of the slums and the middle and upper class buildings is significant, but their lack of communication is even more so. Geographically, they are almost concomitant, but in practice they don't come into contact. We built *O primeiro dia* around this idea, this need to, at least in the utopic space in the film, create a possibility of communication, of an encounter between the characters that don't look at each other anymore. In a way, it is also a film about the question of looking, re-learning how to look at what people can't see anymore." Daniela comments that "The city is being filmed as a maze; the city is a prison, the apartment corridor, the narrow entrance to the slum, and this labyrinthine quality of the city is the image of the inability, in a way, to look at the other. Only at the end do we see a city of beaches, of sea – until then, it is just a labyrinth."[41]

The image lights up from within the dark screen. Arising like a whisper, a deep breath after a long time without air. Until then the camera snuck among corridors, cells, alleys – no horizon in sight. What emerges from the dark that ends a nocturnal scene with fireworks in Copacabana is an open image, a composition of the horizon. In it, very small, is the figure of a seated woman facing the sea. The man next to her, lying on the terrace of the building, goes unnoticed. She breathes deeply; the air breathes deeply, as well – the

---

[41] Walter Salles and Daniela Thomas, *"O navio, o minhocão, o corredor e a urgent necessidade de reaprender a olhar,"* interview to Josè Carlos Avellar, Icana Bentes, Carlos Alberto Mattos and Geraldo Sarno in *Cinemais* 19, September/October 1999. The interview is partially reproduced in the documentary series *A linguagem do cinema*, produced by Riofilme and directed by Gerardo Sarno: *Walter Salles and Daniela Thomas: a construção do filme em torno de uma imagem*. The question mentioned in the text was proposed by Ivana Bentes: "Two characters that connect *O primeiro dia* to *Terra estrangeira*: The old man, the grandfather played by Nelson Sargento, and the character of Laura Cardoso. They are characters that die in the beginning. They are characters that don't see. He does not see the First, the arrival of the year 2000, nor does she see her native land. It is very interesting.... There is this idea of redemption, someone is going to see the arrival of the First; someone is going to get there."

wind blows and whistles. The short lines of the characters are an extension of this respiration, words in the wind. He speaks as one who thinks out loud: "It's the First! Look at that! Man, I didn't think I would see this day!" He speaks as though he were speaking with grandpa. He looks up to the sky and asks: "She's my forgiveness, isn't she, old man?"

This short conversation in which the two characters speak more to themselves than to each other, might seem to Walter to be "rooted in the Freudian desire to go beyond the father, beyond the point at which the father was, to overcome the paternal territory. I think that, in *Terra estrangeira* as in *O primeiro dia*, this built-in desire, is in there." João, for example, continues Daniela, "fulfills the dream of the old man when he gets to the terrace of the building in Copacabana." Walter and Daniela comment about the similarity between Paco's mother in *Terra estrangeira* and the grandfather in *O primeiro dia*: both characters die in the beginning of the story without fulfilling their dreams of going to San Sebastián (hers) and seeing the year 2000 (his). "In these two films there is, in João and in Paco, the desire to see what the other, though no longer there, did not get to see." João in the beginning of the film had given up on everything, Daniela reminds us, "He says that two thousand, three thousand, fifty thousand are all the same, but after the death of the old man, he embodies the desire of the grandfather, it is as if he had won the desire of the other as a gift. And he goes after the realization of this desire."

As a question left open, suggested but not entirely formulated, it may be suggested here that the son, by reinventing the father and in this way inventing himself, unconsciously fulfills the desire of the grandfather, does what the father of his father was not able to do. The question in suspension: in the morning light in *O primeiro dia*, the colors of the sea and surges through the window of Maria's apartment, which had been closed until then, with an intense white, is a gesture in suspension. Just like the car that crosses the border in *Terra estrangeira*. Like Dora's teary smile in *Central do Brasil*. Like the sea before Tonho in *Abril despedaçado*. The children, here, are like Oedipus in front the Sphinx or in front of blind Tiresias.

VI.

To this picture of recent dialogues/confrontations with the father/country, *Rocha que voa* (2000), the documentary that Eryk Rocha made from statements that his father, Glauber, recorded in Havana in 1971, approaches from a new angle. Walter Salles's *Diários de motocicleta* (2004) presents another, revolutionary angle (there may not be a better way to describe it): here it is the son who creates, invents, generates and educates the parents.

Eryk defines *Rocha que voa* as a film through Glauber. It isn't exactly about Glauber, but *through* him.[42] The father, here, is not a character invented by the son or a character that the son disregards. He is not the one that conducts or the one that oppresses. He is part of the historic context in which the son exists. He is a point of reference, a wild man who speaks, who dreams, ahead of his time and his country. The son no longer needs to confront him in order to constitute himself. On the contrary, the father is the one who allows the son to invent his path freely, in the same direction or in a different one from that chosen by the father, but, nonetheless in continuity with the project of freely inventing the self. The son can freely invent himself from the recognition of starting from a coherent/contradictory

---

[42] This definition can be found in the introduction to the book *Rocha que voa* (Rio de Janeiro: Editora Aeroplano, 2002) along with the two complete interviews with Glauber in Cuba in 1971; one with Janime Sarusky and the other with Daniel Diaz Torres, which were used as the base for the narration.

movement that preceded him. It is part of a whole that asks of him that he invent himself *through* his father, through the critique of the experience of his father – especially because, in this case, the father was more a son than a father.

Walter Salles's *Diários de motocicleta* (2004) is, even more radically, a film less *about* than *through*. Through a character guided not by a relationship (of acceptance or conflict, of continuity or refusal) with the father, but by a process of learning from the relationship with the brother. Inventing himself, defining himself, transform himself from the inside out ("I am not myself; at least, I am not the same as I was before," says Ernesto at the end of the trip), not taking the father figure, or the country, as a reference. The *Hino Nacional of Drummond* becomes broader: *There is no country*, or, at once simpler and more complicated to say: *there is no father*. Only after finding his brother was it possible to constitute his own identity – "one single race, from Mexico to the Strait of Magellan" – it becomes possible to build a centre, a country, a father as product of the free invention of his children.

In the same way, that an artistic expression, as an expression, only exists after the reality meant to be expressed through it; in the same way that an artistic expression can anticipate a reality and express something latent, express an idea that has yet to materialize a reality not yet manifested. In the same way, the son here is the one that anticipates the father and the mother, the one that is born before his parents' birth. Not only in the narrative approach, which first shows only the son and then the father, but because, as in *Central do Brasil*, what we know of the father is mainly from the description of the son, who does not know him. The son, then, is the father of his father. Without forgetting the remarkable differences between the two stories, and not wanting to suggest that the second may have been consciously thought as a complement of the first, it may be possible to say that the adventure of Ernesto in *Diários de motocicleta* picks up where *Central do Brasil* ends: Josué between brother confident of the father's return and the one who is sure that the father has disappeared for good. Just as Josué's father, even without being seen, is at the center of *Central do Brasil*, Che Guevara (not the Ernesto that we see on the screen but the Che that Ernesto finds inside himself during this tour of South America) is at the center of *Diários de motocicleta*. Let us watch these films as they really are: as ex-centric constructions, in which what happens off-screen is just as present as what happens on-screen.

Another eccentric construction, in *Rocha que voa*, Glauber is always at the centre of the image. He is the narrator, the restless voice that proposes an artistic language as poetic expression that anticipates a still non-existent reality, the one who dreams the cinema "as the art that is capable of transforming and unifying South America," as the art that requires the Latin American intellectual, before anything else, "to completely demystify themselves, leave the role of interpreter, of critic behind" without a "concrete, political participation in the story," that requires the artist to "abandon his elite position" and identify himself with the working classes, because "then his art will develop more in depth; it will be better." Glauber, yes. But the one who really speaks is the son, Eryk, in the reorganization of the father's speech and his organization of the language of the image. The son speaks through the father. He talks about him, what happened in Latin America in 60's and 70's, thinks that the impulse that was born yesterday is a challenge today: "Bringing the aesthetic back into contact with the political." In a short testimony, Miriam Talavera reminds us what Glauber proposed during the preparations for *História do Brasil* (1974): "The history of Brazil does not exist. Let's invent the history of Brazil here and now." Eryk does almost the same: Glauber does not exist; let's invent him here, now. Inventing the father, the son adopts a gesture not forgotten, the creative impulse of the father's generation.

VII.

One must not forget what the title-image suggests; *Linha de passe,* by Walter Salles and Daniela Thomas (2008), refers to a way of playing soccer in which the ball is passed from foot to foot in the air, without touching the ground, before a kick to the goal. The title, at the same time, shows the conditions in which people live at the outskirts of the city, expelled from it as Oedipus was expelled from his father's house; this defines the gesture of the son that disregards and reinvents the father's figure as a process, as a moment like the one in which the ball is in the air, on its way to the foot of the next player who will or will not make the pass. This is the way the characters live, looking to balance a life in the air, like the ball in the pass line. This the way that the narration is constructed: the film passes from one character to the other like a gaze that follows the ball in the air, from foot to foot. From the belly of a pregnant woman, we pass to an enormous flag inflated like a ball in the stadium; from hands that shake in the air to welcome the players, to hands that rise to God in the temple; from the players dribbling in the stadium, to the winding motorcycle races in the street; from the enthusiastic scream of the fan to the striker – "Go on, son!" – to the son training to become a professional player; from the scream of goal from the fans in the stadium, to the metallic scream of the small radio where the driver is listening to the game while driving his bus.

There is no father. There is no country. There is a son who invents his father. There is a son who does not know how to invent himself as a father.

Denis, Dario, Dinho and Reginaldo live with the mother, Cleuza, in a meager house half in, half out of São Paulo. The mother, pregnant for the fifth time, works as a maid and is afraid of losing her job because the lady of the house hires a second cleaning lady and suggests that she take time off to take care of the baby that is coming. Of the four children, Denis crisscrosses the city transporting small deliveries by a motorcycle, Dinho works at a gas station, Dario wants to play soccer professionally and the younger boy wants to meet his father.

Cleuza's four children, and the fifth that is about to be born, are from different fathers, all absent. In school, Reginaldo fights with his classmates, who call him "Big black guy, son of the bear." At home, he doesn't believe what his mother says, that his father died and watches him from heaven, and imitates her way of talking in front of the bathroom mirror: "Your father is watching and protecting from where he is, my son. This was his dream for you." He doesn't believe: he is sure that the father forgot that he exists, that the father speeds in his bus in the city streets to make a living, trying not to drop the ball. That's why he spends the days traveling by bus, but only buses whose drivers are black like him. He doesn't get off at the last stop, but repeats the ride to learn from the father that he invented. Learning how to step on the accelerator, how to switch gears, how to turn the steering wheel. He observes the driver attentively like the younger boy observes Fabiano in *Vidas secas,* dreams with his eyes open like Josué standing before Jesus in *Central do Brasil.* Cleuza repeats that the father died (like someone who knows that parents die before the birth of their children). He died, he is in heaven. She doesn't like to see her eleven year-old son leaving the house like this, without any warning. "Where do you think you are going?" – but he is decided, "I am going to look for my father." The father, he imagines, might be one of the black drivers at the bus depot not too far from his house. Without listening to what his mother is screaming at him - "I am both your mother and your father" - like the father, he seats at the steering wheel, turns on the engine and drives the bus by himself along the avenue.

Also on the avenue, Denis races his motorcycle like someone who knows that, for him, the city is made of blind alleys. He, who did not know his father, now has a son, just a baby, who does not recognize his father. Denis goes to visit him, and the baby cries, scared of the stranger that smiles at him from the other side of the window. He is so scared that the mother comments: "Wow! It's like the boy's just seen the devil!"

Almost at the end of the film, Denis repeats what he said earlier through the window to his son in his cradle: "Look at me!" This time, there is no sign of sweetness in the whispered voice that looks for the baby's attention, but there is the anger of a son looking for the attention denied by his father; not a request, but a scream, a command: "Look at me!" The scream comes at the end of a desperate race through the city that ends in an empty space almost outside its limits, an improvised soccer field on packed dirt without grass, wooden poles stuck in the ground as goalposts. From the open field it is possible to see from far the city big buildings. In his search for a way to pay off the motorcycle that he uses for work and get some spare some money for his ex-wife and infant son, Denis decides to take part in robberies. Cars stuck in traffic jams, stopped at red lights; the motorcycle passes quickly and he grabs the bag left on the seat near the driver.

Everything happens very fast: two on the motorcycle, the impact on the car window, the hand that grabs the bag before the driver recovers from the scare, the start, the sudden turn at the corner, the accomplice's fall, the police siren, the car that comes out of nowhere, the accident, the destroyed motorcycle, its driver on the ground, the fright of the car owner, "Don't you look where you're going?" The hand in the pocket though there was a weapon there, the scared silence of the man and the motorcycle driver's command, his face still covered by the helmet: "Get in the car!" and then another command, and another, and another – "Move ahead! Turn to the right! Faster!" – to the improvised soccer field from which one can see the distant city.

The stopped car, the driver's fear increasing as the motorcycle driver removes his helmet and commands what no thief or kidnaper would ever command: "Look at me!" He repeats the command, angrily. "Look at me! Do you see me? Look at me!" The driver shakes with fear as though he had seen the devil. Everything happens very fast (as it happened on the day of the encounter between Oedipus and Laio?) And with a lot of force.

Not because we are watching a film, not only because the motorcycle driver looks at the same time at the driver at his side and at the spectator, when he says "Look at me!" Not because the object of his gaze is forced to keep looking. But because "Look at me!" is half verbal image, addressed to the character at Denis's side: the camera on Denis's face, the line addressed directly to the spectator. In Denis's face the spectator realizes that (like Oedipus when he met with Laio?), in reality, the aggressor is more victim than the aggressor. What is not seen, what is expelled from the picture, what does not have an image – what the father does not want to see – is present here; it shows its face and (unlike Oedipus, who destroys his own eyes) firmly, looking the country in the eye, says with all the rage in the world: "Look at me!"

Peru: Films for After a War

Ricardo Bedoya

1992 was a difficult year for Peru. President Alberto Fujimori suspended the Congress of the Republic in order to govern without opposition while he created a new institution to suit his needs: one based on permanent reelection. Meanwhile, the violence that the Maoist group Sendero Luminoso (Shining Path) had been unleashing on the country since the 1980s hit the capital city of Lima with an attempted bombing on a central street of the residential Miraflores neighborhood. In September of that year, the ideologue and political leader of the Sendero Luminoso, Abimael Guzmán Reynoso, alias "Comrade Gonzalo," was captured. This marked the beginning of the end of the internal warfare, or, rather, the beginning of an unexpected period of calmness that has lasted to this day.

That same year, an authoritarian liberal reform was enacted on the economic system of the country. Among other measures, the Executive Branch repealed the film law passed in 1972 by the military regime of General Juan Velasco Alvarado, which allowed the production of sixty feature films and nearly twelve hundred shorts, all of which were granted mandatory screenings in movie theaters and public funding.

The early days of political peace coincided with a moment of uncertainty for Peruvian cinema, which lost its legislated support from one day to the next. From that time on, each film would have to arrange its own microsystem of production, whether by applying for state subsidies – set aside by a film law passed in 1994 that is still in effect today, though it is frequently ignored – international funding, or private investments large or small, according to the scope of each project.

In a cinematic corpus as discontinuous as Peru's, it is difficult to find family resemblances, follow genealogical lines, or map established traditions. Nonetheless, it is possible to follow the traces left by the experience of recent years in the way political violence is addressed as a recurring event. I would like to examine five Peruvian films made during the period of pacification: *Bajo la piel*, by Francisco Lombardi; *El bien esquivo*, by Augusto Tamayo San Román; and *Días de Santiago*, by Josué Méndez, as well as *Madeinusa* and *La teta asustada*, by Claudia Llosa. Though some of these do not deal directly with the matter of political violence, all do so by refraction, ricochet or tenacity, making the effects of the trauma felt, each in its own way.

The ancestral blade

In 1996, Francisco Lombardi released *Bajo la piel*, an allusive, elliptical thriller that follows the disciplined and precise narrative created by screenwriter Augusto Cabada. Lombardi's film presents a penetrating glimpse into the climate of impunity fostered by the government of Fujimori, which offered amnesty to a paramilitary group known as "Colina," which was responsible for crimes against the country's citizens in the early nineties. The plot is of a genre very much in vogue: a serial killer leaves his victims in a deserted town along the northern coast of Peru with their heads cut off. *Bajo la piel* locates criminal activity within a specific place and time: the murders are carried out with a "tumi," a pre-Columbian ceremonial blade used in the sacrificial rituals of the Moche, which took place on the northern coast of Peru more than a thousand years ago.

The crimes in the film refer back to the violent past of the former inhabitants of Peru, but they also look to the present. The serial killer, an archaeologist who works for the museum at the site, reveals himself to be a sensitive man stifled by the narrowness and mediocrity around him. The technique he employs in removing the heads and eyes of his victims is similar in its perfection to the refined art of his ancestor, the *Degollador* of Túcume, a figure depicted in the art of the region. The figure of the intellectual in the provinces stirred to violence by the mediocrity of his life is similar to that of the marginalized student in *Sin compasión*, Lombardi's previous film, who follows the same path. The feelings of resentment and suspended desire lead them to enact violence in the name of a particular idea of justice, a central preoccupation in Peru in the nineties, when it seemed the country was being consumed by the flames from which it would emerge, renewed, according to the millennialist vision of the Sendero Luminoso. The agents of this fundamentalist violence were, for the most part, youths from the lower or lower middle classes, or sometimes intellectuals from the provinces or the capital frustrated by the limited opportunities for development presented by their environment. Inspired by Jim Thomson's novel *The Killer Inside Me*, *Bajo la piel* delves into the subject of the moral duality of power, embodied by the Chief of Police for the area, who is also a criminal and is beyond the reach of the law. Like Chabrol's portaits of the provinces, though without their sardonic humor, *Bajo la piel* brings the hidden tensions and relationships within a small town to the surface, articulating them through a criminal impulse that implicates all its inhabitants.

Bajo la piel was made at a time when secret graves filled with the charred bodies of students and workers killed by government-backed paramilitary groups were being discovered in Peru. This is the reason for the recurring imagery of the tombs that are discovered, opened and emptied throughout the film; this is the reason for the little skeleton that splits the visual field in the police car, imposing a deathly horizon on the frame; this is the reason for the final shot of the film, which presents an idyllic image of domestic harmony founded on the suppression of past crimes and sins. At the end of the film, one of the killers, who also represents police authority, talks about how happy he is as he reclines in a hammock. He is the head of a family and has been forgiven all his crimes, just as he forgave the lies of his partner. After focusing on him, the camera descends in a travelling shot to pierce the ground of his garden, digging under the grass and the trees fertilized by the bodies buried there. The portrait of the family – which is also one of the country – painted by *Bajo la piel* is based on denial and impunity, and leads back to the central question of those years: how can something solid and lasting be built on the denial of the obvious, the suppression of crimes, compromised ethics, and the impunity of those in power?

Mestizaje, unresolved

El bien esquivo (2001) does not deal directly with social violence at the end of the twentieth century in Peru, but it is marked by a sense of disorientation, of post-traumatic stress, an erratic search for identity and the feeling of living in ill-fated times after having experienced chaos or getting the impression that the end of days have arrived. In other words, it recreates a past moment in order to compare it to the tumultuous present.

It is the story of Jerónimo de Ávila, the *mestizo* son of an indigenous woman and a Spanish man who returns to Peru to look for written proof of his mixed ancestry. The tempestuous days of the conquistadors' arrival, when it seemed to the indigenous population that the world had fallen into absolute disorder and chaos, have come to an end. It is a time of cultural imposition and the eradication of idolatry, designed to eliminate native beliefs and replace them with the cult of Christianity. At the heart of this confusion, the main character tries to claim his heritage and gain proof of his lineage. He experiences, tragically, the impossibility of uncovering his true identity.

El bien esquivo is one of the Peruvian films that explore not only rhythm and fluidity of exposition, but also the ways in which history is represented in Peruvian cinema, with the greatest sense of awareness. The first images of the film, which show the empty "huacas," or ancestral grave sites, the scorpions running across the ground, the greedy men in search of gold that oppress native religions while the indigenous population struggles to protect what is left of their culture, present an approach that is different from that of the average historical film. This movie is not the edifying biography of an exemplary figure or the depiction of the picaresque and licentious lifestyle of the viceroyalty in Lima; nor is it the recreation of a tradition, a literary work, or a pious hagiography, as many other "historical" Peruvian films have been. *El bien esquivo* tells the story of a *mestizo* without a heritage that returns to Peru to find a country fallen into darkness, devastated by fanaticism and cultural violence.

The visual treatment of this tumultuous world favors torchlight and the darkness of the caves in which the prohibited indigenous rites are performed, the ghostly light of a monastery cell and the glint of metal. It is the iconography of a moment of historical inflection and perpetual violence. If there is any trace of the "swashbuckler" film to be found here, it is that the action moves slowly, as though suspended or picking its way through the debris of a recent catastrophe.

The action is situated in the past, but also in the present, not only because the issue of unresolved *mestizo* identity is still of central importance, but because the film invents compositional devices that place it squarely between the old and the new. It favors, for example, the artificiality of representation. Not adornments, glitter, or masquerades; an awareness of the creation of illusion through the mechanisms of cinema. The dialogue spoken by the actors has an obvious literary quality, though it remains clear and convincing; characters are presented in medium or group shots while the background is left dark, shadowy, with a touch of tenebrism or austere expressionism; the acting gives the impression of a final performance, a parting gesture, as though each intervention announced something terrible to come.

Anticlimax is the hallmark of this film; the search leads nowhere and the genealogy is derailed forever. Jerónimo de Ávila watches in silent and serene tension as the evidence of his lineage is destroyed, and bears out the unresolved question of his mixed provenance, which is joined to a sense of being an orphan. Over the course of the story, the fate of the characters falls out of sight. We are in an opaque world: documents neither prove nor indicate, they are burned and proscribed. On the journey toward personal insight, words, order, personal expression, and lineage are all useless paths. Just like identity, the conclusion, affirmation and accomplishment are illusive; this idea is expressed in the very texture of the images and in the ghostly immateriality of the chiaroscuro.

El bien esquivo is an unusual film in the panorama of Peruvian cinema. Not only because it does not hold back in its treatment of the unresolved subject of *mestizaje*, but also for its stylistic cohesiveness, traditionally made yet unequalled in its use of representational modes that evoke the ghostly air of anachronism seen in some of Manoel de Oliveira's films, such as *No, o la vanagloria de mandar*.

The mined city

Días de Santiago, by Josué Méndez (2004), is a study in imbalance: the portrait of an army lawyer, a veteran of conflicts with the Sendero Luminoso and the border wars with Ecuador during the mid-nineties. The narrative point of view is that of the protagonist, a man of iron discipline educated in regulations and strategies, who is unemployed and set loose on the city, which he crisscrosses at full charge as though it were an extension of the field of battle.

Santiago can get neither a perspective on nor answers about his past. He has been made to believe that he is a national hero, but he receives no recognition. His identity escapes him, just as it did Jerónimo de Ávila in *El bien esquivo*. If belonging to a social, national, or familial community presupposes a line of descent that is both accepted and carefully tended, internal conflict breaks these bonds. Santiago is one of the un-reconciled.

The film works from within the codes of the realist tradition, but it unravels the effects of recognition, mimesis and conventional verisimilitude. The hallmarks of urban culture, even the most strident, dissolve in a series of transfigurations that test the limits of normal perception. The city is experienced through an altered, neurotic, point of view that turns the real into the simulacrum of a battle. The film does not denounce a case of social mistreatment or tell a story of "personal interest." It is the journey of a character that feels nostalgia for an anachronistic order and, as such, the journey can be somewhat ridiculous and frustrating.

Días de Santiago calls into question the documentary realism of dramas of social criticism, films caught between raw document and fiction, and also the typical slanted gaze that favors specular effects and urban *costumbrismo*[43] that are so often mined in the filmic narrative realism of Peru. It is Lima in the frame – we recognize it by certain distinctive traits – yet, at the same time, it looks strange because it offers itself to us unevenly, in color and black and white, grainy and smooth, with varying degrees of visual definition. The daylight Lima of the documentary becomes, through a change in visual texture, a horizon of expressionist strokes. *Días de Santiago* distances itself not only from *Cuentos inmorales*, but also from *Gregorio*, the two films that best represent, respectively, the neo-*costumbrismo* of Lima's middle class and social drama influenced by the Neorealists.

Unlike these, it is a split visual object, just like its story, which develops through the sustained tension between contradictory forces. Santiago moves forward, dragged on by the opposing demands of order and disorder, in a schizophrenic duplicity that his consciousness obliges him to hold together; this is the reason for his refrain: "You have to analyze, get your bearings, plan your strategy." The chaos of the environment rejects the precise commands of military regulation. The city resists and bubbles over. The result is Santiago's paranoia; the film brings the difficulty of telling his story – or the impossibility of telling it in order – to the fore. Not even time is a reliable marker; it is, instead, a flow altered by the subjective consciousness that molds it.

Días de Santiago is like a jigsaw puzzle made up of heterogeneous blocks of time irreducible to any sort of symmetry.

---

[43] TN: The aesthetic interpretation, often exoticizing, of local culture, manners and dress.

Somewhere in the Andes

Madeinusa, by Claudia Llosa (2005) does not need to name the experience of political violence in order to situate itself at the intersection of feudal authority, superstition, poverty, and many of the constitutive components – the ferment, almost – of the recent war. Peru's history is there, subsumed within the plot of the film, even without any mention of real events, not even a date or any other concrete reference. Everything is converted into fiction and exposed in a way that had never been seen before.

It is also a transgressive film. It abandons the verist or documentary approach to the Andean world in order to present itself as a cruel fable. Llosa invents the Andean town of Manayaycuna in the sierra of northern Peru, the foothills of the Cordillera Blanca. This is where the action of the film takes place. There, relationships based on the exchange of tokens and favors on both an economic and sexual level prevail. The action of the film begins as the inhabitants of the town await the arrival of "Holy Time," a period that begins at three in the afternoon of Holy Friday and lasts until six o'clock on Easter morning. It is the time during which Christ lies dead and is unable to see the collective excess. A time of pain turned *carnaval*, when people can do as they please behind Christ's back, without his judgment and out of his sight. The mayor of this town lives there with his two daughters, one of whom is named Madeinusa (Magaly Solier). The house is plagued by rats on the outside and by tensions on the inside, including that of incest, which will come to a head within hours. It is a space ruled by a double patriarchy: that of Christ, who dies on the cross and takes his eyes off his children once a year, and that of the biological father, who decides to take the virginity of his daughters for himself. There is no escape from these fathers except by way of violence, by facing a power that naturalizes incest, impunity and crime.

Madeinusa examines its place within the tradition of representing the rural Andean world in Peruvian cinema. Is it possible to maintain the starry-eyed indigenism of the Cuzco School or the epic of the Andes in a collective struggle for ownership of the land after experiencing such political violence? Can one construct a narrative grounded in the time of myth and the place of past utopias? Is there still a place for the representation of the peasant as a collective, anonymous, hieratic, impenetrable cipher? Do colorful representations and the broad strokes of the epic of insurrection from the seventies still rule?

Llosa submits the traditional cinematic treatment of the Andes to a profound modification. Unlike other films about peasants, in which the protagonist is anonymous or simply a passive or mass figure, in *Madeinusa*, every event is filtered through the point of view of the protagonist. It is a biased consciousness that struggles not for a collective cause, but for its own survival in a hostile environment. Madeinusa is one of the few female characters of Andean origin in Peruvian cinema that demonstrates complex motivations and mature crafting. The earlier ones are divided between the archetypal "Juanacha" and the no less significant "Kukuli."

Juanacha was one of the main characters of *Camino de la venganza* (Luis Ugarte and Narciso Rada, 1922), the first feature film made in Peru. The embodiment of the pristine values of an ancestral culture, the young peasant girl Juanacha is seduced by the foreman of a mine, separated from her indigenous boyfriend, and taken to Lima, a city of sin, in which she survives through arduous labor. The nineteenth century melodrama is combined with indigenist vindication in the representation of this type of lacerated Andean femininity.

For her part, Kukuli is the protagonist of the eponymous film made in 1961 (*Kukuli*, by Luis Figueroa, Eulogio

Nishiyama and César Villanueva). A peasant girl from the high plains of Cuzco entering adolescence, Kukuli leaves her parents and travels to the festival of the Virgin of Paucartambo, a valley located at a lesser altitude. As she travels down the mountain, Kukuli receives life lessons, learns about her traditions, pays tribute to the Apus and meets her mate. It is a journey of initiation through the most characteristic spaces and myths of Andean culture. She experiences sex, desire, and the mythological violence embodied by the "ukuku," the bear who steals little girls. Kukuli is the embodiment of an image of the Andes as legendary and outside of time.

Unlike these two earlier models, Madeinusa does not inhabit a harmonious world, distant from human conflict and of the purest bucolic beauty. From the opening sequences of the film, we know that she feels herself to be a prisoner in her own home, harassed by the rats and desired by her father, who is saving her like a snack for "Holy Time." *Madeinusa* also alters the representation of the causes of dramatic conflict in films about the Andes, given that the usual approach has been to mythify the order and harmony of the high plains, destroyed by the arrival of strangers to the place in a cyclical and mythical repetition of the historic invasion of the sixteenth century.

Madeinusa imagines a singularity, invents a world and creates laws and characters to fill it. But it does something more: it suppresses the pastoral preconceptions of peaceful coexistence and inalterable order in Andean life. Here, the disintegration is not due to external causes; the seeds for the decay of the fabric of society are already sown from within. They are there in the persistent violence embodied by the proliferation of rodents, parasites and predators that stalk the place and remind us that, beneath the bright blue sky of the mountaintop, there exists a world of extreme need and elemental, violent drives.

The inherited memory of war

Claudia Llosa's *La teta asustada* (2009) offers an account of the memory of political violence from the experience of a subaltern body, that of Fausta, its main character, played by Magaly Solier. Fausta is a pivotal figure in recent Peruvian cinema, one that best embodies the negotiations between the displaced individual and the new *limeño*.[44] In order to realize her transcultural, bilingual project, Claudia Llosa chooses an approach based on allusion, reference and symbolism for *La teta asustada*. The daughter of a woman raped by militants during the internal conflict, the girl suffers from the syndrome of the same name, as described by Kimberly Theidon,[45] having inherited the fear and memories of the war through her mother's milk. She walks around with a tuber inserted in her vagina to protect her from having relations with men, or with her surroundings.

Over the course of the film, Fausta passes between two opposed but complementary natural elemental orders: those of "earth" and "water." In the process of overcoming her old attachment to her mother, whose lifeless body is on its way to decomposition, she breaks her morbid bond with the "earth" in order to blossom personally, affirm her creative potential and explore her sexuality in the open orders of "air" and "sea." Fausta is at the heart of a personal quest, but she also consolidates the symbolic trajectory of a film that offers itself up in the temporality and stages of a story or fable, but also those of a rite of passage.

At first, Fausta is only a voice. She sings to express both the pain of her intrauterine memory of violence and her own

---

[44] TN: Inhabitant of Lima, the capital city of Peru.
[45] Theidon, Kimberly. *Entre prójimos: el conflicto armado interno y la política de la reconciliación en el Perú*. Lima: Instituto de Estudios Peruanos, 2004. TN: In English, this has appeared as "the milk of sorrow."

ability to invent stories, by making up songs that only she ever hears. They are musical lamentations that bind Fausta to her mother and to her inheritance of sorrow, distancing her from the urban landscape that surrounds her.

Fausta is resistant to the celebrations organized by her family. Impassive, her arms crossed, she is outside the emergent and vital world of Lima growing in the settlements and populations that encircle the capital. In order to get the money she needs to bury her mother, she goes to work at the home of señora Aída, a last refuge of the fallen upper class of Lima. A house that looks like a fortress separated from the flood of "rabble" by a drawbridge. There, the girl encounters two characters of opposite natures: the woman with the narrative function of a "guardian angel," who nonetheless reveals herself to be predatory and malevolent, and the gardener, who becomes her benefactor. Her first encounter with each of these characters sets the tone for her relationship with them.

Aída is associated with the experience of the sinister. In her bedroom, Fausta discovers the portrait of a soldier that draws her in and disturbs her, bringing back the memory of the attack on her mother. Her encounter with the gardener, on the other hand, is marked by a moment of amnesty: a conversation in Quechua, the language of their ancestral lands.

As in *Madeinusa*, the plot of which is structured by exchange and reciprocity, pacts exist here as well. Fausta establishes contracts with both Aída and the gardener. The first is explicit: Fausta receives pearls from the *señora* in exchange for her songs. The critic Emilio Bustamante, citing Luis Millones and Hiroyasu Tomoeda, has explained one meaning of this exchange and of the siren song intoned by Fausta: "The belief exists, in Andean culture, that certain musicians make a deal with the sirens as they would with the devil; they perfect their instruments or endow them with talent in exchange for their souls. The length of the musicians' lives is counted out by the siren in the grains of quinoa the tempted individual gives over to her. When the count is finished, the musician's life comes to an end and the siren carries his soul to the bottom of the sea (or to hell)."[46] The other contract into which Fausta enters is implicit and belongs to the order of the unspoken: the gardener helps her to blossom, ridding her of the weeds that had built up inside her and awakening her emotions, desires, and drives.

The final segment of *La teta asustada* clearly takes a turn for the symbolic. Without the potato inside her, Fausta observes one final contract of a cosmic nature: she offers the body of her mother to the sea in exchange for the cleansing of a soul led astray by violence. The final image of the film depicts Fausta enjoying the scent of a potato plant in flower. The camera follows the straight stalk downward and ends its journey at the rounded forms of potatoes poking up from the ground. Fausta is open to new sensations and possibilities that do not exclude the presence of the phallic. She is no longer afraid, but perhaps still retains the inherited memory of war.

---

[46] Millones, Luis y Tomoeda Hiroyasu. "Las sirenas de Sarhua".*Letras*. LXXV: 107-108, 2004. 15-31, quoted by Emilio Bustamante at http://paginasdeldiariodesatan.blogspot.com/2009/02/la-teta-asustada-por-emilio-bustamante.html

Mirrors on the Periphery

Marcos Loayza

Many things in Bolivia are difficult to understand or explain; it is a country that is still in the process of coming together as such, and because it is a complex, mixed society in which different social classes with their own social pacts coexist and fail to coexist. It is a country where more than thirty nations come together in different ecological strata. A country that has lived nearly its entire history immersed in different crises.

Things do not happen in this society as one might suppose, according the theories of various schools of social science, nor do they happen as the laws of economic science would dictate. This must be because the territory has not yet found its center. In terms of our life as a republic, for example, every so often we move the capital or its center, despite the paradox of being located at the center of this part of the continent. Or perhaps it is for other reasons that we have not yet been able to digest, which have turned us into a deeply provincial society with a unique way of seeing and relating to Western hegemonic centers and a unique, contradictory way of looking at itself. Nor should we overlook the fact that ours is a society that, as many of us see it, is not in touch with monotheism, capitalism, and many other tenets of Western thought; or, at least, it interprets them in its own way. It is a society in which, despite its unquestionably being a part of the Western world, absolute truths do not exist, family and social ties are of great importance, and the mythical, the spiritual, the ceremonial and the festive permeate the day to day.

It is also difficult to understand or to explain a society that, in spite of itself and its potential, seems condemned to poverty. Yet, despite all this, at the moment it is working toward change and toward finding itself, having only recently begun to see itself through its own eyes. Finally, it is important to note that it is a society whose transformations throughout its history have happened so quickly that the majority of its intellectuals and many of its artists have not been able to keep up. For all these reasons, as well as others that are doubtless better suited to other contexts, I believe that these are not times of absolute truths or organizing principles. We should refrain from these if we do not wish to fall into schematics or ideas that, with a few respectable exceptions, have only done us harm.

The world has changed in this new century: it has become globalized, and we are a part of these changes, though it would appear that we remain at the margins of the process. Modernity reaches us in a filtered state, creating distortions and new scenarios. To give just one example, what is condemned, sought out and penalized as piracy in other countries is organized here into legal unions that pay taxes and represent an economic activity that touches nearly all corners of society, and in which everyone takes part, whether they want to or not. This distortion means that the infrastructure of the culture and entertainment industries either does not exist or functions badly.

We have yet to understand or approach these distortions in a serious way, just as we have yet to understand how to integrate globalization, how to relate to the hegemonic center from this marginal space on the border of the global village, and how we are to occupy and survive in this space. It is not only a matter of taking stock of our situation, but of resolving certain practical and logistical issues; for example, in this country there is no way to make commercial transactions over the internet, which means that the entire transaction needs to be routed through some bank in Miami or Switzerland. Yet despite the fact that the world is so far from us, although it reaches us through television channels, the internet, and the few texts that are brought in from outside the country, people make the strangest effort to get close to it, belong to it, make it theirs.

For all these reasons, we may see the cinema – the subject of interest here – in a skewed way, but with greater clarity, as a result of reaching rock bottom, of needing to weave a future from a point of disillusionment, with empty hands, and of having to work without aspirations, without manifestoes, at the margins of commercial spaces and screens.

We sense that the ways of distributing, screening, and viewing cinema has begun to change, that it will not be as we know it today and will never again be as we knew it in our childhood: an almost magical world inhabited by artists, specialists, cinephiles, critics, directors that made artistic productions and hard-to-find films that could only be seen at special screenings. This sense is born from the observation that, today, humble street vendors in all Bolivian cities selling *api* (a warm, corn-based drink) for breakfast screen a pirated copy of the most recent action movie to come out of the major studios as a little bonus for their customers; or how travelers going between the provinces are offered the latest martial arts movie on board during the trip; it is also born from seeing how the number of viewers purchasing tickets and the number of movies being released in theaters goes down every year; above all, it is born from seeing the reduction in the number of quality films being offered. That is, it is becoming harder and harder to release a film that was not made with a big budget or produced by one of the big companies; yet, paradoxically, people are watching more movies than ever. Yet this is a completely pragmatic market that allows all movie theaters, even new multiplexes, to premiere works shot on video and presented on lesser formats, such as DVD.

Aware that the phenomenon of cinema has its natural complexity, its variety, its characteristics that are particular to every society and historical moment, we can assert – taking these traits simply as tools to help clarify our position – that there are only two ways of making films: on the one hand, there are those who make movies by investing money with the primary objective of gaining utility from that investment, and then there are those who have a need to express themselves and invest money or seek out investments in order to satisfy that need. It is based on this reasoning that one can infer that it is more difficult for the former to achieve expressive success; conversely, it is more difficult for the latter to achieve commercial success. That which we call the film industry is a giant machine that the former manipulate according to their interests, with greater or lesser artistic sensibility, and which the latter try to make their own through whatever interstices they can find or are allowed them by this immense economic organization. This apparatus has been perfecting itself in order to make even more money from its productions; in the time of globalization and the internationalization of capital, its territories of exhibition have grown to the point that now, in contrast to the golden ages of cinema, the mathematical possibility of not recovering a capital investment no longer exists; these are no longer the days in which the film industry rested on seven desks at seven major companies. Now the capital is spread throughout the marketplace and the organizations have created complex networks that include all sorts of businesses: those in which the artists who appear on the screen work, factories that make televisions and DVD players that will be used to watch the movies, publishing houses that produce the novels on which they are based, biographies of the actors that appear in them, and interviews with their most "visible" directors and producers. There are also the magazines that spread gossip about its most famous protagonists; servers, portals and websites where one can read about projects and premieres, read reviews (positive, of course, or at least only slightly unfavorable), see the clothes worn by the stars and anything else that could arouse our curiosity. This enormous apparatus includes, in addition to the banks that lend the money to fund the productions, foundations that help raise funds to meet the entire budget, fast food chains or mass-market breakfast products to run promotions featuring characters from those movies that need promoting, teams of lawyers, representatives and lobbyists and – as though it were really necessary – small and independent production companies, alternative distributors, television channels on which their products are discussed as news, channels that show *reality shows* based on these movies and those that air movies all day, that buy the rights and air the films in their collections. The apparatus would be perfect, were it not for one thing it has not been able to conceal: boredom.

But there is no reason to give in to disillusionment completely; it is an industry that also includes a space for those who do "more daring," more "independent," more "artistic" work, who have created a smaller network for select groups of consumers that fall into market niches that offer magazines, supplements, websites, festivals and prizes that continually turn out new stars, new discoveries, iconoclast actors, new talent, alternative directors, rediscoveries, local cinema and art-house films. We should not forget that cable and the internet make it possible to transmit signals simultaneously, appealing to a wide range of tastes.

To this should be added an equation that factors in production budgets, which have a tendency to go down, and the costs associated with publicity and the release of a film, which go up every day. This equation is, furthermore, related to the fact that nearly every state has its own policies of protection, subsidy and support for its local filmmakers; as we all know, capital has transcended national borders for years, which means that the same stories are being told with the same money in the same way, just in different languages and with different cities in the background. In other words, it would seem as though it were only a matter of making capital circulate.

Yet because Bolivia is an insignificant market due to its limited number of inhabitants and its reduced acquisitive capacity, it is of little interest; the industry's efficient infrastructure works in a unique and distorted way. An example: action figures made in China that entered the market in the United States are the first things to make it to us, then a pirated version of the *Play Station* game based on the movie, then remaindered clothing like the styles worn in the movie four years earlier and, finally, if we are lucky, the movie itself, in a pirated version or on some cable channel, for a few viewers only. Yet it is important to remember that digital technology is reducing the cost of production and exhibition, both through the low cost of digital video equipment and through easier access to the latest sound, editing, and special effects software in pirated form. Since movie theaters are also in crisis, projection in digital format seems a more and more viable option, and there are many other options for exhibition that present themselves every day.

The question is: what is being made? We feel as though living in this space has required of us certain types of filmmaking that have varied according to the moment. In the 1970s, they wanted films from us that reflected the revolutionary spirit of Latin America, films that denounced the difficult political and economic situation of the dispossessed, often overlooking the real expressive needs of Latin American art that permeated the continent at the time, following the triumphant Cuban Revolution, the student protests in France, the 1968 massacre in Mexico or the presence of the guerilla fighter Ernesto Che Guevara in Bolivia. Shortly thereafter, the works that were best received were those that were able to bring to the "big screen" the same ideas that had worked in the so-called "Boom" of Latin American literature. In this way, we turned into the locus of the marvelous real, a paradise of magical realism, our screens populated by characters that defied every imaginable law of physics.

Later, to coincide with the quincentennial of the encounter between the new and old worlds, a number of opportunities arose to co-produce works and many screenwriters created characters that were Spanish or came from the First World and who, to varying degrees of success, spent time in these lands, experiencing a reunion with a South American family member or an adventure at the furthest reaches of the continent, or who stayed on to live here permanently. In the following years, films that reflected the difficult living conditions of the marginalized, of life on the streets, the exoticism and the barbarism of those that act outside the law, like drug traffickers. Now it would seem as though filmmakers are being asked to make experimental works that reinvent, or appear to reinvent, the language of cinema, without taking into consideration how much they may be alienating the viewer, as though a bridge had been built that directly connected Parisian film critics with provincial directors.

There are also directors that make films in the hope of producing the same type of movie produced by the major studios, the ones they see in the movie theaters and on television. Since they have neither the technology nor the budget, what they end up producing is no more than poor imitations of romantic comedies, of dramas, of science fiction, detective movies whose only originality lies in the exotic backdrop of our cities, Latin American poverty, or the gesture of depicting this society as a peripheral region of global society inhabited by extreme, marginalized characters: drug traffickers or "bananero" revolutionaries.

I believe that every society, according to its own specificity and stage of development, needs its own stories and someone to tell them and present them in a particular way in order to be able to project itself and understand itself as a society; for this reason I believe that, given the struggle that making a movie in my country represents, the only option left is to try to offer our society films that might be useful to it, in the broad sense of the term. In order to achieve this we do not need formulas or paths, but we will need to examine ourselves, reflect on our position at the margin of any sort of capital, almost at the limit of the Western world to which we belong; it is also necessary to recognize that there are things that we cannot leave behind, such as artistic integrity, one's respect and love for one's culture and the society. For this reason, I believe that the social engagement of the artist – beyond subject matter and the different ways of representing it – should be an engagement with excellence. The more fully realized the work, the greater the benefit it can bring to society.

In a country with meager cinematic output, in which there is no company dedicated to the production of either narrative or documentary film, in which the majority of audiovisual work is produced for advertisements or institutional communications, directors are practically forced to create their own production companies in order to make their films. Though some may co-produce their work, they do so in collaboration with similar businesses in other countries, rendering their relationship with the film industry nearly inexistent – a fact that becomes obvious when the time comes to distribute and screen the films; one could say that, by definition, all of our locally produced cinema falls under the category of independent film.

Yet, due to a variety of causes, our country has seen profound changes in both the way production is approached and the way stories are told from one generation to the next. The creation, more than twenty years ago, of the International School of Film and Television (EICTV) at San Antonio de los Baños in Cuba meant that every year one or two filmmakers who had recently graduated from the school would return, ready to work in an audiovisual field that barely existed. On the other hand, the lack of training in the rest of our nations quickly became evident; in response, a number of private film schools and programs administered by foundations were created in our most important cities, the fruits of which we have recently begun to see.

Following the 1979 premiere of Antonio Eguino's *Amargo mar*, there began to be more reflection on the importance of being able to depend upon state support in order to maintain stable production and create a "mirror of our own." During those years, the Bolivian Cinematheque gathered momentum, the national Cóndor de Plata and municipal Amalia de Gallardo prizes were established, and a number of books about film were published. Among these, *Cuadernos de cine*, a series edited by Luis Espinal, a Jesuit priest who was later assassinated by the dictatorship, stands out. These years are also marked by the rise of the "Juvenil" and "Luminaria" film societies.

Throughout the following decade, and coincident with the restoration of democracy, a struggle was taking place to pass a series of laws that would create a fund to encourage film production and establish measures to protect that production. Yet when the moment was finally conducive and the conditions right for the parliament to approve these laws, when filmmakers were united under the shared mandate of the "Ley de cine YA" and a lobbying group had been established – with the valuable help of artists from other sectors, including actors and musicians – the continent and, above all, the country found itself in the throes of neoliberal politics that called for the elimination of all taxes and subsidies that were not "absolutely necessary." As a result, in 1992 a film law was passed that, though it created the cultural entity known as the Consejo Nacional de Cine (Conacine), it was accorded neither the power nor the budget to assume responsibility for all the audiovisual production of the country. Though it establishes a fund to support film production, its terms are similar to those of a bank, with 8% annual interest rates and late payment fees that can exceed 30%. The effect of this process was a small boom in 1995, with more than five mass-market premieres and some twenty international prizes. From there, production declined little by little until the market was left in a disastrous condition completely unfavorable to those who make films, with nothing left in the support fund and a large number of its directors deeply in debt. The only thing that kept the fund alive was Bolivia's participation in the Ibermedia program, the tenacity of the filmmakers, and the drive of a new generation of directors.

Though there is still a need to change the film laws and the agreements with distributors and theaters owners, a new generation of young directors is beginning to emerge that, through sheer will and the use of digital formats, have continued to produce films. The quality of this work varies widely, but the results inspire optimism nonetheless, reaching an average of three premieres each year. It is no accident that one of the greatest box-office successes in recent years was a digital production that came out of a film school, Rodrigo Bellot's *¿Quién mató a mi llamita blanca?*

Yet in terms of the content of these stories, the cycle appears to be much slower and more profound. The different approaches to the subject matter that has been filmed over the course of our brief history of cinema can be summarized – understanding the risk that this implies – by the concept of a love-hate relationship between the countryside and the city. The social revolution of 1952 tried to solve the problem of multiculturalism and social difference by proclaiming an "alliance between classes." As a result, those who lived in the country stopped being Indians (whether they were Aymara, Quechua, Guarani, Mojeño, Tacana, etc.) and became peasants instead. In the field of cinema, the Bolivian Institute of Cinema (ICB) was founded, which – in addition to making pro-government newsreels – facilitated the production of the first films of modern Bolivian cinema. These films examined this new relationship, in which the perpetuation of racism and social differences became paradoxical; their directors trained their urban eyes on the countryside. Such is the case of the Jorge Ruiz's emblematic documentary *Vuelve Sebastiana* (1953), which looks through the eyes of a girl from the Chipaya, an overlooked nation on the high plateau that refuses to disappear. It is also worth mentioning the work of Jorge Sanjinés, which attempts to act in the service of that "clandestine nation" and its parallel existence. For example, the tragic persecution of the Aymara peasant who seeks to avenge himself again a *mestizo* aggressor in *Ukamau* (1966); the peasant's unfortunate visit to the city in search of medical help for a loved one in *Yawar Mallku* (1969); or the story of Sebastián Mamani, a renegade peasant who returns to his community in search of forgiveness in *La nación clandestina* (1989). In one of his last films, *Para recibir el canto de los pájaros* (1995), Sanjinés constructs a metaphor for the quest that defined his career by sharing a bit of his own life, which shows the culture shock that faces a group of directors making a film that seeks to reflect and portray indigenous society.

It is no accident that the genre most often adopted by filmmakers, from the most traditional to the most innovative members of the new generation, is that of the *road movie*, a sustained attempt, from the perspective of the city, to set eyes on a different type of citizen, find the nation in its vast reaches, find the road that society lays out ahead, all the while sensing that we are headed toward the unknown. In *Mi socio* (Paolo Agazzi, 1982), a truck driver from the West travels across the land accompanied by a Young man from the East; in *La nación clandestina* (Jorge Sanjines, 1989), the protagonist returns from the city to his community to find redemption through the ceremonial; in *Cuestión de fe* (Marcos Loayza, 1995), three characters transport a statue of the Virgin deep into the jungle; even in *Dependencia sexual* (Rodrigo Bellot, 2003), one of the stories is about one boy's journey from the provinces to his studies in an important city in the United States. In *¿Quién mató a la llamita blanca?* (Rodrigo Bellot, 2006), a couple low-level drug traffickers from the plateau travel to the East and, finally, *Lo más bonito y mis mejores años* (Martín Boulocq, 2005) depicts the impotence of one of its characters who is unable to emigrate out of the country.

We could also approach these different bodies of work in terms of certain recurring situations or scenes that have become emblematic. In Italian cinema, for example, it is common to see scenes that take place at weddings or funerals, which may be due to a strong Catholic influence. In North American love stories, action movies and comedies, the car is frequently used as a means of kindling romance. In nearly every film made in Bolivia, the characters always end up drinking in a bar for one reason or another, or drinking as though they were in a bar. In Tonchi Antezan's *El cementerio de los elefantes* (2008), the protagonist decides to go into a bar and drink himself to death. I believe that, beyond the depiction of a society that drinks in excess, this is due to the fact that this is a society that needs rituals in order to come into contact with the darkest reaches of its being, to be able to live with its own uncertainty and to be able to establish social bonds and relations. We can cite Antonio Eguino's *Chuquiago* (1977) as an example, which takes the Aymara name of the city of La Paz – a fact revealed to us by the character Carloncho, a charismatic public employee, as he gets drunk with his co-workers. Or Paolo Agazzi's *Mi socio* (1982), in which the protagonists gives confession to himself in a bar alongside the highway. *American Visa* (Juan Carlos Valdivia, 2005) tells the story of Mario, an ominous figure and a teacher at a mining school, who exists as different characters and lives at the bar.

Yet, unlike other societies, audiovisual production has always held a privileged place in Bolivian culture. Making a film is difficult work that could not be realized without the help of those associated with the production team, which makes it impossible to take the practice lightly. There is tremendous pressure from friends, family, sponsors, and the rest of those involved, and I do not think they would forgive it if there were nothing worth salvaging in the work. In the same way the public, though it gets smaller every day, demands and wants to see films that are socially engaged, above and beyond the quality of the story and how it is told.

Over the past few years, our audiovisual production has become democratized and has managed to put out more than twenty films, which – due to their precarious conditions of production – are largely destined to be forgotten, and justly so. The only works that really stand out are *Zona Sur* (2010), by Juan Carlos Valdivia, a courageous piece about the decadent upper class and *El Ascensor* (2010), by Tomas Bascope, a new project out of Santa Cruz.

Even at the periphery, we can sense that cinema is changing in meaningful ways around the world. It will soon be different, despite new technologies and because of piracy, social networks, downloads, *YouTube* and *Vimeo*, because of the public's new viewing habits. Film is changing the same way music changed when it faced the impossibility of continuing to sell albums and had to make a shift from disc to concert sales. The audiovisual, however, does not know where to go. It is haunted by the ghost of television. It is haunted by the ghost of opera, a niche art form that not all cities are able to offer.

Finally, it should be said that in the time since the restoration of democracy and the simultaneous emergence of video as a format, the past twenty-five years have seen the parallel activity of indigenous groups organized into non-governmental organizations, which have continually produced and screened audiovisual works as part of a project of recovering and affirming their cultural identity.

Argentine Cinema: a State of Affairs

Jorge La Ferla

> *Larry King: You're investing in land around the world. In Argentina, for example. Why?*
>
> *Ted Turner: I like to fish.*[47]

New Cinema for a New Argentina

The arrival of this, the second decade of the third millennium, has been marked by good news. News of a promising new direction one decade after the country's most recent crisis, from which we have now recovered. Building on a foundation of steady economic growth and a public image rooted in both the local and the international, the country has recovered its confidence since the debacle at the end of 2001. These good tidings have their correlate in the growth of Argentine cinema, which – in the year of the Bicentennial – has won its second Oscar.

The political stability of our economic system, like the achievements of our seventh art, speaks to a period of growth and relative stability. Nonetheless, this circumstance is tied to the polarization of the industry and the absolute concentration – by a handful of multimedia corporations – of the production and distribution of audiovisual material in Argentina. New laws passed in 2009 governing the

---

[47] The Larry King Show, CNN. December 13, 2000.

audiovisual media seek, in part, to counteract this situation despite the strong opposition of the media and parties tied to their interests. The subsequent standardization of the imported cinematic messages shown in multiplexes, the consumption of television through both the networks and cable, and the entertainment offerings *online* lead us to ask certain questions about mass media and independent audiovisual production, focusing on the idea of the authorship of artistic works and cinematic composition in particular. The peripheral condition of Argentina in the so-called global marketplace influences all the goings-on of politics, media, and the audiovisual arts, as these are seen as pertaining to a country that produces raw materials and services, with an extremely limited internal market.

Experts in cultural studies, some with forgotten revolutionary pasts and golden exiles, dream of a strong, national, popular culture industry, and a national cinema that finds success in local and global entertainment markets in a world ruled by free trade and finance. The discourse is either laudable or demagogic; but it is certainly questionable in terms of actual practice. This discursive gesture, which takes a euphemism like the concept of a "culture industry" as its point of departure, is analogous to the arguments that profess the expansion of tourism. Both take for granted a moment of development and industrialization – in the sense of the production of consumer goods, as well as autonomous, stable and sustainable capital goods destined for use in Argentina and around the world – which in reality does not exist. The contradictions become apparent when we consider the formative role of Peronism, which emerged in the mid-twentieth century and created, in both concept and action, an idea of national industry that would come to be destroyed during the nineties. This paradox reveals, looking back over the history, a phenomenon that those who have studied Argentine political history and Peronism in depth have seen time and again.[48] It is something that remains in Argentine society even after the disappearance of its founder in the mid-seventies. Paradoxically, it is this same society that played a notable role in the dismantling of local production and public, state-run businesses.

In matters of politics, Argentina often pretends to follow in the footsteps of its European mentors while faithfully adhering to lessons learned from Washington. This is something that the geopolitical alliances of Mercosur, under the leadership of the Brazilian government, have tried to counteract in the first decade of the new millennium. Both the horrifying military dictatorship and the government from 1990 to 2001 reduced even oppositional thought to a meaningless consensus, one by means of weapons and execution and the other by means of democracy and the media, that went hand in hand with the systematic sale of the economy, the industry, and the wealth of an entire country. In the new century, the democratic State has tried to change some of the rules of the game in economic, social and media terms, despite always being led by the same party, ballot boxes in tow. This movement accentuates the processes of readjustment after the crisis of 2001, following the rampant privatization of State businesses, the destruction of the national apparatus of production, the decade-long forced convertibility of the peso with the dollar and unjustifiable, interminable foreign debt.

The current state of the Argentine economy, after the debacle of 2002, meets the conditions of the 'grape theory' of development, which states that if a country like

---

[48] The works of John William Cooke, Ezequiel Martínez Estrada and Salvador Ferla are eloquent on this point.

Argentina, endowed with extensive natural and intellectual resources, does not meet the demands of its people to attain higher standards of living, and if the enthusiasm to forge a greater nation is replaced by resignation, resentment and corruption, the country will be condemned to dry out slowly, irreversibly, like a grape. This vision of Argentina, pronounced by President Arturo Frondizi in the early 60's, may yet haunt our country even at the dazzling turn of the new millennium and the conclusion of our Bicentennial celebrations.

This nation, conceived by the Creoles in the 19th century, reinstituted by the immigrants at the start of the 20th, and led toward what seemed to be its great historic destiny by Peronism from 1945 on, is currently experiencing a crisis of identity that has brought its focus to stagnate on mediocre, transient goals established by political parties and competing media properties. This stagnation would mean a return to submissive and participatory support, to an economy completely determined by the policies of centralized economic groups in major world markets, to money laundering, industry based on factory production, and amnesty for all wrongful acts committed during the military dictatorship and the government of the 90's. An eternal return to being an agricultural and service economy – we are currently an exporter of genetically modified soybeans that feed Chinese livestock, led by an administration whose formal governance is determined by the international financial system – in which speculation drives lawmaking and poverty and marginalization appear on a staggering scale.

It proves interesting to locate, within this panorama, the dream of an industrial, national, and powerful Argentine cinema, which was conceived in the mid-20th century and was always presented as a project of mass culture to accompany the political and economic ups and downs of

Argentine policy.[49] A cinema that was reduced to its most meager expression during the military dictatorships and the decade of the 90's, that was reborn in the democratic transition of the 80's and that, after the crisis of 2001, is now regaining its spark.

Over the past two decades there have been two central variables to consider: on the one hand, the radical shift in the business of film distribution and screenings and, on the other, the new technologies for film production on the market. Local independent distributors, a group of entrepreneurs that at its peak consisted of around twenty members, slowly began to disappear and their participation in local and regional markets was reduced to a bare minimum (within a market considered insignificant on an international level for the meager profits it can offer). The lack of State control over the business of screenings, as well as the circuits of independent movie theaters and distribution, led to a near complete collapse of this activity, except in what has really become the only option: the internationally-owned multiplex theater.[50] This critical phenomenon, rarely studied even today in Latin America, is one of the factors that contributed to the dramatic decline in attendance of local cinema, together with other factors like widespread access to DVD burners coupled with a savage and expansive parallel market of pirated films sold in public streets or online. In this scenario, Argentine cinema is left without any guaranteed quota of screening space, aside from active laws or resolutions. Other factors

---

[49] Coscia, Jorge. *Del estallido a la esperanza*. Buenos Aires: Corregidor, 2005.
[50] The present danger is that of following in the footsteps of Santo Domingo, capital of the Dominican Republic, and the increasingly prevalent model it presents: the capital of a Latin American country in which practically the only option is less than a dozen international multiplexes. All with the same programming.

have also contributed to its falling out of favor with local audiences. High production costs have made Argentine cinema dependent on the backing and credits provided almost exclusively by INCAA (The National Institute of Cinematography and the Audiovisual Arts) and, to a small extent, by San Luis Cine, dedicated to promoting film production in the province of the same name. In a few cases, external funds for co-production, usually coming from government agencies and private producers rather than commercial entities, are employed.

The investors who were able to operate outside the credits and international aid mentioned above no longer exist in Argentina. The independent producers who, in a local context, bet on a commercial product. It is worth noting that this is the situation in all of Latin America, where cinema is being produced that is certain to be an economic loss, without paying dividends or even making enough to pay back initial investments. Exceptions, of course, do exist, such as the case of Fabián Bielinsky, a director of quality commercial films who, in his brief career, made a public event of his two feature films *Nueve reinas* (2000) and *El Aura* (2005). It is the same phenomenon seen today in Juan José Campanella, whose film *El secreto de sus ojos* (2009) swept the box offices, even surpassing the numbers of Hollywood heavyweights and joining, in this sense, the ranks of the "blockbuster" – in the slang of the medium – having exceeded attendance figures of 2.5 million viewers in Argentina.[51] It was an unusual case that sparked euphoria among mass media critics and stupor among the educated classes, as well as in certain academic

---

[51] "There are films whose relevance is more related to their status as cultural phenomena than to their aesthetic value. A perfect example of this among the Argentine public and later at the Oscars: the discussion surrounding *El secreto de sus ojos*" states Eduardo Russo in *La Tempestad* (May/June 2010, 12-72).

circles, students of the seventh art and those in charge of programming independent film festivals. This distance and disdain, however, was not accompanied by an analysis of the situation to examine the success of this film at the box office, compared to the rest of the films produced in the country (which obtained paltry attendance figures in the same year).[52] Aside from this exception, it is the increasingly uniform *Made in USA* cinema that continues to be the favorite among the Argentine public.

The fact is that in Argentina cinematic production is not profitable, and there is no industry for it, except in very unusual circumstances (certain products for television or advertising, international productions made within the country). This implies that commercial films and those that are not, the independents, present themselves as two opposing camps. Independence marks a difference, then, from those films geared toward a large viewing public, generally lacking in meaningful compositional elements. These films present themselves with all the semantic weight of the authorial and the artistic. On the other hand, another entelechy situates itself within that of independent film: that of New Argentine Cinema.[53] These are relative terms, of

---

[52] The figures: 1- *El secreto de sus ojos*: 2,410,000; 2- *Las viudas de los jueves*: 538,.000; 3- *Papá por un día*: 497,000; 4- *Esperando la carroza 2*: 375,000; 5- *Música en espera*: 235,000; 6- *El Ratón Pérez 2*: 226,000; 7- *Cuestión de principios*: 168,000; 8- *Felicitas*: 128,000; 9- *Anita*: 122,000; 10- *El corredor nocturno*: 96,000; 11- *Boogie, el aceitoso*: 85,000; 12- *100% lucha: El amo de los clones*: 79,000; 13- *El niño pez*: 55,000; 14- *Amorosa Soledad*: 18,000; 15- *La ventana*: 15,000; 16- *Tres deseos*: 13,000; 17- *Poema de salvación*: 13,000; 18- *Mundo Alas*: 13,000; 19- *La sangre brota*: 11,000; 20- *El hombre que corría tras el viento*: 10,000. http://www.diarioelatlantico.com/diario/2010/01/03/6621-el-secreto-de-tus-ojos-exitosos.html

[53] "The critic Horacio Bernades, in his contributions to *Página/12*, has not only employed the syntagm 'New Argentine Cinema,' but has also proposed the acronym NCA, revealing precisely how, in reality, the denomination has the character of an identifying mark." Aguilar, Gonzalo.

course, only denominations that do not correspond to any deeper concept. All Argentine cinema is produced outside the industry, and nearly all of it is made possible by subsidies and credits from the National Institute of Cinematography or by foundations and production companies outside the country. Yet in this sense, the cinema is not independent at all, in that it is only possible because of these entities, at least on a material level. This is especially laudable if we take into account that we are talking about cultural and artistic production, which should not depend on the pseudo-market dominant in Argentina. It is striking that powerful companies tied to multimedia conglomerates also rely on these sources of public finance when making their rare cinematic productions, which tend to be quite deficient in their creative proposals. In any event, Argentine film production is comparable in economic terms to the solicitation process whereby the State chooses a contractor to perform a service. Yet without this assistance it becomes nearly impossible to make a movie.

We recognize that those categories that appeal to novelty, independence/freedom, and authorship/art do not tend to address fully the phenomenon of the country's film production. A polemic issue, without question, precisely because it is this type of journalism, these manifestos, declarations, and expositions that support these categories.[54]

Otros mundos. Un ensayo sobre el nuevo cine argentino. Buenos Aires: Santiago Arcos Editor, 2006.

[54] *Otros mundos. Un ensayo sobre el nuevo cine argentino*, by Gonzalo Aguilar, is a wealth of information on Argentine cinema, due to the way it attempts to systematically examine a complex and heterogeneous phenomenon over the more than two decades of production that have yielded several hundred films.

New technology for New Argentine Cinema

A country without cinema is like a house without a mirror.

INCAA slogan

The issue of film equipment is also central to thinking about cinema in terms of the hybridization of media and the disappearance of photochemical film. The gradual, excessive and inevitable development of computer technology has called into question not only all aspects of the production and reception of these works, but also those academic propaedeutics based on the specificity of the formats and their languages. These radical changes – hybridization and the use of different formats – were not accompanied in Argentina by a theorization that considered the appearance of digital technology and its relation to the audiovisual media that came before it, particularly film. Nor do the tentative discussions that apologetically accompany new technologies and thought on changes in format, the interactive and the virtual, examine the history of film and video as a precedent, given the historical cross-pollination between photochemical, electronic and digital processes. Even today, this topic continues to be ignored or, at least, poorly addressed; sometimes due to ignorance, sometimes to an attempt to maintain a discourse devastatingly affected by the loss of the noble machine specific to the cinema.[55] A posture that coexists with the eternal sales pitch that

---

[55] "Without the images of drama, of adventure, of comedy, of natural and artificial events printed on the film, there would be no cinema; there would be nowhere from which to draw its history; there would be nothing left to cinematology. In its place would be fixed (photographs) or transitory (electronic) images. This is what video confirms: a civilization that is captive to the nightmare of its visual memory no longer needs cinema. Because film is the art of destroying images in motion." (Cherchi Usai, Paolo. *La Muerte del cine*. Barcelona: Laertes, 2005).

goes along with new technology that has accompanied the history of media over the last two hundred years: the discourse of novelty.[56]

It is essential, then, to consider the variety of technological resources over the course of this history and the current preponderance of digital format in all aspects of cinematic production. The presence of the computer and of digital codification in filming and post-production – in the storage, transfer and, later on, exhibition, transmission and reception of cinema – should be considered part of a process that facilitates the simulation of cinematic effect. As was the case, in its time, of the other widely ignored medium of video, this crossing and hybridization of film with different technologies, which has been going on for decades, has not been addressed in Argentina, either by theory or by a praxis that takes into account the emergence of the electronic and digital image in their own terms and in relation to cinema.

For example, the notions of takes and editing are archaisms in the context of the filmic construction of a narrative grounded in the possibilities of digital capture and post-production. Faced with the imminent disappearance of the material aspect that makes cinema, in the purest sense, which will culminate in the absence of silver-coated celluloid, it is interesting, at least, to think about this cinema that is made less and less on the machines of cinema. Some call this expanded cinema, others, post-cinema.[57] The

---

[56] "This rhetoric of the new is the vehicle of a well-defined double ideology: the ideology of *ruptura*, of the *tabla rasa* and, consequently, of the rejection of history. And also the ideology of continual progress. The only historical perspective to adopt this discourse is that of teleology. Always more, further, stronger, more advanced, etc. Onward, always!" (Philippe Dubois, "Máquinas de imágenes: una cuestión de línea general" *Video, cine, Godard*. Buenos Aires: Libros del Rojas (UBA), 2000.

[57] Youngblood, Jean. *Expanded Cinema*. New York E.P. Dutton & Co. Inc., 1970; Machado, Arlindo. *Pré-cinémas & pós-cinemas*. Campinas: Papirus,

process of digital conversion is irreversible and is taking place throughout all analog media.

We once again call attention to the limited analysis of this critical issue, despite the production of a number of important films and videos that take a creative approach to cinema, using digital and video devices. A paradox, in a country like Argentina, which boasts the highest concentration of film schools in the world. In any event, several filmmakers conducted pioneering, high-level experiments in crossing film with electronic and digital technologies. We can cite the work of Juan Antín, Albertina Carri, Leonardo Favio, Gustavo Galuppo, Fabián Hofman and Fernando Spiner, among others.

In the late eighties, when digital systems for the manipulation and control of video were starting to appear, a process of technological reconversion began that was marked by the corporate policies of different businesses. These devices changed the way we work with the medium by offering peripheral controls and a wide range of ways to manipulate an image digitally. In the early nineties, the combination of video and digital format, like Sony's D1, along with different configurations of equipment and programs for the manipulation of audiovisual data, like Quantel, offered new possibilities for expressive work with an image, but often ended up being used to create special effects for advertisements. Post-production companies established themselves in the market in Buenos Aires, offering elaborate options for what quickly ceased to be traditional editing and became instead a creative practice of post-production.

Filmmakers working in video, along with the directors of commercials and music videos, immediately began

---

1997 and Machado, Arlindo. *El paisaje mediático. Sobre el desafío de las poéticas tecnológicas*. Buenos Aires: Libros del Rojas, 2000.

to incorporate ostentatious displays of special effects in their work, many of which were based on the new possibility of superimposing images within a frame shot in real time. These days, from the personal computer to the most sophisticated apparatus, there is a whole range of opportunities in post-production to transfer material to film format at different levels of quality. Faced by the diverse and expanded uses offered by this technology, a number of filmmakers conducted important experiments in the combination of different audiovisual devices. 35mm and 16mm Moviolas were replaced by VHS/S-VHS/U-Matic, Betacam and Betacam Digital video editing equipment. Then came the gradual shift from recording, mixing and post-production on video to, at the editing stage, a completely digital post-production process with devices and programs based on different configurations of *hardware and software*, to HD equipment (to name just a few of the variables in an endless spectrum of electronic and digital products that present themselves as a simulated prosthesis of a cinematic device on its way to disappearing). For some directors, this is already something worthy of serious consideration: the innovative use of video and digital as part of the process of composition. A creative practice that involves the filmic, the videographic and the photochemical, from pre-production to the final transfer, always taking into account the expository possibilities that each of these has to offer. Due to this hybridization and the conversion of photochemical and electronic images to a numerical format, everyone found themselves obligated to transfer their work to a computer for post-production. Many directors did so without considering this new reality from a creative perspective. And so the same approach that had been taken with video was repeated: stick with the old notion of editing based purely on film, even when working with a different format or technology.

But there were also works that, after long processes of creative trial and error, became touchstones for their experimental proposals. We can cite *La sonámbula* (1998, Fernando Spiner), *Los rubios* (2003, Albertina Carri), *Perón, sinfonía del sentimiento* (1999, Leonardo Favio), and *Pachito Rex* (2001, Fabián Hofman), the aesthetic proposal of which includes the creative manipulation of cinematic formats expanded to include video and computer science. The rest of the production barely addressed these technological variables, despite making use of them, leaving all possible developments – both aesthetic and expressive – in the hands of the technicians on his crew and, in the best of all cases, trying to simulate something that had been impossible up to that point: giving video and digital the texture of film. We should also consider that the majority of works shot on film and video formats are kept, first and foremost, in digital format as soon as post-production is complete. Conversely, the majority of projects made in HD, especially features, end up being transferred onto film. Many still consider this irreversible reality to be a disadvantage when compared with the purity of the filmic process alone.

Other projects do not pass through the stage of being shot on film and are recorded directly as digital video. One might wonder about the sense of transferring to film a project made in digital video, something that is not actually of the cinema, but rather of television. Nonetheless, we can cite *Carancho* (2010, Pablo Trapero), which, through *transfer*, was presented under a filmic veil, yet stands out for not aspiring to simulate the aura of the photochemical image, and for its exploration of the potential of digital technology. It thus achieves a texture that plays with different chromatic values and an image harmonious with the compositional gesture and the dark, artificial tones applied to actions largely carried out indoors or at night.

The part of the production that is still shot on film is inevitably transferred to digital from the negative. Once post-production is complete, it can remain in digital video format or be transferred back to film. Either way, it can easily be projected from a computer onto a screen or shown on a television without the need to be converted to a print. There is no justification, in most cases, for a theater premiere, except for the commitments established by INCAA. This seems as though it will change at some point, that is, that it will be possible to show the material in the format in which it was originally created. An important assertion made by many directors and film producers that is, for the moment, being channeled by the DVD format, which is not well-suited to projection in movie theaters. The growing trend – overt but, at the same time, hidden – of presenting film premieres at movie theaters and charging full admission to watch a movie in DVD format under the shabbiest of conditions, is disturbing indeed.

Beyond the discourse surrounding the 'filmic' and the 'non-filmic', considering the possible combinations of different audiovisual devices and formats, as well as the processes that come after registering, shooting, or recording, allow us to focus on other conceptual, expressive and narrative mechanisms that emerge from the inevitable contact with digital format and the potential for the manipulation of image and sound. Yet these processes, in all their different forms, only influenced the way a few directors thought about composition in their works. The privilege of still being able to "roll" film is an increasingly rare exception to the rule that, when it does occur, remains one of the most intense experiences of the entire process of feature filmmaking.

Shooting on film is still transcendent because of the implications of using a device designed specifically for the medium, but it is a process that will, unfortunately, disappear. For many directors and producers, it is no longer a viable option due to its cost, though it continues to be one in terms of the formal and aesthetic possibilities it creates. The transition from film to digital should not simply attempt – as is so often the case – to create a perfect and imperceptible simulation of the cinematic in its use of editing and sound mixing. The incorporation of other technologies, for the miniscule number of directors that have done so, is considered to be a value added to the process of filmmaking on a conceptual, aesthetic and operational level. The previously mentioned cases of Antín, Carri, Favio, Hofman y Spiner are a testament to this, as is the audiovisual work of Gustavo Galuppo, Iván Marino and Marcello Mercado, who have all created internationally recognized works grounded in experiments in combining film, video and digital. Many of these artists propose a broader field for cinema, one which extends to installations or interactive documentaries online, in projects generated by the creative manipulation of technological hybridity. A phenomenon that few critics or professors want to address or analyze within the academic framework of traditional film schools. The complete denial of the subject has led to the widespread schizophrenic acceptance of thinking about computer-based audiovisual technology as a prosthesis, the rarely-achieved primary function of which is to emulate film. An inexcusable error, of course, which has become pathological in Argentine cinema.

Despite innovations in post-production, and with the exception of transfers from digital to film and a few advertisements, there have not been many directors on an international level who have demonstrated creative processes based on the opportunities offered by extra-cinematic technologies, either. Some of the work of Michelangelo Antonioni, Jean-Luc Godard, Peter Greenaway, and Wim Wenders has presented interesting examples of experimentation in the use of video and digital. Already in the late seventies – we insist on the question of temporality, as it is relevant to the discussion of the early articulations of this new discourse – these artists were creating a breach in their careers as film directors through the combination of and friction between different audiovisual formats. Recently, other filmmakers like Alain Cavalier, Mike Figgis, Abbas Kiarostami, Agnès Varda, Lars Von Trier and Thomas Vinterberg – to name just a few – have produced works on video that are impressive in the way they propose a range of compositional possibilities through the use of mixed media, thus creating a specific aesthetic through their fusion.

A symbolic and transcendent example in Argentina is the saga *Perón, sinfonía del sentimiento* (1999). Leonardo Favio developed a project that produces meaning and is realized on a material level through the electronic and digital manipulation of both recorded and archival audiovisual material. This documentary hybrid marked by visual synthesis is based both on an aesthetic of combining multiple images within a frame and on the animation of many of its sequences. In an exhaustive labor of post-production, Favio shatters traditional concepts of editing. It is now also a matter of manipulating the archives, creating animations, and generating a project outside the frame that transfigures any archive or dynamic image that occurs in front of the camera. In this way, Favio creates a revolutionary work that would never have been possible using only devices made for film. The imagery of this anthological series can be explained by the hybridity of the formats used and by the genius of its director, who expanded the field of filmmaking by challenging the entrenched formulas of Argentine cinema, including the ideology of the partisan political machine that commissioned and funded what was supposed to be a traditional, didactic film. *Perón, sinfonía del sentimiento* remains a little known and little-researched work.

Cultural studies and culture industries

The past quarter century of democracy has found in Argentine cinema a practice that stands out in the field of culture and the arts and which remains, in quantitative terms, one of the most important on the continent. But consideration should also be given, in this state of affairs, to incentivizing the production of quality films that are innovative in their composition and retain their value, unlike so many movies that are, from an academic or experimental perspective, the mere repetition of stories and clichés. Taking their specific aesthetic proposals into account, only a few films stand out among hundreds of local productions. This is logical, of course, since these works (those that offer some innovative value) do not tend to elicit the same reception from both critics and the public. However, they do make possible the construction of virtuosic imaginaries and admirable works. The rest is made up of uniform productions that adhere to the materiality of the cinematic spectacle and the step-by-step processes of making a film: writing a literary script, transcribing it as a technical one, producing it, shooting it, editing it and screening it. All this tends to come across as filmmaking based on the literal transcription of the literary, something taken from a concept of film writing as a testimony of the choices and worldview of the director.

A great body of work, fascinating for its breadth and dubious for its haphazardness, was generated upon the return to democracy as one of the critical incentives, as we indicated, of State policy. It was especially during the notable tenures of Manuel Antín (1983/1989) and Jorge Coscia (2003/2005) at the helm of INCAA that these policies offered the greatest incentives and facilitated the consolidation of an international brand for Argentine cinema. Within this sponsored cinema, a few creative works with expressive and narrative proposals appeared, breaking with traditional cinema meant to entertain or fulfill a political purpose. These, however, were exceptions. The discourse that insists on the category of New Argentine Cinema is redundant and instrumental because it produces interest in new works by young directors. In their day in the mid-eighties, Cristian Pauls, Gustavo Mosquera and Fernando Spiner (Martín Rejtman would be added to this list in the first years of the following decade) were the first to be singled out by critics as young directors of what at the time was called "the new promise of a new Argentine cinema." A discourse that is decades old, yet tries incessantly to fill its slots with new talent that, to the extent that time marches on, does not last long as such. Young directors inevitably get old after being enthusiastically received as the representatives of a new cinema; establishing continuity after their first work becomes a genuine challenge.

Attendance figures for national cinema are strikingly low: they range on average from 5,000 to 15,000 viewers per film. This fact may not seem particularly meaningful when considered in terms of cultural and artistic policies, given that the State has assumed the role of fostering this crucial element of the culture. But if we think about it in terms of the so-called culture industry, the issue becomes alarming. Add to this the challenge that these directors and technicians face, trying to make a living in this particular field (unless they take on other work in commercials, television, or foreign film productions).

Another complex variable is film distribution. Indeed, it requires courage and political will to solve this pressing problem, as well as that of screenings, due to the lack of regulation by relevant State and corporate agencies, which is reinforced, moreover, by the silence of many close to the film industry. If we go on this way, there will be nothing but multiplexes showing films from major international cities, in which it will not be possible to show national or unconventional foreign films. The agencies in charge of culture and the arts have not been able to preserve screening rooms and theaters that might constitute a cultural and ideological alternative to films meant for consumption in multiplexes. Changing this situation remains essential, though it is generally regarded with suspicion as a lost cause; without this call to action, the panorama would be even more uniform and without prospects.

In any event, if this issue were addressed through its possible solutions – a utopia, of course – the preference of the Argentine viewing public would not necessarily switch to local cinema (which is not necessarily a problem in and of itself). One cannot expect the viewing public's mass consumption of Argentine cinema to be based on the sole appeal of its being a local production. These days, there are two types of movie complexes. The private multiplex, which falls within the framework of exaggerated consumption and the aseptic *fashion* of an assortment of shopping malls and airport duty free shops, on the one hand; and on the other, the state complexes, named according to their distance in kilometers from the National Congress. These publicly funded screening rooms are in a state of technological collapse; this is true of their equipment, to say nothing of the facilities themselves. This deterioration and neglect of public resources, despite the government's enormous reserves and budgets, is consistent with the policies held in the sectors of audiovisual production dependent on the State. State television, for example, with its anachronistic structure, is ignored by most television viewers, who prefer a more vile form of retinal massage to boring and mediocre official discourse. Most viewers prefer the trash of multimedia conglomerates, either in foreign or corporate hands, to the state television monopoly. All of these, both public and private, offer a dismal level of programming, possibly in response to the taste of its audience. And there you have it: one of the great achievements of Berlusconian post-republican democracies of the third millennium.

For this reason, it is important to dedicate even a small amount of space exclusively to quality audiovisual products not appropriate, perhaps, for the masses, but which would guarantee the survival of forms of artistic and cultural knowledge in danger of extinction, such as those of cinematography, video, television and multimedia production.

The dedication and sacrifice of actually making a film in Argentina is, for many directors, the result of persistence. This titanic effort does not necessarily imply the production of artistic or auteur cinema. Festivals are often the best showcases, ideally catapulting a director toward his fifteen minutes of fame through a prize, a mention at the podium, or a good review in some paper. But these feats are not enough to attain a lasting place in the difficult world of audiovisual production. New Argentine Cinema is made up almost entirely of first-time directors.

Encouraging the production and funding of a creative body of work that is all our own, within the limits and difficulties that our country can at times present, continues to be an inescapable challenge and an ongoing task of educational institutions, INCAA, and other foundations seeking to promote quality filmmaking. This is an attempt that, in a small, marginal way, fosters works that experiment with certain formal and narrative parameters within the framework of the development of an artistic voice. These creative laboratories were supported at first by the Fundación Antorchas, which set an important precedent; they are currently being carried out in Argentina by Fundación TyPA and outside the country by the Sundance Institute, the Talent Campus of the Berlin Film Festival (currently in collaboration with the University of Chile), the Film Foundation of the Cannes festival, Cinergia, and others.

The program mentions its laboratories, or workshops, for scripts, for working through narratives and personal criteria and values in the context of mise en scène. This work on a completed version of a script is part of the *work in progress* of the writing process, in which options and production choices are made under the guidance of experts in the field. In the case of nearly all these films, the participation of foreign producers is important.

Artistic or auteur filmmaking rarely produces a consensus. Nonetheless, some critics have tried to create a different kind of consent, defending the entelechy of New Argentine Cinema. It might be useful to recall a few milestones in the history of our national cinema, such as *Pelota de trapo* (1948, Torres Ríos); *Las aguas bajan turbias* (1952, Del Carril); *La casa del ángel* (1957, Torre Nilsson); *Crónica de un niño solo* (1964, Favio); *La hora de los hornos* (1968, Solanas y Getino); and *Perón, sinfonía del sentimiento* (1999, Favio), which are still significant today, over and against the transitory discourse of novelty, which represents no more than a rhetorical effect (without a conceptual foundation) based on an unfounded project of renewal that negates the important history of local cinema. From this perspective, Lucrecia Martel is an heir to the tradition of Argentine cinema, which cares little whether something is new or old; rather, what matters is the quality of a work and the expression of the ethics of an artist.

It is to this body of resistance to a system that promotes transitory work, ignoring an entire tradition, that the contributions of a few particularly memorable Argentine directors will be added for their uncategorizable work in the expressive and artistic field, far removed from the banalities of New Argentine Cinema. The discourse of novelty or independent film does nothing more than propose indefinable categories and concepts that mask a production that is contingent, dependent on the State, and made by directors that struggle to make a second or third feature. The few that do cross this threshold, in general, only manage to repeat that which might have been an innovation in their first films.

The only mass industrial offerings remain those coming from the United States – now a vast majority, since the astronomical rise of production costs – which will continue to consolidate certain economic parameters, narrative discourses and directorial approaches that are increasingly uniform and lacking in interest. Despite the precepts of the financial industry, it remains true that the greater the investment, the lesser the aesthetic risks taken; a fact that is reflected in the low quality of these products of mass consumption. Trying to imitate these mega-productions would be impossible, and useless, in Latin America; even more so if one is trying to make quality work. Hollywood has always had a quota of *ethnic* Latin American directors. At the moment, the longevity of Robert Rodríguez has been taken over by Alfonso Cuarón, Alejandro González Iñárritu, Fernando Meirelles, and Walter Salles, who offer weighty productions based on sterilized, politically correct stories. A number of their compatriots have tried, with varying success, to work within the Hollywood system. It is worth mentioning a few diverse experiments, such as *Deadly/ The Stranger* (1986/87, Adolfo Aristarain); *La casa de las sombras*, (1976, Ricardo Wüllicher); *Gringo viejo* (1989, Luis Puenzo); *La casa del lago* (2006, Alejandro Agresti) and *El beso de la mujer araña* (1985, Héctor Babenco), to name just a few of those who tried to perform the difficult task of producing Californian work. These were high-budget films according to local standards, but they were low-budget according to the parameters of Hollywood. Some, with highly paid stars and films coming from "Latinos for *export*" with the affect of quality, have realized the dream of many: to work near Hollywood. It must certainly have been worth the time spent in the local independent film circles of Argentina, Brazil and Mexico to accomplish such a feat.

Nonetheless, even in this difficult situation, in a quarter century of governments elected at the polls, there has always been a very interesting space for the development of a personal body of work, a space in which several first films have taken on the role of formal manifestoes. A few emblematic cases have included *Diapasón* (1986, Jorge Polaco), *Picado fino* (1993, Esteban Sapir), *Sotto voce* (1995, Mario Levin), *La ciénaga* (2000, Lucrecia Martel), *Los rubios* (2003, Albertina Carri), *La libertad* (2001, Lisandro Alonso), *Hamaca paraguaya* (2006, Paz Encina), *Tan de repente* (2002, Diego Lerman), and *El desierto negro* (2007, Gaspar Scheuer); all examples of foundational first films that give an idea of future explorations of directorial style and, despite the difficulty of the situation, provide a sense of optimism about the emergence of strong creative personalities in Argentine cinema.

The teaching and practice of audiovisual creation is a complex task that requires programs different from the established curricula of most instructional institutions. This means thinking about different approaches to the structure of audiovisual education, as opposed to the traditional structures that continue to dominate most of the country's institutions. Beyond simply fulfilling the soft *diktat* of what a new and independent cinema might be, it is important to promote a vision of filmmaking that reveals the elective processes that go into the composition of a film, something that remains attractive to a number of foreign producers and is desperately sought by film festivals and institutions dedicated to supporting quality works of cinema. One of the biggest draws for those teaching centers should be the promotion of experimentation in works that, in their directorial approach, demonstrate a personal exploration and ultimately something different in the face of so much uniformity and cliché. *La ciénaga, La libertad* and *Los rubios* may be the three films most emblematic of this line, which consists of subtly revealing a country and an environment riddled with decadence and conflict. They are, quite possibly, an extension of other notable first works, such as *La hora de los hornos, Crónica de un niño solo* and *Invasión*, all milestones of Argentine cinema. Three films made nearly at the same time by three directors who left their mark on Argentine cinema and who, forty years later, are still making films. And who were, without a doubt, the new Argentine cinema of their time, but whose work is unknown to many of the directors of New Argentine Cinema. Favio, Santiago and Solanas were able to keep making interesting work, even as adults and after their novelty had worn off. On a regional level, there are a number of names that have made history by carrying on the intense subjective proposals of their first films, such as Mario Peixoto, beginning with *Límite* (1931), Raúl Ruiz with *Tres tristes tigres* (1968) and Glauber Rocha with *Barravento* (1962).

Argentine cinema is still alive and well. As long as Argentines continue to be born, there will always be a new cinema made by the young that, in turn, will guarantee the dose of the elixir of youth needed in order to speak of New Argentine Cinema. Yet it is a conceptually weak entelechy, and one that does not resonate with the category of independence. In any event, the rhetoric surrounding the new does not denote any real difference, in the same way that the political discourse of a new Argentina does not.

Changes in technology and the disappearance of celluloid in production processes, problems with distribution and changes in screening policies, the lack of clarity in the allotment of production subsidies, the lack of access to television as a medium of diffusion, the political dependence and internal discord of film festivals, the tremendous power of INCAA and the government over the audiovisual media, the lack of standards for and debate about the approach to teaching, the scarcity of research and analysis on the audiovisual arts in general and Argentine cinema in particular; these are a few of the important issues that affect production and will need to be worked through and discussed on all its levels, including the political.

Regardless of the situation, there will always be an Argentine cinema that, through important works removed from any idea of novelty, presents a vision of the country through its mise en scène. The role of educational centers, critics, scholars and functionaries within the field is to keep this history of great works with individual directorial proposals, which do not adhere to the parameters of the homogeneous system of commerce and the spectacle, alive.

The only national context in which it makes sense to speak of independent cinema is in the United States, the uncontested master of a monstrous feature machine and of the financial manipulation of the media (in its versions of film, television and multimedia). For this reason, it is always worthwhile to remember the life and work of certain North American filmmakers who earnestly confronted the entertainment industry and, as such, fought with conviction against the system. The cases of John Cassavetes and Robert Kramer are emblematic, as they were directors whose work was never sufficiently disseminated due to its minimal commercial impact in the United States. Some were forced, at different moments in their lives, to work from outside the country, specifically in Europe. Instances of harassment and even of censorship wrapped them up in a continuous struggle that left behind it a long and uncompromising body of work, created under great adversity and sustained over time. We are talking about non-commercial films that inscribe themselves with rare eloquence within the most important works of the twentieth century, and which shaped the character of independent auteur cinema.

One might also wish to consider other models in order to define, as a counterpoint to the category of auteur cinema, a cinema directed at a broad public and produced within the country or region that considers and captures an audience hungry for escape, entertainment and consensus. A product that would be, without question, of great political value, but which is currently monopolized by movies from the United States. Argentine television, for its part, provides a dose of spectacle necessary for the survival of our democracy.

Argentine cinema has its own versions of these rare but fundamentally important, uncompromising directors who create timeless films far removed from any trend or generational classification. The idea is to energetically promote this admirable work, radical despite its limited reach, and its films that endure for their aesthetic position, their directorial ethics and their connection to the transcendent moments in the history of national cinema.

Memories of New Argentine Cinema

Andrés Di Tella

I.

At some point in the 80s, I found myself sitting in a half-empty screening room on calle Lavalle in Buenos Aires, as the images of an Argentine film whose name I do not care to remember paraded before my eyes. To combat the typical sensation of frustration and impotence that the Argentine cinema of the time tended to produce, and in my condition as a budding filmmaker, I attempted to distract myself with a game of the imagination: I tried to think of other ways of telling the story, with different dialogue, different acting, different images. But I couldn't; it was literally impossible for me. I was trapped within national cinema. As though making an Argentine film were impossible without imposture, rhetoric; without the grammar of shots and reverse angles in which the weight of an entire crew moving reluctantly from one camera set-up to the next. The effect generated by these movies was that of scripts transferred onto film, for better or worse, far removed from the expressive potential of cinema. I came to meet one of these directors, and was surprised by his apparent lack of interest in cinema and complete ignorance of even the names of the most important filmmakers of the time. Behind his stance of viewing cinema as simply one profession among many, he gave the impression that he really could have been pursuing just about any other profession. In fact, one might have thought that the only art a filmmaker needed to know in those years was the art of navigating the halls of official buildings in search of their paychecks. I know that generalizations of this kind are ridiculous and that it would be unfair to take them too seriously. But I am, clumsily, trying to explain a sensation. When I hear or read that someone doubts the existence of a "new Argentine cinema," I remember the sensation I used to get from watching national cinema and have no doubt that something, something profound, has changed.

II.

For me, that something began to change when two UFOs appeared in the heavens. Martín Rejtman's *Rapado* was made with minimal resources in 1991 and shown five years later in a screening room of the Tita Merello Complex (which is not a new Freudian syndrome that plagues the filmmakers of Buenos Aires, but rather the name of a government-run theater). According to the director himself, the film was grounded in a negative proposal: not to do anything that national cinema had been doing. For the first time, *Rapado* showed the world of middle-class teenagers and young adults, whose problems could easily have seemed insignificant in the context of the hyper-dramatized psychological universe of Argentine cinema. But Rejtman's sagacity in observing human behavior, coupled with his visual and narrative creativity, allowed the minor incident of the theft of a motorcycle to convey, better than any deliberately meaningful story, what life in Argentina is like today. It was nothing less than what Vittorio de Sica did with the beginnings of Italian neorealism. In addition to this new form of realism, which changed the way we saw the world as we stepped out of the theater, paradoxically, Rejtman imposed his own world upon the viewer, one that followed its own rules and existed only on the screen. In other words, we were looking an *auteur*. The movie may have lacked the formal ease and sublime humor of the later *Silvia Prieto*, also by Rejtman, but it was his first film and, watching it, one got the unmistakable sensation that someone had finally managed to escape the prison of national cinema. It is no coincidence that he frequented Buenos Aires' Chinatown in search of rare videos and was a regular at the retrospectives at the Sala Lugones. Unlike the national cinema that came before, and on which he turned his back, his work was in dialogue with the world.

The other unidentified cinematic object was Esteban Sapir's *Picado fino*, shot in 1994 with a Bolex on 16mm black and white film and shown for the first time 4 years later (also, I believe, in the smaller theater at the Lorca; the fact that these films were screened in marginal theaters speaks to their place in national cinema). His was an aesthetic language diametrically opposed to Rejtman's austere rigor, which had a freedom with respect to the image that brought to mind the unexpected combination of experimental film and the new Argentine comics of the 80s. But this was a film whose condition as cinema in its purest state, which was, nonetheless, able to illuminate the experience of the everyday in a way never before seen in our country, left its viewers speechless. You walked out of *Picado fino* or *Rapado* with a heavy dose of cinematic adrenaline running through your veins. It was a feeling that is difficult to convey, and one that will probably not be recaptured by watching the movies over again on video or DVD; not because the films have aged, but because the context is no longer the same. They no longer seem like UFOs. Like Rejtman's, Sapir's movie was made outside the system of finance and production (and, so often, *fraud*) typical of the then-National Institute of Cinema, later re-baptized under the acronym INCAA (National Institute of Cinema and Audiovisual Arts).

III.

Toward the end of the 90s, I received a call from the government of Buenos Aires asking me to organize the first independent film festival there, the BAFICI, which was a critical forum for the development of New Argentine Cinema. Incidentally, I never felt completely comfortable with the term "independent cinema," which David Lopérfidio, the Secretary of Culture of the city at the time, gave the festival – in part to differentiate the it from the one in Mar de Plata, which was organized by the government of Carlos Saúl Menem and was more attached to the glamour and big names of the past, like Gina Lollobrigida and Alain Delon. The Buenos Aires festival also had a certain oppositional dimension to it; this was reflected in its somewhat radical programming, which also revealed the blind spots of the national politics of cinema, promoting the young directors that INCAA overlooked. The adjective "independent" may have been unnecessary and in fact sparked numerous debates. It was a term that had always been used in the context of the theater. Yet, at the end of the day, Lopérfido's idea of invoking the spirit of independent theater, with its grimy floors and little sandwiches in the dressing rooms, was not such a bad fit for this new cinema that was beginning to appear at the margins of official and commercial circuits. One of the first films we watched for that first festival (1999) was Pablo Trapero's *Mundo grúa*. We watched it in the home of filmmaker Eduardo Milewicz who, together with the aforementioned Sapir, made up the first "artistic committee" of the festival (nor does it seem an unimportant detail that the festival was created by filmmakers). It was a *work in progress*, a VHS tape produced on a computer without mixed sound or so much as a final cut. Even with its imperfections, we immediately saw that there was something genuinely new about it. Adrián Caetano and Bruno Stagnaro had already shown their *Pizza, birra, faso*, with all its audacity and the powerful presence of the street kids that would start the trend of using "non actors" in New Argentine Cinema. But Trapero's film, which was essentially the beginning of the international scope of the movement, had something more to it. Rulo, played by an electrician friend of Trapero's father who was acting for the first time, was a new, unexpected character that no one could have thought up, had he not actually existed. Yet the spontaneous charm of the protagonist, the affinity between character and individual, occur within the framework of a story that transcends the constraints of the documentary through intensely lyrical rhythms and images, as well as its combination of grainy 16mm black and white film with the austere beauty of the settings and landscapes. Yet again, one might be tempted to say "of course" – the movie was made outside official channels, supported by the Manuel Antín Film School (it would be impossible to overstate his importance *backstage* in all this) and by a modesty subsidy from the Hubert Bals Fund of the Rotterdam Festival (idem what was said about Antín). Instead of waiting for an official transfer of credit, which he would certainly not receive, Trapero went out and started filming. Later, Lita Stantic (ibid idem) would take over the production and make sure that it made it into the right hands, this time with official support – first from BAFICI and then from INCAA itself. You might say that things began to change with *Mundo grúa*: it became possible to get official support for "independent" film.

IV.

I am talking about the memory of movies that, in some cases, I have not seen again. But I remember that I had a sensation of revelation in the presence of each "new" film worthy of the name. And there were more and more of them. Like a recurring miracle that restored my faith in the possibility of making original Argentine film. Unlike the films of the 80s, and even those of the 90s (though there may have been minor exceptions to the rule, these were only minor exceptions), these films demanded the attention of the audience, as it was almost impossible to anticipate the next shot or the next line of dialogue. Each movie seemed to be proposing its own set of rules, which certainly had something to do with the fact that each film had to make its own way. No one had ever done anything like *La ciénaga*, or like *La libertad* or *Tan de repente*. And each filmmaker forged their own strange path, which did not appear in any manual and which was theirs alone to discover: from the nearly 200-page script written by Lucrecia Martel to the absence of any script in the work of Lisandro Alonso, via the unrecognizable adaptation of a short story by César Aira at the hands of Diego Lerman. The differences were also enormous in terms of production. While Lita Stantic assembled, for *La ciénaga*, a production team that included such unexpected members as producers from Mario Pergolini's famous show and the Japanese network NHK, Lisandro Alonso used his own money to film a sort of minimalist *home movie* on land owned by his family in the province of Buenos Aires, with a field worker as his only protagonist. Lerman first made a black and white short film with friends and later expanded it into an unexpected feature with the help of Lita Stantic herself, the same producer working on a very different scale. And just as these directors embodied the freedom to seek their own methods, the sense was that a cinematic language stripped of the burden of the old was becoming more and more common. It was also becoming more common to feel a breath of truth coming from these films that made you turn around in your seat as though someone had opened the door to the theater. While it is not such a surprise anymore (the fact is that New Argentine Cinema, after ten years, is no longer a novelty), certain films still have this effect on me, just the same.

V.

As a director, I consider myself to be a bit outside the phenomenon of any "new generation" of cinema, due to my age and also, for a time, my role as the Director of BAFICI. But most of all, it is because I make documentaries. If one of the novelties of New Argentine Cinema had to do with its way of incorporating the real, and even with a certain documentary tone in some cases, the genre of the documentary did not really seem to undergo a similar renewal. I myself, after making documentaries that, though they were not conventional, still clearly belonged to the documentary tradition, searched for years to find a way to make a documentary different from anything that had been seen before. The innovation of *La televisión y yo* was, for me, the decision to show my hand, to reveal the comings and goings of the investigation and especially the failures of the director (me), which can sometimes be better at "talking about" something than any so-called success. Without intending it, I had introduced in Argentina the rich genre of the film-essay, or as I prefer to call it, essay-and-error. But I soon realized that I was not alone in this winding and lateral quest and that I was not the only one to put this new idea of the genre, which transcended the genre, into practice. The film that in my opinion best represents the new documentary is *Los rubios* by Albertina Carri, in which the director, daughter of two of the dirty war's *desaparecidos*, had the courage to confront her parents' story in all its complexity, with an unprecedented degree of sincerity and personal exposition. Through the combination of documentary, animation, autobiography, reenactment and fiction, *Los rubios* demonstrates a level of conceptual sophistication and formal freedom that changes what one can expect from a documentary. And, at the same time, she changed the terms of the national debate over the recent past (three years after its release, the film is still generating intense debate). This is no small thing. You could say that *Los rubios* transcends its place not only within the documentary genre but also within cinema itself, entering into dialogue with other cultural areas as few works of any kind have done. What is most evident in the documentaries illustrates a characteristic of all the New Argentine Cinema: the fact that these new films were not made according to existing models, sometimes not even according to a script, but instead by finding their own way as unique objects; each with its own narrative and aesthetic system, far from the influence of the formulas that dominate so many productions around the world.

VI.

Where did (and do) all these filmmakers come from? The spirit of independent film would seem to be at odds with the academy. Nonetheless, with a few important exceptions, the vast majority of them come from the new film schools that, beginning in the 90s, have turned Argentina – and particularly Buenos Aires, into a place with one of the greatest densities of film students. According to certain statistics I have read, at the moment there are nearly 15,000 students in film school or related programs. Even if these estimates are exaggerated, they shed light on at least part of the mystery: quantity makes for quality. The fact that there are thousands of potential filmmakers trying to get their projects made means, almost inevitably, that at least some of them will be fairly original. On the other hand, the absence of a true "commercial" industry originating from the marginal position that local cinema occupies in the market, means the appearance of an unusual number of "non-commercial" projects, which apparently contributes to their originality as well. Many probably study film because they do not see any more stability in a career in engineering, let's say; nor should one underestimate the influence of numerous professor-filmmakers that have no reason to subscribe to the ideas predominant in Hollywood. In this sense, and perhaps for the first time in the country, there has been an organized transmission of information from one generation to the next. And do not forget the key fact that Argentina has very strong policies supporting the cinema, particularly the Film Law of 1995, which, among other things, allots ten percent of all proceeds from ticket sales to the production and distribution of national cinema. Of course, the decisions made by the authorities at INCAA are often questionable, and invaluable opportunities to promote Argentine cinema on a global level have been lost, almost deliberately, due to a lack of affinity between the authorities and representatives of New Cinema. A certain corporate function that privileges political accords between union and business interests over the quality of the projects or the young people who have done and continue to do so much to change the face of national cinema. In any event, the atmosphere of fostering cinematic production puts Argentina in a privileged position with respect to other countries in the region, even though local filmmakers have a hard time believing it and often feel exposed, left to fend for themselves. It should be said that this same feeling of perpetual uncertainty, created by the political and economic crises that have recently shaken the country, could also become a factor that, though undesired, fosters creativity.

It was in this context that – from the very first years of the independent film festival – we tried to open up the playing field, provide information that had previously only been available to a select few, and bring together a host of young people with a hunger for the cinema. This was not only to expose them to specimens of independent film from around the world that could serve as examples of paths they might follow though the presence of young Korean, Chinese and Japanese directors, ignored by the critics because of a certain Eurocentric strabismus, was an incentive for some. The first retrospective of the hero of North American independents, John Cassavettes, which also included members of his team, was a major discovery for others; the "dogma" of Lars von Trier, who participated in a workshop during the first festival, had the same effect on others, even through their rejection of it. And so on. The idea behind these encounters was never to present the latest trend, but rather to reveal cinema as a process, as an activity carried out by beings just as human (or just as brilliant) as the guy next door, not by untouchable magical beings. Further still, in the second year of the festival we shared, through the memorable *Fight Club* and its representatives, information on a number of European funds that some had been keeping secret and that, with relatively small sums, helped to finish films that had been languishing away on VHS or, on the other hand, provided a space for that critical moment in the development of a project, something that was often overlooked by the National Film Institute. Funds like the Hubert Bals in Holland or Fond Sud in France were immediately inundated with Argentine projects and, in recent years, Argentine directors have almost always made up the majority of award recipients. Once again, quantity makes for quality.

We also created spaces for local and international filmmakers to share their experiences and, in collaboration with Américo Castilla and various international foundations, formed a workshop for Latin American film projects that, fortunately, has survived the many different directions the festival has taken, including the disappearance of the Fundación Antorchas, which was its primary source of funding. One of the advisors on the first workshop, Ilse Hughan of the Rotterdam festival, let her enthusiasm lead her not only into taking over the workshop, but also into organizing the Buenos Aires Lab (BAL), gathering of filmmakers and producers that takes place as part of BAFICI and is the perfect complement to the project workshop, which was first called "Bariloche" and later "Colón" after its geographic location. It was sometimes hard for us to explain what the workshop really was, apart from the experience – enriching in itself – of getting away from the world for a week with a group of Latin American filmmakers in a remote area of Patagonia or a bucolic town in the province of Entre Ríos. It was not a screenwriting seminar or a production workshop, but rather an opportunity to think about the best way to proceed with a project, which was different for each director, from the ability to write a good synopsis or film treatment, to the competence skill needed to present a film to a producer and, above all, to examine something as elusive yet as perfectly tangible as the true relation between a director and his project: the knowledge that it is that one person, and no one else, that will make the film. That same unique sensation that the best films of New Argentine Cinema transmit. Among these are some that came out of this very workshop, like *Ana y los otros*, by Celina Murga; *Los muertos*, by Lisandro Alonso; *El custodio*, by Rodrigo Moreno; or Paz Encina's Argentine-Paraguayan co-production, *Hamaca paraguaya*; all of which have won awards at the most important festivals in the world.

VII.

I cannot make a list here of all the Argentine films that had an impact on me in those years, nor is it my intention to do so. But if I think about New Argentine Cinema, I cannot help but think of Lucrecia Martel, who, in my opinion, is one of the most important directors of our time (not only in the context of Argentina, but of the "world"). Even though Martel, when they ask her, refuses to be included in the flock of New Argentine Cinema. Daniel Burman, who realized the myth (and apparent paradox) of the independent director who makes films that are at once increasingly 'commercial' and increasingly personal, would certainly say the same thing. Nor would Fabián Bielinsky have considered himself a bird of a feather with the rest. But few recall that his megahit *Nueve reinas* started out as a project that could not get produced. I understand that it was even rejected by the same producer that ended up working on the project, almost against her will, after it unexpectedly won an award in a screenplay competition organized in response to the phenomenon of New Cinema. There had never before been a Bielinsky. In a way, Bielinsky is both a part and a product of the phenomenon. Alejandro Agresti, who directed Keanu Reeves and Sandra Bullock in Hollywood and who began his career as a young man in exile in Holland, was never a card-carrying member of new independent cinema. Nevertheless, he left a few films along the way that seemed to announce something new, like *El amor es una mujer gorda* and *Buenos Aires viceversa*. He was even ahead of his time in his connection to Holland, though not necessarily in his move to Hollywood. When he made *Historias mínimas*, Carlos Sorín said that it was the younger generation of filmmakers that inspired him to step away from the comforts of mainstream cinema and return to the Patagonian roads he had traveled some twenty years earlier in *La película del rey* (one of the *exceptions* to which I alluded before). In all the countries where it was shown, to great success, it was described as the next chapter of New Argentine Cinema.

The critics who were able to see what was different about these new films and fought with their editors to get good placement for articles about, for example, an exceptional but decidedly difficult movie like Lisandro Alonso's *La libertad*, also played an important role. I don't think that they would consider themselves part of New Argentine Cinema, with the exception of someone like Juan Villegas or Sergio Wolf, who were daring enough to step out from behind their typewriters and make their own movies. *Sábado* (Villegas) and *Yo no sé qué me han hecho tus ojos* (Wolf, co-directed by Lorena Muñoz) are significant works. I would venture to include (without telling him) a stage director like Federico León, who has also made his own films and who also develops and provides actors for other films, like those by Diego Lerman or Ezequiel Acuña. (One of the best-kept secrets of Argentine cinema is its close relation with the theatric panorama of Buenos Aires, upon which it feeds.) Nor would Mariano Llinás care to be associated with this horde, after his radical provocation that questioned any trace of *bourgeoisification* on the part of the new generation of directors and his incitement to make digital films, without funding, outside the system. Not even the historic figures of the early *Historias breves*, a collection of short films compiled in 1995 and thought by some to have started New Argentine Cinema, would admit to being part of it. And that is not to mention lone wolves like Raúl Perrone, the Jim Jarmusch of Ituzaingó, honored by BAFICI with a retrospective, or Ana Poliak, who became the first Argentine winner of the international competition of that same festival with *Parapalos*, which was still never able to secure a commercial release (this is another story entirely, which deserves its own chapter). Nor would veterans like Edgardo Cozarinsky, the great writer-director repatriated after a charmed but solitary exile in Paris, or Rafael Filippelli, the Zen master who leads the new generation from his position at the University and from the halls of BAFICI, identify themselves with the new cinema. And of course neither Sapir nor Rejtman sees himself as the precursor of anything, though the latter, true to his exceptional nature, once admitted that there might be something called New Argentine Cinema, and that he might be considered an example of it. As though he were saying, defiantly, "So what?" There are many others we could discuss and that, at the moment, I cannot recall. What is remarkable is precisely that there are so many others. It is hard to imagine, for those that do not remember it, how little there was to talk about when it came to Argentine cinema from "before." I would go so far as to say that it is hard to remember even for those who do remember it. And yet, it is perhaps in this very impossibility of belonging that one may ultimately find a unifying characteristic of this movement-that-is-not. *Eppur si muove...* As Groucho Marx would say: "I refuse to join any club that would have me as a member." Such are the 'members' of New Argentine Cinema: no two are alike, and neither are their films.

2. Singularities in Context

In this section the perspective shifts toward (and from) the filmmakers. The concept of the auteur has enjoyed a long critical history that today coexists with the consecration of the director within *mainstream* production. Many directors have become brands that add value in the audiovisual marketplace and, as such, allow themselves to be put to corporate use as a guarantee for films that inundate theaters the world over. Nonetheless, the category of the auteur must be considered on another level: that of the struggle for the development and support of a desire for cinema. This desire is a driving force of those who, under different conditions – and often in resistance to opposing forces – give shape to their own form of cinema. The auteur, then, is able to represent the act of taking a stand, work at the margins of accepted practice, even situate him- or herself outside the system, to the point of radicalization.

Two filmmakers representative of these remarkable paths are studied here by scholars that delve deeply into their bodies of work. Mauricio Durán brings into focus the surprising figure of Luis Ospina, a filmmaker who was once part of a collective that established a utopia based in Colombia and in the seventies reconsidered and tried to reformulate certain modes of cinematic production in Latin America. With a trajectory that became more solitary and silent, but always demonstrated his passion for cinema, Ospina has become a referent for new generations; much like Cristián Sánchez, whose work is addressed by Jorge Ruffinelli in a study that examines what makes the director, whose cinematic production has developed with unexpected vitality under the most adverse conditions, so exceptional. Both texts offer a combination of analytic rigor and the passion for cinema that both Ospina and Sánchez still convey.

In terms of radicalization and consequence over time, it is hard to compare to the trajectory presented by Lisandro Alonso of Argentina over the past decade. His tetralogy is examined for signs of an extreme approach to cinema through his composition, not only within his films, but in the state of cinema he persists in showing. Like the figure of Janus, something in Alonso seems to be looking in two directions, noting at once a breaking point and a mutation that could salvage longstanding cinematic forms, along with other possibilities for the future of cinema.

At the dawn of the new century, Latin American cinema proves – like the construction of identity itself – to be a continual process. Paz Encina reflects on the experience of making *Hamaca paraguaya*, the influence of Ozu cinema, and the anima of a remote country that has rarely, if ever, been seen (and so memorably heard, in this case, through the Guaraní language) in theaters. Written with a clarity that establishes a profound, loving engagement with its object, the text inserts itself within the bonds that join the subject to a communal plane, personal history to a collective that has stood the test of time and is designated by a *we*.

Luis Ospina and Colombian Cinema: Independence or Resistance?

Mauricio Durán Castro

> *In Colombia, one sets out to make the film one wants and ends up making the film one can.*
>
> Luis Ospina

Independent of what?

How can one speak of independent cinema in a country without a film industry? This type of cinema is only possible in countries with an industry from which certain directors can become independent. In Brazil, Argentina or Mexico, the most consolidated Latin American movements – Cinema Novo, Third Cinema and Other cinema – chose to work at the margins of the industry. They needed to come up with strategies to reduce production costs in order not to have to meet the commercial demands of the industry and have more freedom in the way they worked with subjects, stories, and narrative forms. But in a country like Colombia, even the slightest expense implies an extraordinary effort, literally one of "tearing the house apart to make a film" as Camilo Correa, José María Arzuaga and others have done.[58]

Although Colombian cinema played an important role during the time of the silent film (1922-28), with more than twelve feature films distributed throughout various Latin American countries, the arrival of the sound film and the

---

[58] Henao, C. "Entrevista con Luis Ospina" *Kinetoscopio 67* (Medellín, 2003).

immense challenges and production costs that came with it gave the advantage to the distribution and screening of foreign films. From 1928 to 1948, most production was of newsreels and silent documentaries, which fortunately form part of the country's historical record today. Many of these productions were essentially official films financed as propaganda by the government: in 1908, General Rafael Reyes imported a French cameraman to record presidential outings; Ospina Pérez (1946-50) and General Rojas Pinilla (1953-57) hired Marco Tulio Lizarazo to make films about their politics and the works of their administrations. Despite the difficulties surrounding the production of other types of cinema, between 1928 and 1960 nearly a dozen feature films were made, as well as the short *La langosta azul* (1954), a piece unusual in its desire to create an expressive form that did not necessarily require an audience. This "film on vacation," as its creators Álvaro Cepeda Samudio, Gabriel García Márquez, Enrique Grau, Nereo López and Luís Vinyens called it, is one of the first works of auteur cinema, without strictly being independent.

In the sixties, other forms of audiovisual production, such as television and films commissioned by state entities or the private sector, were established. Among these, the efforts and accomplishments of two important directors stand out: Julio Luzardo and the aforementioned Arzuaga. At the end of the decade, the project of New Latin American Cinema was being taken up, producing films of urgent political militancy, images that denounced social injustice and revealed "the presence of the people" in every shot. The ethnographic documentaries of Gabriela Samper, the militant cinema of Carlos Álvarez, the documentary *Camilo Torres* (1967), by Diego León Giraldo; the mise en scène documentary *Chircales* (1966-72), by Jorge Silva and Marta Rodríguez or the counter-informational *Oiga vea*

(1971), by Carlos Mayolo and Luis Ospina demonstrate these tendencies.

The resistance to official cinema

In 1971, a surcharge law was passed, which protected the local production of short films by mandating they be screened in all theaters that showed foreign films. This state protection increased the production of short films from 10 in 1970 to its peak at 103 in 1976. The audience paid the surcharge, which was shared between the theater and the producer; however, adding insult to injury, not only did they have to pay, they had to sit through increasingly bad short films, despite the creation in 1974 of a government body in charge of quality assurance. Producers and directors of narrative shorts almost immediately adopted the *tics* and actors of a national television only recently established: stories that were no more than well or poorly told jokes, travel documentaries, or worse, so-called exposés that did nothing more than repeat the cheap formula of shooting misery and marginalized subjects accompanied by a voice-over, without any research, sensitivity or imagination. What is more, the theaters reused these shorts for years on end without the intervention of the producers, until they decided to corner the market by producing them on their own. For Luis Ospina, this is what gave Colombian films a bad name in the eyes of the public, who naturally rejected local cinema.[59] Nonetheless, this gave many the opportunity to learn the trade and gain the experience they would use to make the feature films of the eighties that were produced through the state entity FOCINE (1978-1993).

Other directors preferred to work without state support in order to address subjects that were being censored by

---

[59] From an interview with Ospina on Wedesday October 4, 2006 in Bogotá.

the office of quality control, making films that were twelve minutes and longer on 16 and 8mm stock. Groups and cooperatives emerged to make films at the limits of the (surcharge) law. Silva and Rodríguez continued to make the most politically engaged cinema of the time, without allowing its poetry to be eclipsed by the rigor of its ethnographic gaze: *Planas* (1970), *Campesinos* (1976) and *Nuestra voz de tierra, memoria y futuro* (1982). In Bogotá, groups like Mugre al Ojo and Cine Mujer came together on the basis of form and language. Arturo Jaramillo and Ignacio Jiménez in Bogotá, as well as Víctor Gaviria in his early work, promoted Super 8 as an experimental alternative. Another group was organizing film societies in Cali, publishing a journal and making films. This collective, which shared cinematic ideals and aesthetic affinities, centered on the writer and film critic Andrés Caicedo and the filmmakers Mayolo and Ospina; together, they created a movement that would also reach the theater, literature, photography and the visual arts.

The Cali group

In the sixties, Cali ceased to be an average, unassuming city and became a vigorous industrial center with significant social problems. Its rapid growth and transformation was due to industrial developments that attracted immigrants and peasants displaced by the violence in the countryside, all of whom sought refuge in its abject suburbs. At the end of the sixties, Hernando Guerrero founded the Ciudad Solar, an independent cultural center that was the site of 16mm screenings from the film society created by Caicedo and Ospina, the staging of experimental theater projects, Miguel González's art gallery, a dark room for photography, the production offices of *Oiga vea* and of *Angelita y Miguel Ángel* (1973), and a commune for artists and wanderers, in which Caicedo lived for a time. The playwright Enrique Buenaventura, the filmmaker Carlos Mayolo, the photographers Eduardo Carvajal and Fernell Franco, and the visual artists Ever Astudillo and Oscar Muñoz all held meetings there. In the mid-seventies, Guerrero traveled to Paris and Ospina used his home as the 16mm screening room for the film society, the offices of the journal *Ojo al cine* (1974-1976) and the location for a few of the scenes in *Agarrando pueblo* (1978) and Caicedo's video project *Angelitos empatanados* (1975). Just like Ciudad Solar, this was a sort of commune for Ospina, Caicedo and Carvajal. The Cali Film Society and the journal *Ojo al cine* contributed to a rich and passionate discourse on the cinema in the city and in Colombia as a whole, promoting its taste for certain North American genres like horror films, comedies and westerns, as well as European directors like Buñuel, Truffaut, Chabrol, Pasolini, and Polanski, and dedicating extensive interviews and essays to Colombian directors of the sixties and seventies, like José María Arzuaga, Julio Luzardo, Jorge Silva and Marta Rodríguez.

The other passion of Cali's youth was music, exalted in Caicedo's novel *¡Que viva la música!* (1975), which tells the story of the movement of its heroine, Maria del Carmen Huerta, from her home in northern Cali and her preference for the Rolling Stones, to the south of the city and her encounter with the music of Richie Ray and Bobby Cruz, and comes to a close in a brothel. It narrates her high jinx and her downfall: from rock to salsa, from the north to the south, from her bourgeois roots to her eventual disgrace, as a choice. In its final pages, María del Carmen offers her reader, perhaps another adolescent, some words of advice: "Make impulsiveness and contradiction your standards of behavior [ ] There is no better remedy for the hatred that the censors have instilled in you than murder. For timidity: self-destruction [ ] If you leave work behind, die happy, trusting in a few good friends."[60] In 1977, days after the novel's publication in the collection *Obra en marcha* by Colcultura, its author committed suicide at the age of 25. The influence of the work, however, would continue to grow among future generations of cinephiles, fans of teen literature, music lovers, and bohemians.

In 1986, Ospina made the documentary *Andrés Caicedo: unos pocos buenos amigos*, looking for the marks he left on the city, friends and acquaintances, his music, his writings, and the unpublished fragments of his stalled film project *Angelita y Miguel Ángel*. This narrative feature, conceived by Caicedo and Carlos Mayolo based on an idea of the former, was left unfinished when the latter decided that he wanted to turn it into more of a documentary. The recovered scenes demonstrate, despite their poor condition, Caidedo's taste for the stories of youths and a measured compositional style, removed from the clichés of naturalist representation to which the national cinema still adhered. As in his novel, the story moves from the bourgeois origins of its protagonist to contact with the popular, from the north to the south of Cali, to the street, salsa and dance. *Angelita y Miguel Ángel* reminds us, in its story and its fresh cinematic approach, of its contemporary, *Palomita Blanca* (1973), by the Chilean Raúl Ruiz.

The vampires of Cali

The attempt to recreate this lost Cali can be seen in the narrative features *Pura sangre* (1982), by Ospina; *Carne de tu carne* (1983) and *Aquel 19* (1985), by Mayolo, in the documentary series *Adiós a Cali* (1990) and *Cali, ayer, hoy y mañana* (1995), by Ospina or in the performance of Caicedo's play, staged by Sandro Romero. The ghostly

---

[60] Caicedo, Andrés. *¡Que viva la música!* Bogotá: Norma, 2001. 203-206.

spirit of the city was uncovered by Caicedo in short stories like "Infección," "Vacío," "En las garras del crimen," "Calibanismo" and "Los mensajeros" – a city that "doesn't open its doors to desperate men" – as well as in his masterpiece, *¡Que viva la música!* Cali appears, to its adolescent protagonists, as a space of uncertainty, of appearances and disappearances, combined with characters taken from Poe and Lovecraft, zombie movies, vampires, detectives and criminals. More than just the imported imaginaries of other narratives, the monsters and monstrosities of thousands of displaced persons proliferate within them, alongside the indelible traces of the rural violence of the fifties. This identification with vampirism and hardboiled fiction is carried over in the films of Ospina, Mayolo, Oscar Campo and Jorge Navas. This ghostly and evolving Cali is where the generation of the Cali group lived out their adolescence and youth. In 1956, the city was shaken by the explosion of several trucks loaded with dynamite, which destroyed one of its nicest neighborhoods. Ospina remembers this moment, which is also when he met Mayolo: "We lived nearby, in Versalles, and the explosion knocked down part of our house. So we went to live with my grandmother, in Centenario, and Carlos Mayolo lived across the street. I was seven at the time and I remember that one of the first things we did after we met was go up the hill of the Three Crosses and light a candle."[61] This historic event was portrayed by Mayolo at the beginning of *Carne de tu carne*. Another story that circulated among the children and teens of the city in 1963 was that of the Monstruo de los Mangones, Cali's version of "M," which Ospina used as part of the plot of *Pura sangre*. He recalls his impression at seeing one of the victims of the infanticide: "One morning

---

[61] Pérez, C. and Gómez, S. A. "Entrevista con Luis Ospina" *Kinetoscopio* 22 (Medellín: 1993).

I looked outside to see a gathering of people a block and a half from my house. There was a naked boy, apparently raped, with a hole near his heart. The legend was that the Monster killed little boys, drained their blood through that hole and raped them. I started working with that idea because, for someone my age, the Monster was like the bogeyman. If you weren't careful, he would literally eat you alive."[62] In 1964, at fourteen and with his father's home camera, Ospina makes his first film: a silent short of about five minutes called *Vía cerrada*. A young man is bored and takes a train from Cali to the outskirts of the city; he gets off at a ranch and finds a rural cemetery with a gravestone in it that bears his exact name. This story, which today seems rather trite, reveals his early preoccupation with one of his central themes: death.

Learning outside

From 1968 to 1972, Ospina studied film at the University of Southern California and UCLA. He experienced the counterculture movements of the late sixties in the United States: hippies, psychedelics, the struggles of ethnic and cultural minorities, the student revolution and the protests against North America's intervention in Vietnam. He also got to know the underground film promoted by Jonas Mekas: from the films of visual artist Andy Warhol to the political cinema of Emile de Antonio. During this time he made *Acto de fe* (1970), *Autorretrato dormido* (1971), *Bombardeo a Washington* (1972) and *Oiga vea*.

Acto de fe, the first project he made at the university, is based on Jean Paul Sartre's story "Erostratus." A man sees humanity as a swarm of insects from his sixth floor balcony; his voice expresses his disdain for the anonymous masses

---

[62] Ibid.

and the individual human being, addressing the public with the words "You may find it agreeable, but it makes me sick." He sees men, squashed against the ground, make horrifying gestures as they eat, leave theaters as though they were floating on air, dazzled by the movies they just watched. The protagonist of *Acto de fe* wants to shoot someone, "maybe you," he says, looking into the camera by way of a mirror. He steps out into the street, revolver in his pocket, and passes through the crowd until he achieves his objective. Like the protagonist of *Taxi Driver* (1976), he sees the crowd through a windshield and later exerts his revenge upon it. Both come from one of the most profound descriptions of the soul of a man of the urban masses, of the consciousness of the individual trapped in the abyss and the disjuncture of great societies, which appears for the first time in Edgar Allen Poe's story "The Man of the Crowd." But if Scorcese's Travis justifies his actions through his moralistic delirium, Ospina's Eróstrato sees only the absurd in both society and human existence. He ends up locked in a public bathroom unable to decide between killing himself and going back out into the world. The short presents the image of death through murder and suicide, which Ospina will repeat in the avenging heroes of *Asunción* (1975) and *Agarrando pueblo* (1978); even the eccentric one of *Pura sangre* (1982). He also begins to establish his own language while filming on the streets of Los Angeles, combining mise en scène with shots taken in a more documentary style; editing the material, making use of voice-overs.

Ospina filmed *Autorretrato (dormido)* on a three-minute reel of Super 8 completely on his own and without any edits. He set the camera to automatically shoot one frame every ten seconds while he slept, thus compressing ten hours of sleep into three minutes. The idea came from *Sleep* (1963), in which Andy Warhol filmed John Giorno for five hours as he slept, but Ospina decided to cut out the "dead air." It is also the first film to be made by a sleeping man, a method that would have gotten the attention of the surrealists. Although its impetus had been a joke – "to respond to that film as a bit of a joke, which was what Andy Warhol was doing, was a joke about a joke"[63] – the documentary filmmaker in him can be felt in the need for an understanding of that which we cannot witness. What happens to our bodies when we sleep? The answer surprised him by demonstrating how his body (breathing rapidly) becomes pure vibration.

Another exercise from his years at school was *El bombardeo de Washington*, in which a story is told in one minute using images from the archives edited together: a bombing attack on the Capitol. It joins the Dadaist technique of the "objet trouvé" with the cinematography of Lev Kuleshov, Sergei Eisenstein and Dziga Vertov, which shows how new meaning can be constructed by extracting a fragment from its environs and coupling it with another context. Ospina translated a number of Vertov's texts from English to Spanish and, more recently, has returned to these techniques in *Un tigre de papel* (2007), which includes, as a relevant self-reference, *El bombardeo*. In this brief exercise he explores his interest in different documentary forms and for the work of film editing.

Return to Cali

For his final project at UCLA, Ospina was permitted to make a documentary outside of Los Angeles, completely in Spanish and in collaboration with Carlos Mayolo. *Oiga vea* began as the desire to make a documentary that would show what the official documentary of the sixth Pan-American Games in Cali would not: in their words, "a documentary of

---

[63] From an interview with Ospina on Wedesday October 4, 2006 in Bogotá.

counter-information." Mayolo's 16mm camera captures the directors of the 35mm official documentary from behind, along with their shirts that say "Official Cinema," while Ospina asks people on the street what official cinema is. *Oiga vea* depicts the preparations for the games, the costs and benefits they bring to the city, the participation of the residents, without the directors drawing any conclusions in voice-overs. They are images of the work, its billboards, athletic scenes seen from outside, events in the street, working-class neighborhoods and the sounds of the radio, the television, the opening remarks of President Misael Pastrana Borrero, sports ballads, salsa music, and interviews with the people of Cali, the editing of which leads the viewers to come to their own conclusions. With a tape recorder and a spring-wound Bolex, Ospina records the sound and Mayolo the images. The name of the film alludes to a Cali localism ("Listen, look") and alerts the spectator to reality and how the images attempt to present it. Yet it also alludes to the minimalist team that made it: one "listens" and the other "looks"; meaning is later created through Ospina's audiovisual editing. Without a script but with a "starting-point of view: the point of view of those who could not get in to see the games."[64]

Jean Vigo expounds upon his idea of the "documentary point of view" through a text in which he explains his approach in *À propos de Nice* (1930); Fernando Birri put this into practice in his documentary *Tire die* (1956-58), an important landmark in New Latin American Cinema. *Oiga vea* shows its "point of view" several times: one take shows a diver on the Olympic pool's diving board – as he jumps, a *zoom out* quickly reminds us of our place where the shot was taken: outside the stadium. The sound insists on this point of "view" as well: the opening ceremony and

---

[64] Pérez, C. and Gómez, S. A."Entrevista con Luis Ospina" *Kinetoscopio,* 22.

the events aired on the radio, the commentaries and answers of everyone excluded from the games. In *Oiga vea*, cinema "puts itself at the service of the people, so that they can express themselves. In a city like Cali, without any form of audiovisual record, it was important to capture the way the people speak, what they say, their humor."[65] The community is not interpreted by a distant voice-over, but rather through a microphone held right up to it. It is asked about its participation in the Pan-American games, the benefits of the transformation of the city, the costs associated with the games and who paid them, what official cinema means. The answers are juxtaposed with other images and sounds, such as the opening remarks by the President of the Republic. The directors' commentary, their tone and sense of irony, is most clearly expressed in the audiovisual editing: the repetition of the President's voice as it declares "the sixth Pan-American Games are now open" alongside images of the people, caught outside the athletic scene; the exploration of official cinema followed by images of the film itself and the sound of a military march; the projection of slides of the buildings constructed for the games, accompanied by the sound of the projector mixed in with that of a cash register.

With *Cali de película* (1973), Ospina and Mayolo make another documentary about their city, this time at the Cali Fair. Whereas *Oiga vea* was made with their own resources – black and white 16mm film – and was 27 minutes long, they now found themselves with financial backing, a 35mm camera and color film stock; they produced a final cut that was 14 minutes long, which allowed them to show it commercially. They were trying to make a piece of direct documentary cinema, but without an Eclair camera and a Nagra audio recorder.

---

[65] From an interview with Ospina on Wedesday October 4, 2006 in Bogotá.

Disdain for the surcharge

Ospina and Mayolo made their only 'surcharge' short in 1975: *Asunción*. It is the story of a domestic worker whose employers leave her in charge of the house for the weekend; she throws a party for all her friends and ends up leaving it wide open and in complete disarray. For showing how the "class enemy at home"[66] exacts revenge, the film received the censure of the bourgeois viewer. The allusion to vampirism in the moment when the woman cuts herself and lets her blood run into the soup she is making for her employers reveals the vulnerability of the bourgeois family. Just as in *Pura sangre*, this is a metaphor for the exploitation of labor that does not resort to the Manichean and literal approach of exposé cinema, as many surcharge documentaries do. Its subversiveness and the fear of incitement led to its censorship, which was attributed to "poor quality." Ospina found the argument of the quality control, that "the film lacked artistic direction, that the editing was abrupt and that the technical work was insufficient,"[67] to be completely incomprehensible.

Agarrando pueblo is the masterwork of the Ospina-Mayolo collaboration, and does away with many of the bad habits that local cinema had acquired. Its very format assured that it would not only be a critique of the surcharge but also impossible to commercialize: "At the time, there wasn't a place for 16mm films that were 27 minutes long. We worked through the help of friends: painter friends who donated a painting to sell, people who would do our developing for free or send it through under the table at their jobs."[68] It is a decidedly independent and resistant

---

[66] Ibid.
[67] Ibid.
[68] Pérez, C. and Gómez, S. A."Entrevista con Luis Ospina" *Kinetoscopio*, 22.

film about the manic fixations of so-called "exposé" cinema that degenerated into "misery porn": the "stolen image," the tricks used to get footage of the marginalized and their misery, the obvious commercial exploitation of the product and, finally, the voice-over that reiterates the abstract causes of these social conditions: the system, society, the state, the government. It is the story of a film crew making a typical "misery porn" documentary. The voice-over of the fictional documentary offers a caricature of their rhetoric: "the corollary is unavoidable; these are cases of child abandonment, dementia, juvenile delinquency, prostitution, malnourishment and illiteracy." The director of the documentary – played by Mayolo himself – says to his cameraman that "we seem like vampires," and in the final sequence of the film they are caught "community-snatching" by the owner of the ranch on which they are creating their false reality. In the final shot, Mayolo and Ospina interview Luís Alfonso Londoño – who plays the man that surprises the crew filming on his ranch – about this type of cinema that only wants to seize on a community. The film maintains a rich tension between reality and its representation, documentary and fiction, between the real unmasking of a situation and the ideological construction of a documentary, using the juxtaposition of color and black and white, documentary and fiction. More than a "fake documentary" (undertaken later in *Un tigre de papel*), this is cinema within cinema, in the tradition of Fellini's *8 ½* and Godard's *Contempt*.

The longer works, in short

In more than twenty years, Luis Ospina only managed to make two feature-length films: *Pura sangre* (1982) and *Soplo de vida* (1999). Among other things, because the debt he accumulated with FOCINE in order to make his first took him out of the running for a long time. FOCINE was founded by decree in 1978 and operated until 1993, financing and producing 130 mid-length and 29 feature films, of which Ospina's was one of the first to receive a loan. Based on a script he wrote himself, *Pura sangre* tells the story of the Monstruo de los Mangones, interweaving the sensationalist account to the legend of an ailing millionaire who needs continuous blood transfusions. The vampirism takes place in a local social context, making ironic allusions to the sugar industry in Cali and the manipulation of information by the media. As in *Asunción* and *Agarrando pueblo*, the exploitation of labor and the machinations of the media appear as forms of vampirism. But its stylistic refinement and references to other films, which turned a predictable horror movie into a vampiric allegory, were not to the public's liking. What the director was left with: "it did not get into the public's veins, so I was left with nothing but a bank account in the red."[69]

Only 17 years later did he return to the narrative feature with *Soplo de vida*, a detective film based on a script written by his brother Sebastián that addresses, allegorically, the veil of mystery that obscures the crime and the disappearances that take place in our country. It begins with the Armero tragedy, which took more than 20,000 lives in 1985, and concludes in a rural cemetery, a journey that implicitly alludes to the links between paramilitary forces and the political classes. It recounts the journey made by the ashes of a girl known only as "la golondrina" (the sparrow) on their way to their final resting place, and the mystery that surrounds her death. It pays homage to North American film noir in its refined cinematography and use of flashback in the narrative structure, introducing a new social context.

---

[69] Ospina, Luis. "El fracaso de una ilusión: una historia común y particular del cine colombiano". *El Malpensante* 38 (Bogotá: 2002).

As he did in *Pura sangre*, Ospina demonstrates exquisite cinephilic pedigree alongside his documentary concerns, yet without ever getting into "the veins of the public."

To document and preserve

In 1985 Ospina collaborates with Jorge Nieto on *En busca de María,* a short film about one of the first feature films to come out of Cali: *María* (1922). It is an investigation into this lost film – only 24 seconds have been preserved – through interviews with a few of its contributors and film historian Hernando Salcedo and the reconstruction of its filming, in which Mayolo and Ospina play the roles of the two directors of the silent film: Máximo Calvo and Alfredo del Diestro. Ospina has found, in the documentary and in video, the possibility of constructing, rescuing and preserving the memory of artists and works that were condemned to be forgotten: *En busca de María, Andrés Caicedo; Unos pocos buenos amigos, Antonio María Valencia; Música en cámara* (1987), *Ojo y vista: peligra la vida del artista* (1988), *Arte sano cuadra a cuadra* (1988), *Fotofijaciones* (1988), *Nuestra película* (1993), and *La desazón suprema: Retrato incesante de Fernando Vallejo* (2003). Documenting the daily life of Vallejo and rescuing Caicedo and Valencia from the grip of death come from the same drive: to resist death and forgetting. *Andrés Caicedo* opens with an examination of the memory of the writer retained by the youth of Cali that ultimately uncovers their lack of familiarity. Caicedo and Valencia were artists who gave their work to a city that has forgotten them; the fragments of the film *María*, the photos of Carvajal and the encounter with the character filming in *Agarrando pueblo* serve the same purpose. In his documentaries one can see the same ontological essence that Bazin saw in the photographic image: that of stealing an image for the future from the grasp of time and death.

But perhaps the most dramatic moment in this desperate, losing battle is the testimony of *Nuestra película*, which Lorenzo Jaramillo, dying of AIDS, asked him to make to record his final days. Together they make 'our movie,' in which they talk about art, life and death; about film, color and food; about music, Michaux and the theater. The document slips neither into sensationalism nor melodrama, thanks to Ospina's modest approach to the private world of Jaramillo. Similarities with *Nick's Film – Lightning Over Water* (1980) by Wim Wenders and Nicholas Ray are not accidental; the German filmmaker was also deeply engaged by the idea of death and of film as a trace of "death at work," as Jean Cocteau has stated. Wenders and Ospina share the sensibility belonging to a generation that gave birth to rock and roll and watched the death of film. Video is just this to Ospina: the resurrection of the audiovisual from the ashes of celluloid. "The filmic medium is becoming more and more electronic, many films are being shot in digital formats as the chemical process disappears. I like to cover it all; we work in audiovisual – images in motion with sound –the format does not matter."[70]

The conversational documentary

To Ospina, making a narrative film is like hunting, whereas making a documentary is more like fishing: "When you go hunting, you need to be prepared, know what you are going after – bears, tigers, whatever. You have to bring everything, according to the object, like following a script. A documentary is more like fishing: you cast a line and don't know what is going to come out."[71] The documentary seeks to understand a reality on a deeper level; it may

---

[70] From an interview with Ospina on Wednesday October 4, 2006 in Bogotá.
[71] From an interview with Ospina on Wednesday October 4, 2006 in Bogotá.

not show up with preconceptions or scripts, though it is necessary to have a 'point of view' or position from which to approach the problem. He and Mayolo chose the principles of Dziga Vertov and Jean Vigo over those of Robert Flaherty and John Grierson; later they would follow the methods of cinéma verité and direct cinema, without a crew. For *Agarrando pueblo* they have their Eclair camera and Nagra sound recorder. The importance of having the right technology for their expressive choices becomes explicit when they go in-house, from *Oiga vea* to *Un tigre de papel*. Thanks to video, in the eighties he is able to work in a documentary style all his own, in which the chance thread of a conversation seems to guide the narration, as it does in *Andrés Caicedo: Unos pocos buenos amigos*; *Ojo y vista: peligra la vida del artista*; *Arte sano cuadra a cuadra,* and *Fotofijaciones*. Yet this order is actually established in the editing room, in which the themes are made to structure an already edited conversation, retaining, nonetheless, the meandering quality of any dialogue. The conversation moves among equals, among friends, from a place of "giving a voice to the community so it can express itself." Ospina made a documentary trilogy in 1991 about the shoeshines, barbers and taxidrivers he patronized: *Al pie*, *Al pelo*, and *A la carrera*. Each one lasts as long as a shoe shine, a haircut, or a taxi ride: 25 minutes, in which casual conversation reveals the philosophy or the art behind each trade. The world is constructed through a trade to which everyone assigns a specialized gaze: the enlightened conversations of the shoeshine, the tastes and affinities of the hairdresser, the urban legends of the taxi driver.

This type of documentary filmmaking continues with *Mucho gusto* (1997), which examines 'taste' at a moment in which values and aesthetics are being transformed by the rise in drug trafficking. Through editing, Ospina recreates a conversation among professionals that begins on the subject of taste but dissipates into the realms of art, aesthetics, culture, sense and sensitivity, eroticism, pornography, ethics, the monstrous, the horrific, etc. His interviewees are figures in the national scene today: artists, critics, curators, literati, anthropologists, psychoanalysts, neurophysiologists, social scientists, semiologists, television writers. This heterogeneous material is edited together into themed fragments that seem to arise spontaneously as they would in an extended conversation, and which are paced by intertitles and interspersed with images and the song *Sympathy for the Devil* by the Rolling Stones.

Goodbye, Cali

Adiós a Cali (1990) is a different type of documentary, a dyptich composed of *Cali plano x plano* and *¡Ah, diosa Kali!*, each 25 minutes long. The first of these is a sort of urban symphony that shows the city's transformation during those years: from the public buildings and government construction left unfinished or being demolished, to the construction of great glass towers. This transformation is expressed audiovisually through slow pans and tilts on the architecture; slow, deliberate montage; sound based on the noises of the city. The second of these includes the statements of visual artists who retain, in their work, traces of the loss of their city – Oscar Muñoz, Ever Astudillo and Fernell Franco – along with the opinions of demolition experts on their role in the modernization of the city and the same trip made by the director to his childhood home. He superimposes images of the past and of the present: those of the patio and the pool of a house being torn down and the shots in Super 8 of that same pool, in which the Ospina children swam three decades earlier, as though they were diving into a ghostly space in which the present demolishes this fragil, photographic memory. Once again, the thematic obsessions: time, memory, and images obtained and retained through the camera obscura.

In 1979 and 1980, in the Universidad del Valle's Department of Communications, Ospina established a school of documentary filmmaking that directors like Oscar Campo would continue through projects for the series *Rostros y rastros* on University television (UVTV); he also made the documentary series *Cali: ayer, hoy y mañana* (1995), ten chapters of 25 minutes each. The object of these is a documentary "without text, without narration, which has been a constant in my work and in the work of all the film and video directors in Cali who make documentaries: to create their pieces without narration, without voice-over, always allowing the film to create its own discourse, giving the last word to the people."[72]

Video and digital as resurrection

Ospina remembers how, at UCLA, he quickly moved from the Department of Television to the second floor, where the Film Department was. "Video, at the time, was considered ignoble, cumbersome, and conventional. Cassettes had not yet been invented – the only portable equipment were heavy half-inch open-canister Sony portapacks that shot in black and white."[73] Today, video has become the lifeblood of the audiovisual trade, the possibility of working without the high cost of film. From *Andrés Caicedo* on, Ospina no longer sees it as a simple *video assist*, but rather as his mode of expression, a ductile medium better suited to absorb others. With *Ojo y vista*, he opens the space for

---

[72] Pérez, C. and Gómez, S. A. "Entrevista con Luis Ospina" *Kinetoscopio* 22.
[73] Ospina, Luis. "VINI, VIDEO, VICI, El video como resurrección" *El malpensante*, 48 (Bogotá: 2003).

Rostros y rastros on UVTV. In *Nuestra película*, he uses a Hi-8 camera, which permits him the minimal crew required: a cinematographer friend.[74] In 1999, he uses a digital camera to record the footage for the "video art" of *Video (B)art(h) es* (2003), part of a project curated by the video artist José Alejandro Restrepo. He makes the documentary *La desazón suprema: Retrato incesante de Fernando Vallejo* on a Sony digital VX2000 and edits *Un tigre de papel* in his home with young director Rubén Mendoza, 'pirating' a vast amount of material from the internet. His productions grow more and more home-made, thanks to new technologies that make possible Glauber Rocha's dream of making films "with an idea in your head and a camera in your hands" – or that of Astruc, to make film as though writing with a pen. As Ospina puts it: "I felt that I was finally realizing the dream of the *caméra stylo* set out by Alexandre Astruc in 1948."

Lies and video tape

Un Tigre de papel is a "fake documentary" about the apocryphal artist Pedro Manrique Figueroa, pioneer of the collage form in Colombia. The character and work of Manrique Figueroa were supplied by Lucas Ospina, François Bucher and Bernardo Ortiz; his history and anecdotes, by dozens of other characters who invent encounters with the artist. The context of his life is the history of Colombia and the world from 1936 (when Manrique is born) to the early eighties (when he disappears). In the finest tradition of the genre, which extends from Welles's *F for Fake* to Furtado's *La Isla de las flores* and from Allen's *Zelig* to Sorín's *La era del ñandú*, Ospina dismantles the discourses and rhetoric according to which the documentary represents reality and is accepted by society in blind faith as an index of truth.

---

[74] Rodrigo Lalinde and Diego García took turns at filling this role.

He also presents an ironic reading of the public history of his country through the different personal anecdotes presented, which show how the official history is only one among many that bring together fragments of events and facts that seem to be real. The plot, the life of Manrique or of Colombia, goes from dreams and utopias to failures and political, aesthetic and social disillusionment. Farse and truth go hand in hand in the anecdotes, Manrique's collages, the quotations of famous sources and Ospina's editing, which openly shows his lie, quoting the Dadaist Schwitters on collage or Goebbels' "A lie told a thousand times becomes a truth." For Ospina, it was a chance to bring a number of his interests together: national memory, death, disappearance, surrealist 'found object' and bricolage techniques – all on video. He manages to turn video into a medium of renovation and expression; he manages, as a director, to face the challenges posed by making film in Colombia. "By not studying only cinematic language, but also the new possibilities of video, I was able to satisfy a number of expressive needs. Video let me work through a sort of perpetual postmodern collage in which I was able to mix all formats, incorporate texts and include special effects that would have been prohibitively expensive on film."[75]

---

[75] Ospina, Luis. "VINI, VIDEO, VICI, El video como resurrección." *El malpensante*, 48.

Cristián Sánchez, the Stationary Nomad

Jorge Ruffinelli

One of the few films directed by Cristián Sánchez (born in Santiago in 1951) ever shown outside Chile occasioned such an outpouring of critical acclaim that – in any other case – his work would have been immediately consecrated, or at least afforded special attention among his compatriots. The film was *Los deseos concebidos* and the occasion was its projection at the 1983 Berlin Film Festival. The German critic Wolfram Schütte (*Die Frankfurter Rundschau*) wrote: "Of the recent works to come out of the current situation in Chile, [*Los deseos concebidos*] is perhaps the best film of the forum." And, later: "In *Los deseos concebidos*, by Cristián Sánchez, the truth reaches our eyes like a ray of light through the crack of a door left ajar. A work the caliber of Buñuel's *El ángel exterminador* or *Los olvidados*." These words were compiled by writer/filmmaker Antonio Skármeta, who at the time was living in exile in Berlin, in an article titled "Los elogios concedidos." The comparison with the great works of world cinema must have surprised and encouraged the young, solitary Chilean director. In fact, Wolfram Schütte's words were reproduced in the program when *Los deseos concebidos* was screened in Santiago. There was not, however, any substantial change in his marginal position within the film industry (or the business of screenings) in Chile.

Years later, when another of his films (this time *El zapato chino*) was invited by BAFICI to the capital of neighboring Argentina, a young Chilean critic who had been following the legendary film for years finally came face to face with it and, establishing a certain distance between himself and the local audience watching in the same theater, reflected upon the work. The young critic was Ivan Pinto, and he shared his reflections on a website: "I had to find this film somewhere. And it was here, in Buenos Aires, far from home, among people who did not know how to react to the movie (nervous laughter?) and where, I imagined, a few Chileans would laugh in a different way (with complicity and discomfort). The strange thing: the theater was full for the second screening. *El zapato chino* picks up the thread of early Ruiz, with a few more or less sociological touches. As Sánchez himself says, his is a 'bottomless' realism, which does not sound too distant to me from the 'austere realism' proposed by Ruiz. But that is where the comparisons end. This is a veritable anthropology of the margin devoid of political *victimism*; to the contrary, it is charged with keen social observations" (www.lafuga.cl).

Toward the end of 2006, the Valparaíso Film Festival presented an extensive retrospective; in March of 2007 the city of Toulouse did the same with the festival Cinemas de l'Amerique Latine. At the same time, a 360-page publication brought together unpublished and archival materials about Sánchez's films, along with all of his numerous writings on the cinema: *El Cine Nómada de Cristián Sánchez* (Stanford University, 2007). Three and a half decades after making his first films, Sánchez's work seems to have attained, contrary to Márquez's prediction in *Cien años de soledad*, "a second chance on earth."

***

One of the most original directors in Chilean cinema, Cristián Sánchez is, at the same time, one of the least known. His films are endowed with a singular power – by their strangeness, their loyalty to a world all their own, their keen, inquisitive, unique gaze – but they never had the luck that other Chilean films did with respect to theater screenings and critical reception. Nor did they have the financial backing that would have made production relatively comfortable. To the contrary: with low budgets and haphazard technical resources, many works that could easily be called masterpieces depended on the tenacity of a small technical and artistic team loyal, to a great extent, to the vision, the sagacity and the unusual aesthetic and narrative talent of their director.

Although Sánchez's cinematic disquiet predated the coup d'état and dictatorship of Augusto Pinochet (1973–1989), many of his films were made *from within* this dark period and were inseparable from it. Perhaps this is the key to his creation of a unique cinematic language that could evade the risk of censorship. Through this language he created a dark, warped atmosphere that was at once an expressive portrait of the time and an expression of social disenchantment. In this sense, Sánchez (who also wrote the scripts to all his films) managed to effectively present points of contact between marginal social strata immersed in violence and crime, an intellectually anemic middle class and, now and then, the lifeless and decadent strata of bourgeois high society.

From the start, Sánchez's films have drawn inspiration from the directors of narratively distinct and innovative cinema (as opposed to standard, conventional films) on both a global level – Robert Bresson, Luis Buñuel, Eric Rohmer, John Cassavetes – and a local one – the early films of the "enfant terrible" of Chilean cinema: Raúl Ruiz. References to the work of these directors abound in Sánchez's films, whether integrated in the form of posters hanging on the wall behind two characters in conversation, or of scenes that allude to the work of the filmmakers, like in *Vías paralelas*

(1975), in which a young woman says that she would like to adapt the popular novel *Palomita blanca* for the screen, while in reality she is played by the same actress who made that very film with Raúl Ruiz two years earlier.

Sánchez did not turn politics into the message or the subject of his work. It would not have been possible to do so, nor did it interest him. In this sense, his films differed from what was then called the "New Latin American Cinema," the form of politicized cinema that established its hegemony during the Viña del Mar Film Festivals of 1967 and 1969 as a result of the ideological influence of the Cuban Revolution and the anti-imperialist struggles being waged throughout Latin America. At the Viña Festival (1969), Raúl Ruiz himself questioned this desire for dominance, and his films – which he later made in Europe – demonstrated the possibility of working in parallel with a different aesthetic, different subject matter, a different style. Cristián Sánchez belonged to this other strain, though ominous allusions to the dictatorship can be detected in his films, in the form of mysterious crimes, sinister characters and authoritarian acts presented as part of daily life.

While studying film at the Universidad Católica de Santiago, Sánchez made *Esperando a Godoy* (1973), which was never screened, with Sergio Navarro and Rodrigo González, and *Vías paralelas* (1975) with Navarro. After that, he went off on his own to write and direct other films: *El zapato chino* (1976), *Los deseos concebidos* (1982), *El otro round* (1983), *El cumplimiento del deseo* (1985-1993), *Cuídate del agua mansa* (1995), *Cautiverio feliz* (1998), *Camino de sangre* (2003, work in progress). Nearly all his films have been shown in cultural centers or independent theaters and were shot on 16 millimeter film – making screenings in commercial theaters unlikely – while their creator made a living by teaching film theory.

Sánchez's work is that of an outsider, someone who will leave behind him a tradition of rigor and risk – not a specific aesthetic, not a reproducible style. These days it would be difficult, if not impossible, to make a film like *El zapato chino*, with the freshness of the expressive discoveries that its technical limitations may actually have helped it attain. Films like *Los deseos concebidos* (1980-1982) and *El cumplimiento del deseo* (1985-1993) were too personal – without being autobiographical – and belonged to a particular time in the emotional and intellectual life of their creator. They could not be repeated now. And it is unlikely that Sánchez would be able to make a film as lovely and absurd as *Cautiverio feliz* (1998), performed in the Mapudungun language of the Mapuche by their indigenous descendents, who studied 17th century cadence and pronunciation in order to play the role of their own ancestors. The films of Cristián Sánchez seem not to have been simple productions, but rather *events*, happenings that transcended their initial intent, running the risk of failure but turning instead into quiet victories.

The nomad searches in vain for his place

What are the characteristic traits of Sánchez's work? The critic Ascanio Cavallo found a key to this question when he examined his work in 1999 with the concepts of *secuestro*, or kidnapping and confinement, and *autosecuestro*. Having detected various situations of this kind, repeated with variations in *El zapato chino, Los deseos concebidos, El cumplimiento del deseo* and *Cautiverio feliz*, Cavallo concluded that "Sánchez's films suggest that *autosecuestro* is an essential part of Chilean identity, from its origins as a *mestizo* community, to the present moment, infected with frustration and solitude, passing through the periods of violence that have brought about, from the depths of its isolation and semblances, the hidden dementia of routine. If the social implications of this vision are disquieting, its political ramifications could be devastating."[76]

I believe that there exists another possible reading, complementary and also persuasive, a thread that runs through all these films: the motif of being "out of place," which could be read as a modern "nomadism"- a *being out of place* as the essence of the *general malaise of our culture* – one which has come to displace our habitual and comfortable distinctions between the nomadic and the sedentary.

First and foremost, in 1973 the country was thrown off its democratic axis and disjoined from its identity, and nothing was left in their place but a dictatorship. From the initial, excessive attack on the Moneda to its campaigns of extermination – the "death trains," the national stadium converted into a concentration camp, the *secuestro* and murder of thousands of people over more than a decade and a half – Chile was a mangled country forced to survive, resist, and reinvent itself as it went. For the rest of the 70s – the period of the most severe repression – only a few filmmakers were able to press on: Sánchez with his films, Silvio Caiozzi with his own (*Julio comienza en Julio*, 1974) or his joint work with Pablo Perelman (*A la sombra del sol*, 1974, though it was filmed before the coup). Obviously the "subject" of politics was abandoned, though its reverberations in daily life under the regime were not. In the case of Sánchez, who was the most prolific at the time, the fact that politics was "displaced" as subject matter impelled him to search for his own cinematic language.

---

[76] Ascanio Cavallo. "El mundo secreto del autosecuestro." *El Mercurio*, April 11, 1999.

In his films, the characters are always moving from their place of origin toward uncertain and indeterminate destinations. This nomadism is both literal and metaphoric.

In *Vías paralelas*, Kaska (an allusion to Franz Kafka) has lost his job and passes through various workplaces trying in vain to recover it.

In *El zapato chino*, Gallardo rescues Marlene from what we imagine is a brothel (she has displaced herself from the provinces to the capital), and thus begins his travels through the city in search of a place to put her up – without losing sight of her – while he develops an insane passion for her.

Los deseos concebidos opens with R's sister leaving the house of her aunt, followed shortly thereafter by R himself, who begins his own search for his "place" in other people's homes. R is the epitome of the restless and troubled adolescent, exiled from himself; the epitome of the nomad.

El cumplimiento del deseo is remarkable for its inversion of the roles of brother and sister, giving the latter (who disappeared from the screen when she leaves at the beginning of *Los deseos concebidos*) the central role. In *El cumplimiento del deseo*, Manuela abandons her profession as a psychologist, along with her home and her husband, and moves into a house shared with other young people, a house that has a – Dantean – subterranean space (the basement) and upstairs (the attic). These spaces bring Manuela alternately to the brink of salvation and death – beyond the fact that she also travels back and forth between somnambulism and insomnia. From a social perspective, Manuela abandons the place assigned to women by Chilean society (home and husband) to become a nomad.

El otro round tells the story of Dinamita Araya's journey from the ring to the street, from the dream of victory (turned into defeat) to new lives and new businesses that fail, one after the other. The film follows its protagonist from the moment he is cast from his boxing paradise, his *original* place, that which *defines him*, and toward the unforeseen.

Cuídate del agua mansa is, in its way, a story of abandonment and pursuit, this time without the dark and troubled backdrop of the earlier films – it was a different time, socially and personally for the director – something closer to the sentimental comedy as explored by Eric Rohmer in French cinema. Even so, Ignacio, the film's main character, leaves his place (he abandons geology and his wife) and finds, in the house lent to him by a friend, an alternate universe in which the stones of the desert and roadside whorehouses – his past – give way to chivalrous seduction, to the pursuit of pleasure in the company of a young, beautiful, intelligent woman also staying at the house. In this case, one form of nomadism is exchanged for another and, for the first time, the characters and storyline come close to a "happy ending."

To close this list of films, at least provisionally, an extreme example of this exilic nomadism is that of Francisco Núñez de Pineda in *Cautiverio feliz*. There Sánchez expresses the nomadic condition of his main character with a contemplative air, adapting a collection of 17th century of memoirs, already well-known on literary and historical levels, for the screen. Núñez de Pineda, kidnapped by the Mapuche and displaced from his Creole identity, would not only have lived out his "happy captivity" in a space not originally destined to him; his tale of imprisonment would also have implied continuous displacements in order to avoid being killed by tribes unfriendly to his guardians. When he finally is released to "his own kind," Francisco Núñez de Pineda is not able to adapt. Years later, as he writes his memoir, he enacts a symbolic return full of melancholy, to that brief period of happiness. He had experienced a "reverse conversion" from the Creole to the indigenous.

Mad love, or the love of a madman

Of the titles mentioned above, two stand out for the different ways in which they present the question of "nomadism" and, as such, it would be worthwhile to linger over them for a moment. *El zapato chino* is a story of *mad love* in both the generic and literal sense. Because it is about the insane "passion" of a man for a very young woman, a passion met by nothing but the indifference and automatism of the girl. (In a way, this is representative of the traditional dependence of the Chilean woman, particularly before the recent legalization of divorce.) A certain *buñuelian* sensibility can be perceived here, however, far from the aristocracy embodied by an actor with the "presence" of Fernando Rey (in the films of Buñuel), in Sánchez's film the mature character is a vulgar social nomad, marginal despite his job as a taxi driver.

One year after making *Vías paralelas*, Sánchez made this film, with a tighter, more concise and more fully realized plot than his previous work, though not deviating far from the parameters established before, that is, the sense of absurdity, eccentric characters (or ones with eccentric behaviors), all played out against a backdrop of the seemingly mundane. One finds this type of "marginal" character in *El zapato chino*, but by limiting himself to just a few of them and following the currents of their lives, the movie becomes sharper, more direct, shorter and more effective.

To this day some viewers still ask what *zapato chino* – literally "Chinese shoe" – means as the title of a film without any Asian characters. This is not its only enigma. The logic that shapes the action of the film is the opposite of what we are used to seeing on television. The actions of the characters adhere to a certain logic, without question, but they do so with destabilizing ruptures. And the narration, as it interprets the actions of the characters, includes so many ellipses and off-screen actions that the absence of any "logic" of cause and effect is no longer surprising. As in Sánchez's later films, there are murders (seen or unseen by the viewer) that the writer-director makes no attempt to explain. These belong to the nebulous and decentered world occupied by his characters. They are an essential part of a disquieting, unpredictable atmosphere full of risk, though no one knows exactly why. The period itself offers the reason: as long as Sánchez and his contemporaries lived in uncertainty, their context would provide the 'why'.

In any event, the actions are clear despite the fact that their grammar was not. Though he was creating a new language, Sánchez could not fall into the techniques of the absurd utilized by the avant-garde. He needed to find the balance that would make his work intelligible in the end. For example, there is a sense of circularity to the story, an agreement between the opening and the close. In both, a text is read as a voice-over while a static image of the character is presented on-screen, without their physically *speaking*. It is the soundtrack that "speaks." In this case, it is the story of a woman. Her character-axis is a provincial Lolita, a strange, magnetic and dark object of desire, a girl with an innocent appearance and a name of profound cinematic resonance: *Marlene*. Marlene's is the first face to appear on the screen, and hers is the first voice to be heard: the image and sound of the story. She appears, looking straight into the camera, in a shot "à la Godard." She is Sánchez's Anna Karina, the "woman [who] is a woman" in her essential quality of innocence on the brink of inevitable corruption. The child-girl-woman of Vladimir Nabokov and of Juan Carlos Onetti, observed, captured and trapped by the camera (by cinema) at the precise moment her innocence blossoms outside of any obvious sexuality.

From the sound reel, Marlene speak-writes – an oral letter, the kinetic displacement of writing toward sound – to her godmother back home, probably the Madame of a provincial brothel. At the same time, she speak-writes to us, the viewers, who are her true narratees. "Dear Godmother: this may be the last letter you get from me. Don't worry, nothing bad has happened to me, but I lost your letter of introduction and no one is willing to take me in. I look 'round all day, but can't find anywhere to go. So I went to work in a house like yours. But don't think bad things about me. Oh, I can't go on, you don't deserve this shame."

Her story is intertwined with that of Gallardo, the taxi driver who finds her in the brothel and takes her away, wanting to protect her. While he tries to find a place for her in his home, in a pension, or in the houses of acquaintances, his paternal impulse turns erotic, and the erotic becomes obsessive/possessive. Marlene goes from being a migrant (from the provinces to the capital) to being a nomad as Gallardo takes her from one place of refuge to another. These fail, one after the other, because Marlene's transitory space can only be that of the sick, jealous mind of her protector. In the face of the predictable harassment the girl suffers at the hands of younger men, Gallardo (the irony of his name, *Valiant*, should not be overlooked) steps in to "save" her. And, in the process, Gallardo goes "mad" with love for her. Or else, he simply goes mad. His actions push him toward a passive dementia – detected, observed, and commented upon by other characters – from which he emerges, memorably, to have another one of his fits. What today would be called bipolar behavior. The dementia makes him dream up plans or stare fixedly into space. The dementia is sedentary (he succumbs to it when *seated*), whereas his fits involve irrational displacement. In his fits, Gallardo drives (textually, he is a taxi driver) Marlene around with him, hidden in the trunk of the car so his customers cannot see her and, as a result, covet her. A pathology that is not surprising – though it is taken to an extreme – when you consider the feelings of "ownership" and jealousy that the companion of any very beautiful woman might feel.

But Sánchez's "realism" deconstructs predictable human action or, at least, knocks it off its axis. Take, for example, the sequence in which Nano (the son of the owner of the taxi company) takes Marlene to a motel and asks her to undress, yet nothing erotic occurs between them. In its place, two somewhat absurd situations. Someone in an adjoining room asks Nano for a pack of matches. And Nano throws them to him over the wall (perhaps there is no ceiling?) and gets them back the same way. The motel clerk himself spies on the couple, and just a few moments after they enter the room bangs on the door to tell them that their time is up. The entire sequence depicts a sexuality that is misplaced, off-kilter, and suddenly replaced by the grotesque and the ridiculous.

The synopsis of the film, written by the director, summarizes precisely what Sánchez wanted and ultimately what he succeeded in doing: "A taxi driver finds Marlene, a girl from the provinces, in a brothel. He immediately decides to protect her and gives her a place to live in his home. Little by little, his paternal affection becomes a buried passion complicated by the presence of his godson, who is also interested in her. Afraid that someone else might take an interest in Marlene, he hides her in the trunk of his car. Shortly thereafter, he is pursued by murderous creditors who, after a violent interrogation, castrate him. The driver ends up living in the trunk of his own taxi, and Marlene declares that she wants to stay with him forever."

What is so fascinating about *El zapato chino* is not only the tale of "amour fou" so clearly summarized above, but also its development, in terms of narration and style. I mentioned earlier its use of ellipsis which, along with other narrative techniques, demonstrate an attempt to penetrate and describe the reality of its characters in a different way than that dictated by conventional cinema, by the codes of realism. The unusual progressively takes over throughout the course of the story. One of the best examples of these techniques takes place in the final sequence, when Andrés visits a woman in response to "an ad in the paper." The woman explains that she needs a loyal driver and is inclined to hire him. Almost immediately, she invites him to dance (unusual under the circumstances) and a moment later takes him up to her room, where she asks him to remove his tie and the rest of his clothing. What appears to be a seduction becomes a kidnapping as three men advance upon Gallardo in that very room, then beat him and drag him over to a shadowy area where they supposedly castrate him. Though the summary written by Sánchez speaks of *castration*, in the film the visual of the action is replaced by the screams of the man. Once again: *off-screen*, a visual ellipsis. Nor does the narration explain the motives behind the castration. Once again: an ellipsis – or a lapse – in the cause-and-effect logic of the film's action.

The ending of the film brings us back to Marlene, its original "narrator." Another letter to the godmother – and to the viewers – from the sound reel, unaccompanied by any physical gesture; the conclusion of a story that has walked the line between the rational and the irrational, between the logical and the absurd. "So my friend got into the trunk and there was no way he was coming out again. Now he spends all day singing, not eating a thing. The only things he likes are stale bread and rinds, so his teeth started falling out, but he tied them together with his shoelaces and made himself a little musical contraption. He spends all day playing the same song, which makes me sad. The only thing I want is to live with him, forever."

In its time, this film garnered the admiration of both critics and writers. According to José Román (who had a cameo in *Vías paralelas*), "Pursuing his quest through the decantation of an original language all his own, Sánchez has arrived at an important examination of 'the Chilean' that represents a real contribution to the nation's cinema." In 1984, Antonio Skármeta defined Sánchez's "system": "Cristián Sánchez is a master of paradox. He makes lucid films about loony characters and mysterious stories out of situations that have no mystery to them at all." Enrique Lihn sums it up with a brilliant metaphor: "The free gait of *El zapato chino* follows in the artificial footsteps of the real."

The conquest as paradise lost

In 1998 Sánchez took on one of the most daring cinematic adventures in the history of Chilean cinema: to bring Francisco Núñez de Pineda y Bascuñán's work, *Cautiverio feliz y razón individual de las guerras dilatadas del reino de Chile* (*Happy Captivity and the Reason for the Prolonged Wars of the Kingdom of Chile*, 1673) to the screen. Considering the director's early experimental and avant-garde work (from *Vías paralelas* to *El zapato chino*), the existentialist variations on the theme of the Chilean 'soul' (from *Los deseos concebidos* to *El cumplimiento del deseo*), and his detour via the comedy of errors (*Cuídate del agua mansa*), there was no reason to suspect that Sánchez would adopt "indigenous" or historical subject matter, that he would immerse himself with passion and erudition in the culture of "the native peoples," that modern, westernized Chile left behind and to the side.

Though the metamorphoses of Nuñez de Pineda y Bascuñán (1608-1680) were personal, as are those of any historical subject, Sánchez was able to set his sights on a collective national "identity." And on the cultural imbalances that the Chilean sense of self has demonstrated from its inception.

In any case, it was the "uniqueness" of Francisco Nuñez de Pineda y Bascuñán's story that caught the attention of Sánchez. In the account, he found an opportunity to develop his nomadic cinema and to explore, on different levels – historic, cultural, ethnic, psychological – the search for lost spaces and the construction of new ones. Though it would transcend the individual, the film would nonetheless maintain an authorial mark: it closes with a text signed by the director ["C.S."] that indicates, in conclusion, that 27 years after his liberation, between the years 1656 and 1673, "in the midst of personal misfortunes and profoundly disenchanted with the colonial administration, [Nuñez de Pineda y Bascuñán] wrote this work as a testament to his desire to remain part of the Mapuche world, which to his eyes appeared more human than his own. C.S."

The sense of empathy that Francisco Nuñez de Pineda y Bascuñán felt for the Mapuche that held him captive extends to Sánchez's gaze throughout the film. What justifies and gives meaning to Núñez de Pineda's life today is his captivity, but above all the nostalgia that he would feel towards it years later, from the familiar world to which he returned. The story is fascinating precisely because of this memorial, which ends up turning the soldier-writer into the perfect nomad: having lived in both worlds, he was not able to belong to either. And it is this non-space that the filmmaker will inherit.

Over the course of its 118 minutes (there is a longer version, which has never been screened), the film attempts to recreate – more through its contemplative style than through its action – the world in which Francisco Núñez de Pineda y Bascuñán lived, integrating the most authentic indigenous elements into the story, and using conventional sets sparingly, if at all. Thus, the narrative is developed mainly through long tracking shots, the rare medium shot, and a reiterative style (dances, rites, the preparations carried out before going to sleep in the rukas). Though one of the dramatic "motifs" is the possible execution of Núñez de Pineda, given that a few of the tribal leaders, or *cacique*, are determined to kill him – he is, after all, a prisoner of war – while others care for him and want to protect him, even this situation is stripped of any orientation toward "suspense" and entertainment. Rather than make an action movie (there is only one battle, at the beginning), Sánchez wanted to recreate the atmosphere and the circumstances of the prisoner's life. For this, he needed to construct an aesthetic that was closer to painting than genre film.

It was this loving determination to depict a repetitive and mundane existence, in which even sexuality was deferred and withdrawn (by the cultural and religious mania of the historical figure himself), that helped to make this such a singular and unusual film. Upon his liberation, Núñez de Pineda was approached by the other soldiers; because sex was central in the imagination of the conquistador, they wanted to hear about his supposed sexual exploits (the polygamy of tribal leaders was well-known). No one could understand the restraint of a soldier who, when offered the daughter of one of the *cacique* according to ancient custom, would reject her, asserting "I cannot have relations with a woman who is not a Christian." (A qualm not shared by his fellow soldiers.)

One of the objects of *Cautiverio feliz* was to depict the "conversion" of the memoirist to the indigenous world. His memories *were* this conversion. And in order to translate them into cinematic codes, Sánchez needed to immerse himself in Mapuche culture and the Mapudungun language, get the Mapuche together to play their ancestors, and even teach them about the variations in lexicon and pronunciation that shaped the indigenous language over the centuries. Though it was not a film with a large budget for scenery, Sánchez arranged all the details painstakingly and tried to be faithful in his reconstruction, due less to a historicist's search for verisimilitude than to a profound respect for this *other* culture.

It is like the image of the iceberg: what the film shows has an extensive historical, ethnographic and linguistic understanding as its foundation, *none* of which is seen because this is not an academic piece: it is a story on film.

Notable in this story is the expression of feelings, the relationships of love and respect among the *cacique*, their families and the foreigner. As though this affect were out of place; no one expects a prisoner from an army (and a culture) that was decimating the population to be treated with respect. The *cacique* Maulican, in particular, demonstrates an affective and protective bond with the prisoner, the likes of which had not been seen in any film before. This treatment is conscious; in one sequence the Mapuche ask themselves (and Francisco) why they, who are supposedly civilized, do not treat their indigenous prisoners with the same tenderness, or at least with humanitarian decency. Nonetheless, the film does not idealize the indigenous. Violence exists in that world as well; among the different Mapuche tribes there are "doves" and "falcons." The beginning of the film includes a brutal execution, in which a prisoner's throat is slit and his head is stuck on a pike.

What is extraordinary, then, is the ability of *Cautiverio feliz* to make the humanity of the indigenous world seem real without romanticizing it. This required a deliberate rhythm, the unhurried dual labor of image and sound. Had it had any other rhythm or aspirations toward the spectacular, the film would have betrayed its purpose and its meaning.

***

From his earliest films, the nomadic displacement to which I referred earlier – imbalance, the deterritorialization of characters and circumstances – played audaciously and precariously at the limits of realism and the absurd, replacing Cartesian logic with the logic of chaos and the unpredictable. Instead of the habitual order of things, unexpected diffusion. Removed from their axis and their territory, the characters do not behave as one would expect, forcing the audience to come face to face with a world whose order is often strange to us, with no familiar codes but those of a few neighbors or pioneers (from Kafka to Buñuel). In *El zapato chino*, *Los deseos concebidos* and *El cumplimiento del deseo*, Sánchez takes us inside the Unconscious, opening the "realism" of mundane situations up to enigmatic sequences (for example, Mansilla holds two stones in his hands as he sleeps in *Los deseos concebidos*; Manuela somnambulantly peels potatoes in *El cumplimiento del deseo*) and punctuating visual images with noises and sounds from the sound reel that do not correspond to what appears on the screen, like the whinny of a horse or the screech of a monkey, making the atmosphere stranger still.

It is not a matter of imitating the surrealist escapades of a Buñuel or a Ruiz, aesthetics and visions of the real that have their own codes and their own logic. In Sánchez, the rational and causal logic of the action is replaced by a logic of diffusion that questions – by its very existence – our collective idea of reality.

Gilles Deleuze (whom Sánchez has read with great passion for years) reminds us, taking Plato's *Timaeus* as a point of departure, of the existence of two scientific models – which give rise to two visions of the world – denominated the *compars* and the *dispars*. Whereas the *compars* is "the legal or legalistic model employed by royal science [...] the *dispars*, as an element of nomadic science, tends toward material-forces rather than material-forms."

Let us, for a moment, consider the possibility of applying this discourse to the films of Sánchez. Deleuze continues: "It is not a matter of extracting constants from variables, but of placing the variables themselves in a state of constant variation. If equations remain, they are adequations, inequations, differential equations irreducible to algebraic forms and inseparable from an intuitive sense of variation."[77]

This dissipative logic, this substitution of permanent variation for cause and effect, relieves us of the need to explain the actions of the characters "logically." Take, for example, the constant posturing and feints of the characters in nearly all the films. It is not just a matter of the directionless energy of the high-school students in *Los deseos concebidos*, who get into fights whenever they see each other; the adults throw punches, slaps, and threats at one another, like in *Vías paralelas*, or in that memorable sequence in which the characters played by Luis Alarcón and Jaime Vadell fight without touching – pure posturing – in *El zapato chino*. In none of these cases does the absurdity of the "causeless" or inconsequential action exist in a vacuum. A critic has recognized traces of a specifically Chilean idiosyncrasy in these gestures.

Other sequences are just as memorable, and just as significant in their so-called absurdity, such as the visits to motels: the behavior of bourgeois ladies or the women in charge of pensions, the dialogues between friends at the bar The Twelve Apostles, where a sort of cannibalism takes place, and many others in which the strange, the absurd, the grotesque suddenly erupt out of the apparent realism

---

[77] Gilles Deleuze and Felix Guattari. "Traité de Nomadologie" in *Mille Plateaux*, Paris, Minuit, 1980." (English edition: *A Thousand Plateaus*, University of Minnesota Press, 1987).

of Sánchez's story. The logic of the illogical arises all of a sudden from the depths of his films.

The nomadic character of Sánchez's cinema is not defined solely by its literal form, the physical transit of its characters, or by the symbolic displacements denoted by the social and political order. As Vilém Flusser has astutely observed, we all end up as nomads in modern culture since the singular "catastrophe" suffered by Humanity after the Neolithic era – which is known as "the creation of civilization" – a catastrophe that has turned ours into a more and more "uninhabitable" world.[78] Thus it is neither necessary nor correct to identify the nomad only with the migrant. Once more it is Deleuze that steps forward to enlighten us: "To define the nomad by movement is equally false. Toynbee is absolutely right in suggesting that the nomad is actually *he who does not move*. Whereas the migrant abandons a medium turned amorphous and unwelcoming, the nomad is he who does not go, who does not want to leave, who clings to the smooth space in which the forest recedes, in which the steppe or the desert expands, and invents his nomadism in response to this challenge."

I indicated earlier that one of the unique aspects of the cinema of Cristián Sánchez was that it distances itself – gently but firmly – from the strongly ideological presuppositions of "New Latin American Cinema" or at least the social and political criticism levied by the movement and placed at the center of many of its films, rejecting the contemporary intimist cinema of a Torre Nilsson or a Kohon, as the only paradigm for the civic-artistic "duty" of the filmmaker. Sánchez preferred to work at the interstices rather than on the surfaces; he laid claim to the world of shadows better than he did to any discourse of pre-determined ideological

---

[78] Vilém Flusser. *The Freedom of the Migrant*. University of Illinois Press, 2003.

clarity. He explored ambiguity, the undefined pulsations of filmic discourse, without looking to the comfort and support of forms, styles, or content established within the community. He fed off of models (as do all filmmakers) that would help him find the path toward his own form of expression, never trying to keep his work from being uncomfortable, uneven, risky, and solitary. And still, he did not allow any reality to escape him, whether it was social, political, or psychological. Today it is necessary to see his films as an indirect testimony of the time in which they were made, just as the films he makes in the future will embrace different coordinates.

A nomadic cinema that never left Chile, that tried to understand it in all its contradictions. This nomadism, this non-belonging, is without a doubt a central trait of each of his motion pictures. It is also a key to the work as a whole, even given the natural evolution of his technical and expressive skill: the setting in motion of an aesthetic that developed throughout this process. This sensibility was present from the beginning, but it appeared and was approached from different yet complementary angles, in increasingly rich and complex ways. For this reason Sánchez himself can say, speaking openly about the relationship that exists between him and his characters, with whom he shares the extreme and dramatic condition of the nomad, that:

> "The heroes of my films have something of me in them; not in the biographical or psychological sense, but more of an ethical disposition. Their belated and tragic understanding of events situates them within that nomadic destiny at the margins of both country and abode."[79]

---

[79] "El deseo de desear" in Jorge Ruffinelli (ed.), El cine nómada de Cristián Sánchez. Nuevo Texto Crítico, Stanford University, 2007. p. 91.

Lisandro Alonso: States and Mutations of Cinema

Eduardo A. Russo

Preamble: trilogy and method

From *La libertad* (2001) to *Liverpool* (2008), there is a logic to the work of Lisandro Alonso. Each film includes a reading of those that came before it, returning to certain points in order to reconstruct their meaning. This logic seems to have been in place as early as the extreme proposal of his first feature, the manifesto of a programmatic dispossession that not only sheds the mandates that have historically affected Argentine cinema (mainly tied to a broad range of norms and censorship, with the cult of repression as one of its most recognizable family traits), but also several of the more recent tendencies and *tics* of "New Cinema." *La libertad* could call itself 'free' precisely for the way in which it was able to free itself from those mandates: it did not attempt to tell a story, but rather to explore the particular spatial and temporal configuration in which a film is constructed (what falls to the filmmaker: to create, using blocks of time and space the way a writer uses words or a philosopher uses concepts).

Alonso's films demand, as a necessary precondition, the presence and effort of a real film audience. A rare breed in contemporary screening rooms, as Jean Roy recalls in *L'Humanité*, emphasizing the protests of many viewers of *Los muertos* (2004) at the Quinzaine des Realizateurs, when they were confronted by the actual death of a goat onscreen: the cinema had turned into an urban art and *Los muertos* operates outside the sensibilities of city life. Both films create, each in its own way, a time and space. Alonso has pointed out that, had they not included music, these two films could have situated themselves decades in the past or even in the future, insofar as they depart from thematic realism.

Fantasma brought a trilogy to a close, for a time. Some may consider it an episode addressed with relative levity, or in a minor tone: the final work of a trilogy that began with *La libertad* and continued with *Los muertos*. It could also be understood as an *intermezzo* between those two films and *Liverpool*, Alonso's fourth. Yet *Fantasma* was not only the logical and necessary consequence of its antecedents, but also a political commentary on the reach of the cinema that came before the search for other frontiers in *Liverpool*. Let us examine these moments, one by one.

La libertad, or the bare image

The opening is bleak. A lone figure in the middle of nowhere dines on the wild animal he has just pulled from the fire; its remains – a shell, a few bones – appear off to one side as lightning illuminates the night.

Later, in the daylight, this character gets ready for work. The mise en scène does not hierarchize his actions, but rather observes the man within an environment that – as is clearly established in these first minutes – will play as active a role as the protagonist. The character, we quickly learn, is a woodcutter. One might imagine that the film would limit itself to recording a simple task, shaped by a longing for a certain natural existence. Yet Alonso stands on the curb opposite this particular urban perspective. There is no sense of nostalgia for the forest, no flight to an idealized natural realm; we soon see the woodcutter make use of a chainsaw, immediately casting aside the possibility of a retreat into the bucolic. He operates by means of subtraction, leaving the work bare: both that of his protagonist and the essential work of cinema begun by the Lumière brothers. Capturing a visible and audible fragment to later project it, reconstitute it before an audience that, through this process, sees something on the screen as though seeing it for the first time. Just as Jean-Luc Godard wanted: it is a matter of filming in order to see.

The duration of a shot is central to Alonso's aesthetic proposal. Just this side of cinematic language, the way characters, objects, actions and spaces are organized determines what occurs without the dependence on editing. It is the dominion of immediacy, but not because of the synchronic capture of image and sound, or the instantaneity of television. The immediacy in this case is situated between what is presented to the eye, what is registered by the camera, and its inverse: what happens at the moment of projection, when the viewer sets himself before the 'making-present' of what has been filmed. This artifice makes possible, to an extreme, the appearance of reality of the filmic image: the visible has its guarantor, corresponds to something in the world. What is projected is something that has happened, and we are witnessing its presentation – not its representation – that is, we are given access to a new form of presence.

Apart from the radio heard briefly in one passage, about a half an hour into the film there is a dialogue during which we learn the name of the protagonist: Misael. Until that moment, everything had been regulated by physical action and rest, enacted in front of the camera as they had been infinite times before, day after day. Quotidian, cyclical, undifferentiated time. Misael sells his wood, negotiates the price, and talks with his family on the phone. There is no dramatic progression to *La libertad*, nor is there the traditional demand for a conflict, though there may be one nonetheless in the tension between the expectation of the average viewer and the situation to which he is exposed: that of a true purgation of his preconceptions. The film comes to a close, by way of return, with the nocturnal scene from the beginning. A moment much like any other day, as we are led to suspect by its circular structure. Nonetheless, a surprising change in register occurs in the first version of the film.

The deleted final scene shows Misael engaged by the camera from an unexpected angle. Facing the hypothetical gaze of his future audience, he is tempted by an uncontrollable fit of laughter (something similar can be seen in one of the shots not used in *Fantasma*, the unorthodox humor of which was not widely understood, when Argentino Vargas has a laughing fit after watching a piano being tuned and playing a few notes to an empty concert hall).

La libertad is a film about time. In his presentation of the set of DVDs released by MALBA,[80] Quintín observed, as had Jean Roy before him, the circular structure of the film. According to both, this structure stands in contrast to the linearity of *Los muertos*,[81] which, in its trajectory, is a film about space. The draw of the traveling shot is already present in a few luminous stretches of the first film, like Misael's trip in the back of a pick-up truck with a dog. This passion for displacement has been adopted by more than a few contemporary filmmakers (Béla Tarr, Abbas Kiarostami, Hou Hsiao Hsien, or at certain moments, Apichatpong Weerasethakul). It revels in the journey as a pure physical movement that suspends both origin and destination,

---

[80] DVD box set: *Lisandro Alonso, La libertad – Los muertos – Fantasma*. Buenos Aires: MALBA, 2007.
[81] Antín, Eduardo (Quintín). "El último autor," a text to accompany the box set.

highlighting the plenitude of the mobile revealed by a cinema that is, in turn, mobilized by the minutia of its composition.

David Bordwell has commented that, "Differences in taste aside, many critics treated mise en scène as the conscious, albeit natural, display of figures on camera. Many still do. Thierry Jousse reminded his readers in 1994 that recent discussions surrounding the development of polished scripts should not obscure the central issue: 'Parallel to the dramatic construction of the plot, which can be imposed, there is an intrinsic technique, an art of permeation, to the direction of bodies, to choreography, to the occupation of space, to natural movement, which cannot be reduced to a script.' In 2000, when they were asked to explain what mise en scène meant to them, a band of French film critics answered that its central element was the placement of the human figure in time and space. Mise en scène, answered one (Dominque Rabourdin), is the 'demiurgic will to control the entire space of a film, the quest for the perfect and appropriate image.'"[82] In accordance, to a certain extent, with the perspective of these critics, *La libertad* can be seen as a work that draws attention to these foundational contours of film, more like an ontological order than the often-cited language of cinema.

Los muertos, or narrative, suspended

In the beginning, the camera moves across the vegetation of the forest, then turns skyward to the sounds of birdsong and the rustling of leaves. On the ground along its sinuous path, the bodies of two young men are revealed in

---

[82] Bordwell, David. *Figures Traced in Light. On Cinematic Staging.* Berkeley: UCLA Press, 2005. 13.

the underbrush. A hand passes by, surreptitiously, holding a machete: someone has murdered the two men.

An old man wakes up in a room; it takes us a moment to realize it is a prison cell. Just as *La libertad* distanced itself from the conventions of realism understood in socio-aesthetic terms, here the prison designates a space that operates according to its own rules, outside the code of any cinematic genre or of any conventional existence within society. *Los muertos* opens with an ellipsis that spans decades; trajectory will come later.

Writing on *Flowers of Shanghai*, David Bordwell has pointed out the Hou [Hsiao Hsien] filmed the majority of his longer shots between ten and twenty times.[83] He also stressed the difference between the critical reception of this film and the relative indifference to his following work, *Millennium Mambo*. Characterizing the latter as resplendent lacking in plot structure, he repeated the sentence of another critic, who described it as the work "of a stylist in search of content."[84] It is worth pointing out that one of the origins of *Liverpool* is an intense desire to film the snow stirred by a mysterious scene from *Millenium Mambo*: its heroine, Vicky (Shu Qi), visits a small town where a film festival is taking place. While playing with her companions in an icy exterior, she ends up – in a magical moment uncoupled from the narrative itself – leaving an imprint of her face in the snow. It is not a landscape, nor is it the conflict between a character and a hostile environment. It is just a record of the substance that has captured the cinematic imagination ever since the snowball fights filmed by the Lumière brothers, so closely tied to the state of change, predisposed to dissolution and the transition into memory, just like the cinematic image.

---

[83] Bordwell, David (op. cit.) 232.
[84] Bordwell, David (op. cit.) 234.

The additional materials of the DVD include an extended version of the opening shot. Over five minutes, a floating, exploratory camera crosses a forest clearing where three young men, one of them naked and the other two barely dressed, are seen lying on the ground. Two are dead, while the third (who seems younger, almost a child) writhes in agony from a wound in his abdomen. This dark beginning, later toned down in the final edit, demonstrates the extent to which Alonso's editing is subtractive, tending toward the suspension of what screenwriting manuals would call 'information.' Rather than adding to it, these two corpses and the young man in agony would actually downplay the irreversibility of the event and compete with the hand holding the machete for viewer's attention.

Los muertos is not a film about the weight of the past over the present. When asked about his distant crime, Vargas says, almost in passing "That's over now." What is Vargas looking for, aside from his daughter? This is a mystery, from start to finish. The cyclical world of Misael's work in *La libertad* is replaced by an errancy in which lurks a dual condition: on one hand, the ghostly state ushered in by a siesta on a sweltering afternoon. There is something of an atmospheric order, a relation between the human and an environment that allows a glimpse (as in Renoir's *The River*) of a barely-concealed danger: that of an inherently hostile forest wich, just as it offers animals for food, is always silently menacing. All human relations enter into this heart of the darkness barely broken by the small community enclaves, hovering over the settlements of individuals or small groups (families or siblings struggling under the weight of their orphanhood).

Los muertos comes to a close in a way that is unsettling, yet offers the hope of escaping repetition – in contrast to the lyrical circularity of *La libertad*. Vargas turns in the direction he just watched his descendent go. He carries a machete just like the one in the first shot, but he leaves it on a table in the shed before following the boy's path. Alonso does not follow him, insisting on a static shot near the ground, into which two chickens enter by chance, allowing life to inhabit this ending, though it is always at risk of falling apart. It is not the story of a man in search of what remains of his family after three decades of incarceration for the murder of his brothers, but rather simply the demonstration of a few of the forms taken by survival, a poetics of the relation between man and world. There is something profoundly Flahertian about *Los muertos*. Jean-Louis Comolli was asked himself, with regard to *Man of Aran*, "What does the film say to us? Before film, before the gaze, the world is complete, solid, compact, indestructible. Things are there, enclosed in their beings. In the face of these, man would be nothing were he not a relational being (a being of language). His survival, his existence, is joined to the relationships he is able to sustain with the wind, the earth, stones, the sea, fish, algae… and himself."[85] By exchanging certain elements, we find ourselves in the network of relations woven between the protagonists of *La libertad* and *Los muertos* and their elemental, immediate surroundings.

The extensive ninety-minute-long *Making of Los muertos* explores Alonso's work with his actor, Vargas (perhaps it would be better to call him, after Bresson, his model) and his detailed, almost obsessive, attention to the composition of a shot and the potential of the camera. The equipment used for the shoot (complete with crane and canister) is midway between pragmatic rusticity and sophistication in the search for the ideal image. In this sense, Alonso seems to be the Argentine director who has been most conscious in

---

[85] Comolli, Jean-Louis. "L'homme esentiel: *Man of Aran*, de Robert Flaherty." *Images Documentaires* 20 (1995). Translated in Comolli, Jean-Louis. *Filmar para ver*. Buenos Aires: Simurg, 2002.

his choice of the 35mm camera, not so much for the quality of the image, but for the regimen that it imposes upon the work. His work is the polar opposite of the urgency and the lightness of the digital camera, deriving its power from both the weight of the world and that of the machine used to record it. This is not a mania for the format, but rather of the conservation of a device that orders and calibrates events.

Los muertos stretches between the cadavers of its opening sequence and the drive for survival that appears throughout. A survival joined to that of the cinephile, an endangered species. Behind its unsettling, abrupt ending, left in shadow as though to underscore its fragmentary nature, lurks a blind fear of what was just presented, its irreducible mystery. This fear is provoked more by an effect of the cinema than by the film itself. It brings us back to that primordial condition of astonishment and tremors experienced in our earliest encounters with the screen. In the words of Jean-Louis Schéfer: "At the heart of cinema (in its oldest and most brutal state) remains the terror or diffuse fear brought on in our childhood by any film at all."[86]

Fantasma, between specters and survival[87]

The film that was going to bring the trilogy to a close was, in principle, going to be *Liverpool*. *Fantasma* appeared later, inserting itself as a political intervention on the state of film in Argentina, not only from a directorial perspective, but also in terms of its conditions of circulation and reception, forming a stance not only with regard to directors, but also to viewers. The question is simple: What spaces are

---

[86] Schéfer, Jean-Louis. *L'homme ordinaire du cinéma*. Paris: Cahiers du cinéma-Gallimard, 1997.
[87] An earlier version of this section appeared in *El Amante-Cine*, 173 (October 2006).

left to the preservation of cinema today? How can a film engage and, if possible, engender them?

When he wrote film criticism for *Sur* toward the end of the thirties, Borges, in his valiant defense of Luis Saslavsky's *La fuga*, once stated that he preferred stepping into a movie theater on calle Lavalle and finding himself in the Gulf of Bengal or on Wabash Avenue to stepping into that same theater and finding himself on calle Lavalle. With this, he forestalls any claim that his positive evaluation of the film was based on any nationalist zeal. Yet here we step into a movie theater on calle Corrientes, in Buenos Aires, to find ourselves – in the film – in that same theater on calle Corrientes. It is an event unto itself, though it is not all there is to *Fantasma*.

Vargas and Saavedra wander through the Teatro San Martín, around the time *Los muertos* is released. If the restraint of Argentino Vargas makes him a less-than-viable interlocutor, he offers himself willingly to the scrutiny of the theater's attendees. Misael Saavedra, on the other hand, is satisfied to remain a shadow, invisible to all but the viewers of *Fantasma*. The anecdotal justification of their presence is less important than their status as apparitions. Out of place, displaced: the term suits not only these two, but also the viewer confronted by a primordial sense of the uncanny as he perceives the spaces – mundane or vaguely unsettling – in which the action occurs. The San Martín complex seems like a set out of a Fritz Lang film, always almost nocturnal, even in the middle of the day. Its monumental, desolate and inevitably crestfallen modernism is just as ghostly as the two transient figures that pass through it, closer to a Murnau-Flaherty duet than a comic duo. And yet it is not lacking a certain humorous complicity.

Alonso has explicitly pointed out, on a number of occasions, the anti-narrative project behind his films. Nor do his films, in their manipulation of the building blocks of realism, subscribe to the naïve belief in a fusion, a unity between image and reality. In this sense, *Fantasma* is a film of doubles and doubling, as when we see Vargas looking at himself in a poster for *Los muertos* and when later, in the Lugones screening room, he does the same, in the company of a few members of the audience. Not without an unorthodox sense of humor, Alonso opens himself to the question: What is cinema?

This question is presented, in *Fantasma*, in a way that is both extreme and part of this motif of doubling. On one hand, it refers to the content of the film within the film itself. On the other, it turns the Lugones screening room (where it was filmed, had its premiere, and was screened in a limited series of events not unlike a 'limited edition' release) into the ideal space for its viewing; in full awareness of what it is doing, it engages the theater as a physical space one enters in order to watch movies. If the film turns its duplicative effect inward when it shows the theater in which Alonso's previous film is being shown, this experience spreads outward, as well, in that we – as viewers in the Lugones theater – see the theater and the building itself as an extension of the film, in another mise en scène that turns *Fantasma* into an experience at the limits of the art installation rather than belonging to narrative or language (those first cousins fueled by predominant notions of the cinematic); there is, as in the most radical works of Kiarostami, a radical examination of the form. It does not so much qualify as an experimental film as it does an experiment with film.

In *Author and Authorship*, in a rare moment of convergence with the ideas of surrealists like Max Jacob, Ernst Jünger defined cinema as an act of conspiracy: "Film is like artificial flowers, which accumulate layers of dust over time because they do not know death [ ] film appeals to and is congruent with the world of the titans. But the titan cannot die: once he is overthrown, he lives on in the underworld. Today we can conjure the dead upon the screen, through the shadow he emits: it is a spectral art."[88] It is indeed a matter of authorship: Alonso reveals his own to be as personal as it is directorial, just as proud and legitimately distant from the precepts of the spectacle as regenerative – with the help of his two friendly, human, archetypal, filmic ghosts – of a cinema that survives and even has a future.

Returns and origins in *Liverpool*

Liverpool was a way to unravel the effect of closure produced by *Fantasma*, as the final installment of a trilogy. It breathes a different air, not only because it was filmed at the southernmost extreme of Argentina, but also because it presents a new aspect of Alonso's body of work. If, as James Hoberman asserts, his films are defined by their trajectories, here the dynamic is that of the return, from the cargo ship upon which a taciturn mariner returns to land, to the final shot in which we glimpse what this return has allowed him to re-establish.[89]

The gaze of Farrel, his protagonist, is similar to that of Ulysses catching sight of an Ithaca that is both recognizable and unrecognizable. Those who inhabit the land upon his return also vacillate between recognition and non-recognition. Though the scope of this odyssey is, of course, much more modest, the vague form of a new dimension takes shape, not through the logic of the narrative, but rather through poetic correspondences, analogies that invite interpretation.

---

[88] Jünger, Ernst. *El autor y la escritura*. Barcelona: Gedisa, 1987. 47.
[89] Hoberman, James. "Jobber Adrift at Sea Takes Leave in *Liverpool*" *Village Voice*, December 9, 2009. http://www.villagevoice.com/2009-09-01/film/jobber-adrift-at-sea-takes-leave-in-liverpool/

There is no character-based psychology to Alonso's fictional progeny, who at the same time refuses to be the progeny of a documentary. Their opacity situates them at an intermediate point, at once allowing and delimiting an emerging fiction. The word "Liverpool" appears on the key ring the protagonist gives to his daughter; it is not a key, it is not a symbol. It is simply a trace, the mark of a distant place he once was and may have no reason to return to; it is also the vestige of something that has occurred. The key ring is laughable, devoid of all symbolic power apart for its evocation of a distant port. What remains is a film endowed with the "suspended meaning" that Barthes praised in Buñuel, which, far from hampering emotion, joins it to a sense of disruption.

With *Liverpool*, the trilogy becomes a tetralogy, as the filmmaker himself has stated.[90] Perhaps his next film will make it a pentalogy; so profound are the connections between one step and the next. There is reason to believe that Alonso's entire filmic progression preserves – whether consciously or not – ties to its earlier articulations. At a number of events after the release of *Liverpool* (among which we especially recall the public forum at the Cartagena International Film Festival in 2009), the director claimed to have reached an *impasse* after the project. An attentive viewer might disagree: something seems to have been started in its course, although it may take time to develop.

Though the term 'auteur' is used so often these days that its abundance is something of a Pyrrhic victory, ultimately meaning little given the number of them to be found, in Alonso's case it is not only justified but appropriate as a strategic position within the current cinematic landscape.

---

[90] *No Man's Land – The Cinema of Lisandro Alonso*, Nov. 6-8, Harvard Film Archives. See: http://hcl.harvard.edu/hfa/films/2009octdec/alonso.html (accessed 11/7/09).

In his illuminating prologue to a collection of interviews with the directors of the classic cinema of decades past, Serge Daney offered, in the eighties, a lucid evaluation of the concept of the *auteur* at a time when it had become fashionable in the academy to speak of his demise, his death certificate signed by structuralism, as seductive arguments built on the sale of products in the film industry continued to grow. In this context of deterioration, Daney nonetheless detects a liberating function within this idea: "The director, then, would not only be he who finds the strength to express himself in spite of and in opposition to all, but rather he who, in expressing himself, finds the distance needed to speak the truth about the system from which he has distanced himself [...] In this way, auteur cinema would tell us more about the future of the system that produced it than the mere products of the system itself. The director would be, without question, the line of flight through which the system would open up, breathe, have a history."[91]

Thus in the space between unsteady refuge – like the shelter Farrel seems to take in falling asleep beside his bottle of vodka – and exposure, which brings both freedom and an errancy as dubious and risky as that of the character's march into the far reaches of the shot in *Liverpool*, the films of Lisandro Alonso refer back to the state of film today, just as rife with threats to its continued existence as it is rich in the seeds of an unexpected resilience, which it may be more important to cultivate now than ever before.

---

[91] Daney, Serge "Después de todo." Prologue to Jean Renoir et al, *La política de los autores*. Barcelona: Paidós, 2003. 17.

Epilogue: surveying the form, the future of cinema

Through the use of different strategies, the tetralogy comprised of *La libertad, Los muertos, Fantasma* and *Liverpool* represents a true manifesto in support of cinema's power and the right to survive. A claim that is not mournful or tinged with melancholy, but one which recognizes that what it offers cannot be replaced by any part of the totalizing spectacle that has seeped into even the most remote of the throngs of screens that surround us.

Alonso's films do not advocate a return to Lumière – this would obviously be a mistake, the product of an ingenuousness completely foreign to the filmmaker – but rather insist on the importance of the old lesson to maintain a gaze that is as fresh as the objects that inhabit it. They do this within a landscape that is far from auspicious, one that the Brazilian critic Ismail Xavier has described as follows: "Today, the enormous network that is being formed within the production and circulation of images and sound renders more complex the correlation between aesthetic value, political implication and the specific properties of a form, among other things because both the history of that production and its current configuration have demonstrated the necessity of changing our perception of the place of cinema among other forms."[92] With the preservation of the right to a cinematic perspective on one side and the awareness of the shifts necessary to protect a vitality threatened by the present state of normalization and audiovisual programming on the other, Alonso's films draw their strength precisely from their marginal position, not as a lament for a golden plenitude lost among the screens of today, but as a call to push forward into the breach.

---

[92] Xavier, Ismail. *El discurso cinematográfico. La opacidad y la transparencia*. Buenos Aires: Manantial, 2009. 283.

Riding the Storm[93]

Paz Encina

I. Paraguay and the Eternal Silence

> *Cándida:*
> *Did you see it?*
> *Rehecháiko.*
>
> *Ramón:*
> *What?*
> *Mba'épa.*
>
> *Cándida:*
> *A shooting star...*
> *Na'amo ova peteï estrella.*
>
> *Ramón:*
> *As soon as you see it, it glows bright and disappears.*
> *Hëe.*
> *Haimete voi ndajahechái, omimbi ha okañy jeýma.*[94]

Cinema in Paraguay is scarce, inconsistent, almost nonexistent. At present, we are one of the only countries in the Southern Cone not to have a regulated film industry. Perhaps the last, the only one. Our images and sounds are still "to come," and I believe that this silence is a symptom of our history. I wanted to portray it, but how to portray

---

[93] The title of a series by Paraguayan artist Ricardo Migliorisi.
[94] All excerpts are taken from the script of *Hamaca paraguaya*, 11th version.

silence? How to make something ephemeral not seem ephemeral?

Portraying silence was like portraying the wind; it was just as difficult... I felt as though I had to search, with the greatest delicacy possible, for those elements that make up *our* silence. I wanted elements through which I could describe the sensation and not the word itself. It is true that the characters do not speak, but that is not where the silence I was searching for can be found. Not speaking has never been the same as silence to me, and I wanted the silence of *Hamaca paraguaya* to be perceived through a protracted, dead, expansive sense of time, *tiempo*. A time in which solitude and sadness converge with the struggle to preserve a connection, limitless hope, and a search for the meaning of life. It is true that the silence in *Hamaca paraguaya* is political, but I also wanted it to be human. We have a long history of wars lost, others won (but in some ways, still lost), of dictatorships that silenced us and ended... but did not end. These are things that are felt in this country, and it affects the humanity of the people, something sensed more through smell than sight. I wanted a silence that could draw its strength from our particular case, from its cycles, and that would take its time in expressing itself.

II. Autumn has come, and it is still hot...

> **Ramón:**
> *Autumn has come, and it is still hot...*
> *Ro'y tiémpoma ha hakúnte hína...*

Hamaca paraguaya is the story of two farmers waiting for their son to return from the Chaco War. It takes place over the course of one day and the movie begins and ends in the dark; it begins in the darkness before dawn and ends in the darkness of nightfall. All days in one day.

In Paraguay, talking about *tiempo* usually means talking about the other sense of the word, the weather, so when asked about it (*¿cómo está el tiempo?*) the answer will almost always be the same: "Hot" or its variants, that it "Looks like rain" or not. When you talk about the weather, you inevitably get the same answers every time. It seems to me that Paraguay keeps living the same history – with slight variations, but the same one – and I think that this is because the Paraguayan lives in an eternal state of nostalgia for a time in the past that may not have been any better, but at least had one advantage: it was in the *past*. It is as though we were condemned to the fate of always repeating the same patterns, even those that cut us off from our oral traditions and condemned us to a silence that is in no way sublime. My interest in constructing a dual temporality comes from this. I wanted to find the moment between a past that had come to an end and a future that was exactly the same, an after exactly the same as the before, shown through day-to-day situations. I wanted to find this, which is why I wanted the dialogue to happen off camera; that was my primary intention behind using a technique already employed by Hitchcock, Bresson and Godard. I wanted Cándida and Ramón to exist in a time long after the one we were hearing, but a time that was also the same. I remember my ten-line synopsis of the film, that began *June 14 and long after...* those lines capture the film. I wanted two temporalities to be contained within a summary produced by image and sound. Two temporalities, a before and an after, but also something more: the moment between those two times, the point of contact between a before and an after, and the knowledge that what *was* is what *could* (can) be again.

III. Sound as an Axis of Writing

Ramón:
What's the matter?
Mba'e tepa la ojehúva ndéve.

CÁNDIDA is slow to answer, she continues peeling the cassava.

Cándida:
What is the matter...
Mba'éta piko...

Silence.

Cándida:
I can't go on like this, Ramón, moving the hammock around, hoping that dog will stop barking.
Chekuerái Ramón, mboy vécema piko arova ko kyha hendágui, ha pe jagua ñande apysaitépe jeynte oñarö.

She continues peeling the cassava.
Silence.

Ramón:
But you keep moving the hammock closer to the dog...
Ha remo'aguïve katungo chugui la ñande kyha...

Cándida:
What do you want me to do? It's the only shade we have...
Ha mba'éiko reipota ajapo. Ndaipóri otro yvyraguy jaha haguä.

Ramón:
So why didn't you just leave it where it was? Wasn't that a little farther away?
Ha maeräiko upéicharö reru ko'ápe, amo oï haguépe ningo mombyryve kuri ñaime la jaguágui.

Loud thunderclap. CÁNDIDA startles, and stops peeling the cassava. RAMÓN puts his hand on her back. CÁNDIDA goes back to peeling cassava. RAMÓN remains seated on the hammock and takes his hand from Cándida's back. He continues chewing on the leaf. He spits from time to time.

Ramón:
So answer, then...
Nerehendúi piko

Silence.

Cándida:
Isn't it bigger?
Ha tuichave ningo...

Silence.

Ramón:
Bigger?
Isn't what bigger?
Tuichave..?
Mba'épa la tuichavéva.

Cándida:
This shade is bigger.
Ko yvyraguy ñaimeha.

Ramón looks back.

Ramón:
But it's closer to the dog.
Pero jagua ndive ñaime...

The dog stops barking.

Cándida:
That's all I have to say... the dog got quiet, too.

She barks and quiets down, all day the same thing...
Akirirïma... ha péina pe jagua okirirïma avei.
Ha'éko oñarö ha okirirï, manterei.

When I sat down to write *Hamaca paraguaya* I was particularly focused on the word *time*, but was a little surprised because at the beginning only dialogue was coming out. I realized that what I had was a script full of sounds; later, when the New Crowned Hope[95] asked me to write a few words for the catalogue, I discovered something that, to me, was really incredible:

> *When I was four years old, my mother sent me to study classical guitar. I was still too small to use a normal guitar, so they had to make me a special small one. But that is not what matters. What matters is that, over time, I realized that before I learned to read and write with letters, I learned to read and write musical notes, and that was what stayed with me as my studies in reading and writing.*
>
> *When I wrote* Hamaca paraguaya, *it was like writing a score; I tried to be just as careful with it and, without my realizing, the notes flowed onto my computer screen in the form of letters. Quarter notes, eighth notes, and especially half notes and semibreves... and silence. A lot of silence. I was thinking only of the tempo, of the rhythm of the words, and in how two people could make a funeral hymn out of words. That is what I wanted to happen, that these two farmers could express their pain through song, as their voices died out with the passage of time.*
>
> *A few months later, I receive the New Crowned Hope catalogue and see that Peter Sellars considers* Hamaca paraguaya *to be a contemporary lyric requiem.*
>
> *That day, my soul was filled with joy.*
> *And I was at peace.*[96]

---

[95] Event organized in honor of Mozart's 250th birthday, and in which *Hamaca paraguaya* took part.
[96] Personal writings for the catalogue of the New Crowned Hope festival.

I thought, then, of the script for *Hamaca paraguaya* as though it were a score, as though the movie were marked at the beginning with a treble clef. Each scene developed and took form on its own, according to its specific meter, practically without my help. Made of notes and tempo. To shoot the film, I put together "homemade" sound tracks in Spanish, but with all the sounds that would appear later in the final cut because I wanted the sound to be my guide, even on the "physical" level of time... I thought only of how long a word could last, how long I would be quiet after hearing this or that word and so, following an imagined tempo of pain, I conceived of what, for me, would become a melancholy funeral hymn performed as a duet. It was as though the film began with a key in the major scale... and got fainter and fainter until it ended only in chords or barely audible individual notes that reflect that absence – of sound, of gesture, of characters (people) that choose when to mourn an absence that will never be anything else.

Each sound in the movie was chosen according to its proper and just measure. We spent days with Guido Berenblum,[97] just *listening*. Really listening. The tone was very important; for a laugh, there is a story that ends with one of us saying, "*That bird won't work, it's too happy.*" We were there for a long time with our ambition: *we wanted to be able to see the sound.*

Image and sound were structured from the beginning as separate units that come together only in those little moments. Moments that are presented on a visual level under the sign of contemplation, in which their dark, hidden dimensions are revealed. I did not want a silence that would eradicate words, but rather a silence that comes after words, when everything has already been said; that appears when one thing has already been said and the next has

---

[97] Director of Sound for *Hamaca paraguaya*, together with Víctor Tendler.

nothing new to offer. Before and after the word, that was the silence. I wanted to hear it from within, like the sound inside a shell that cannot be heard from the outside, but only from within, where the emptiness resonates. I wanted to hear the emptiness.

IV. Composition

> *Cándida:*
> It's not going to rain. It's not going to rain, Ramón, you're waiting for nothing. There isn't even any wind.
> Ndokymo'äi. Ndokymo'äi, Ramón; reha'arö rei. Ni nda'yvytúi.
>
> CÁNDIDA sucks on an orange. RAMÓN has already finished his, he spreads it open and eats the pulp.
>
> Silence.
>
> *Cándida:*
> There's nothing to be done.
> Ndaiporivéima jajapo va'erä.
>
> RAMÓN gets out of the hammock. He sniffs the air. He continues eating the last of the pulp. CÁNDIDA continues eating the orange.
>
> *Ramón:*
> But it smells like rain...
> Hyakuä ama katuko hína.
>
> *Cándida:*
> The smell might promise it, but it won't rain.
> Ha hyakuä reíntema, ndokymo'äi.

Throughout the writing process, I thought constantly about how cinema was showing less and less of what really happens to people. This really bothered me. I wanted to try to do just that, so when I wrote the script I decided beforehand that each image would last as long as was necessary in order to be expressed, and not as long as it took someone to see it. Little actions begin and end in each shot, lasting as long as they should last. A breath fully exhaled, a fan used until it cools, a cicada unfurling its song, an orange peeled and eaten according to its proper and just measure. Everything needed to begin and end in such a way that it was truly seen. I decided not to be afraid of time, and should say that this was a result of my love of video art. Works like *The Passing*, by Bill Viola and *Sept visions fugitives*, by Robert Cahen have shown me that time does not exist within the image, that everything takes place *at its own pace*. That was the only means I found of presenting a world that felt, more than anything, very personal to me. A slow, reflective, lilting, plodding world. A world of silence, of the time between words, a time described through the word "silence," by which I try to graze the limits of the past and the present. Temporal series superimposed upon one another, not assuming that memory exists, not assuming that memory does not exist. I also spent a lot of time considering how much movement there should be, and could only think about the death of the boy. I could not stop thinking about how much the death of a child would hurt It was horrible, it weighed on me terribly and I spent days not wanting to do anything, but it made me realize that they, Cándida and Ramón, really didn't need to do much; they no longer had any reason to touch one another, no reason to want to talk – they must already have talked about it so often. With the slightest gesture, they could know exactly what the other was experiencing.

All conflict needed to be expressed at the site of the hammock, through long and unequivocal conversations. The arrival at the site, which is itself almost ceremonial, a rite meticulously performed, also encompasses both form and content. Everything seems to have been predetermined by its mundanity: the topics of conversation, drinking *tereré*, peeling the cassava, waiting, leaving. As though it were a place for not thinking, paradoxically, Cándida and Ramón arrive at the site and all these thoughts emerge and conflict swells, and it is in this place, designed to be a place to relax and do nothing that they are betrayed by their memories, and waiting becomes a destiny. If they arrive at this place, it is because a certain kind of conversation needs to be had, a certain kind of memory needs to emerge, and because it is inevitable. Time marks its passing in solitude, an eternal movement forward devoid of vitality, the same story in the same place; things lose their meaning as they go along, without a sense of temporality. Death will try to offer the only meaning in this emptiness, but the characters will fight against it, building up what time tries to diminish.

Distance was another important choice. I had to keep my distance. I had to for many reasons. We are outside of it all and, as the characters were so specifically Paraguayan, I did not want anyone to get caught up in things I was not interested in showing. I was not interested in showing the world how a cassava is peeled, or how we drink *tereré*. I was not interested in anything anthropological. I wanted to show two people facing an inconceivable loss, two people in a state of loss who, if the world did not make a real effort, would never be seen. My feeling is that, although they are in front of the camera for the entire film, they can barely be seen. That fascinated me, because I think that is a bit like our situation. Sometimes I think we don't matter to anyone. That is why I wanted to avoid visual flourishes. Ozu taught me much about that...

> A camera placed at the height of a man seated in a hammock; a very still camera, I do not try to make big movements on behalf of the characters. The film is

structured around the suspension of movement, around the pauses taken to focus on a broken gaze or a hidden emotion. The camera could only be positioned frontally, which meant to me not only flattening the image but bringing the viewer further into the filmic space trying to extend beyond the borders of the screen. The characters are seen only through what they do, perceived only through what they say and it is in this way that the viewer is left with the task of deducing their intentions and emotions and, consequently, of adopting a position relative to them. In this way, the viewer feels almost obligated to "read" the film, to participate actively.

Cándida:
Does your chest hurt, papa?
Hasýiko ndéve nde pyti'a.

Ramón:
There is nothing to be done.
Death is making its presence felt.
Ndaipóri jajapo vaerä.
Mano oñeñandukáma.

Silence.

Ramón:
And if we're wrong?
Ha ndaha'éiramo...

Cándida:
If we're wrong?
Jajavýramo...

It was all this, then, that brought me to make this slow, radical film... but at the same time, something incredible happened to me: I began to believe in myself. I was, for the first time in my life, making the kind of cinema I had always wanted to make, and I felt as though I were "coming to life."

In the beginning, I thought I was only telling the story of the absence of Máximo Ramón Caballero, the son of Cándida and Ramón. Later, almost as though it were a monster, I realized, I saw the history of Paraguay over the past 200 years in the script. That had not been my intention, I had only wanted to show how much these two people suffered but without intending to, one day I found myself with a completely circular space, with two people that flitted in and out of a black hole, in and out of the dark. A single day that spoke of the continuity of continuity, I realized. And that terrified me.

> *Cándida:*
> It's just habit, Ramón, nothing more. What you wait for never comes. I used to think that the less it rained, the closer the rains were to coming, but now I see that the things you wait for, you wait for in vain.
> Péva nde lájantema... ñaha'arövako ndouséi. Che ymámi ha'e avei la a medidake ndokyvéi oky aguï. Pero ko'äga ahechárna la ñaha'aröva ñaha'arö reiha.

3. GENRES, FORMATS, PROJECTS

One of the typical methods of navigating cinematic production is to refer to certain consecrated roadmaps that are as widespread as they are foreign to the specificity of the form. Genre can be a useful descriptor at times; on other occasions it is better to refer to more primordial distinctions, such as the one that separates the narrative film from the documentary. Nonetheless, certain aspects of contemporary cinema break down borders, unsettling the spirits of classification. In these cases, designations are revamped, as has been the case of the category known as the creative documentary over the course of the past two decades. The intersection of a certain gaze and a pronounced authorial imprint, along with the eradication of some of the ethical and sociopolitical mandates of the traditional documentary, denotes one of the most vital and promising areas of contemporary cinema. Carmen Guarini, from her dual perspective as a filmmaker and scholar, looks at certain lines of force within the phenomenon, testing them out through the analysis of a few emblematic cases.

What can be sensed in the documentary at the present moment may not be limited to that sphere, but may instead be a sign of something of concern to cinema in general and to its relation with an outside world still resistant to the totalizing spectacle of late electronic capitalism. Some of the signs of this reconnection between cinema, in a broad sense, and the visible and audible world through a form of observation cultivated to an unprecedented extreme are addressed by Malena Di Bastiano, who examines several emergent Latin American documentary productions close up at the points of intersection between the traditions of film, video, documentary, and experimental work.

Among the categories according to which programs and catalogs are organized, the short film, that younger sibling (though actually, in genealogical terms, it is anything but), stands out. Director and critic Paulo Pécora delineates his aesthetic of the short, which complements the dialogue presented by Daniela Goggi as a curiously effective cinematic maieutics in her article, which is practically a clinical study of the short films regularly produced in film schools across the continent. In addition to examining their objects with acute perceptiveness, both texts can be read as a guide: if not on how to make a short film, then without question on how to be alert to certain automatisms that lurk in a space widely identified with the rejection of pre-established molds.

Not to close the circle, but to coax it into the form of an ever-expanding spiral, Mariela Cantú contributes an analysis of the articulation between cinema and the audiovisual arts from a perspective that originates in the hybridization of the possible, integrating a variety of currents and placing cinema in the context of new perspectives on audiovisual creation. Through this broad approach, she explores the need for inventiveness and adventurousness in a universe where a wealth of trajectories still indicates the promise – and the necessity – of all that is yet to be made.

From the Real to Reality: the Creative Documentary in Latin America

Carmen Guarini

The title of this article implies an objective that is by no means straightforward. The attempt to take stock of the current state of what is known as "creative documentary" production on our continent presents itself as a utopian task due to the very thing, one could say, that has always afflicted Latin American cinema (not only the documentary): its limited distribution.

Essentially, the form known as the "creative documentary" is part of a corpus that has recently been produced in abundance in Latin America, so quickly and with such diversity that it is impossible to understand it in its totality, again due to the issues surrounding the circulation of Latin American cinema. The creation, over the last ten years, of film festivals and screenings specifically dedicated to the documentary in Latin America – among which Brazil's E tudo verdade, Chile's Fidocs, DocBsAs in Argentina, Muestra de cine documental in Colombia, Encuentros del Otro Cine in Ecuador and DocsDF in Mexico stand out – has, however, facilitated the circulation of a handful of important works.

The first titles to come to mind are *Estamira, Edificio Master, El comité, Paradise, El corazón, Por la vuelta, París-Marsella, Arcana, Yo no sé qué me han hecho tus ojos, Grissinópoli, Espejo para cuando me pruebe el smoking...* These are works that I could easily count as part of a tradition of documentary filmmaking defined by a strong authorial presence. There are, without a doubt, many others that have not been mentioned, which perhaps I have not seen; that have been disseminated through unknown channels, yet which nonetheless contribute to the formation of a new kind of documentary in Latin America.

There is a limit, then, to the task I have assigned myself. I will not be able to include everything that would fall under the category or concept of the "creative documentary" to which the title of this article refers, but I will attempt to outline its present state and conditions of production.

I will begin by trying to answer a few of the more obvious questions that come up: what is considered a "creative documentary"? What is the origin of this classification? Can this category be applied to documentaries produced in Latin America?

I will also analyze four examples of creative documentaries, chosen arbitrarily and subjectively. These films correspond to my idea of this type of cinema, and are important because they were made in the early eighties, a time marked by changes in the narrative style of documentaries seen up to that moment in their respective countries.

The concept

The concept of the "creative documentary" or "auteur documentary" (nearly the same thing) appears in the European audiovisual industry in the eighties for reasons having to do with production and the need to establish a documentary form grounded in a treatment of reality that was removed from journalistic habits and preoccupations (informative, educational, institutional reporting).

It all started with the need to assign a name to a type of film that, though it lacked a date of birth,[98] had begun

---

[98] Many will already be familiar with the work of directors like Chris Marker – just to name one well-known example – who always stood out for the

to proliferate as a cinema "of the real" that broke with the models of documentary filmmaking that had in previous decades achieved the greatest circulation (in particular, institutionally and on television) and which, with a few exceptions, was characterized by a strong tendency toward the informative, the didactic and, above all, the explication of the world.

There were, of course, filmmakers like Rouquié, Marker, Leacock, Brault, Rouch, Perrault and Druault, who, along with pioneers like Flaherty, Vertov, Vigo and Buñuel (in the twenties) created a corpus that planted the seeds of the creative documentary.

This legacy is taken up again with great vigor in the eighties and proves itself in the nineties as a form of documentary cinema that emphasizes the idea that the world cannot be explained and that all that can be offered is a subjective, partial, imperfect vision of it, always provisory. It is a cinema mobilized by relative truth.

It is a moment of uncertainty (the seventies and their ideal of a world that could become more just and humane were long gone) and no one knows what to say about it. This new type of representing reality asserts (because something is always asserted) that nothing can be asserted once and for all.

In Latin America, of course, a handful of names stand out, like those of Santiago Álvarez, Solanas and Getino, and Patricio Guzmán, who, inscribed within the specific context of the sixties and seventies, developed a personal record of the political. Yet their works are isolated events compared to the explosion of auteur cinema that has taken place around the world over the past two decades, the

---

pronounced authorial presence in his films. If we delve even deeper, we could speak of the easily recognizable style of Flaherty and Vertov.

diverse subject matter and style of which is impossible to encompass in its totality.

A question of "name"

Almost from its inception, auteur cinema has developed at the limits of a register that took as its paradigm a narrative of the real understood as a product of the author's mind. And this, as we know, was always something associated with fictional cinema rather than the documentary.

In the documentary space, this "authorial gaze" arises as a vindication of a moral, political, and poetic perspective on the world, exposing a cinematic subjectivity that, as the critic and scholar Jean Perret asserts, "turns the real into reality."[99] The concept of the *documentaire de création* appears, then, at the exact moment that it becomes necessary to talk about a style of filmmaking that makes explicit reference to a reality transformed by the gaze of the director. A cinema that emerges with a spirit of innovation, both in its basic concept and in its writing and execution: "Its most interesting characteristic was the combination of the maturity with which its subject matter was addressed and the profound reflexivity that allowed the presence of the director or auteur to be felt."[100]

In an article on Godard and the documentary, Domenec Font examines the form on the basis of the characteristics that define it as non-fiction, asserting that, both in order to distance itself from a purely declaratory and didactic fate and to lay claim to some semblance of truth, the documentary should have established itself, from the beginning, in

---

[99] Jean Perret is the Director of the Visions du Réel Festival in Nyon (Switzerland).
[100] Ixchel Delaporte, "Quelle place pour le documentaire de création à la télévision?" www.humanite.presse.fr.

relation (and in opposition) to the fictional account that is the dogma – according to Font – of the cinematic institution. "Thus its status as an *objet filmique mal identifié*, as described by Guy Gauthier, one of the most respected specialists in the field."[101]

It is well known that in the sixties and seventies the documentary was riddled with concepts like *direct cinema, free cinema,* and *cinéma vérité* that tried – through debate and discussion – to take over a form that was emerging simultaneously in countries around the world, spurred on by the technological innovations of the time (direct sync sound and the 16mm). But with the passage of time and the appearance of digital technology, these concepts showed the limits of their ability to incorporate new ways of capturing the real.

As Font states, "The lack of a territory of its own drives the documentary to invent names and establish distance relative to its object. Obsessed both with the role it has hoped to fulfill and the credibility it has needed for its projects, documentary film has tried to associate itself with all manner of categories. Some of these claims to specificity simply refer back to its descriptive aspect, forming a cohort with the social sciences, such as the ethnographic, sociological, or political documentary. Other, more dubious, formulations divided the history of the documentary according to different organizing principles, such as the four modalities described by Bill Nichols: the expository documentary (Grierson, Flaherty), the observational documentary (Leacock, Pennebaker, Wiseman), the participatory documentary (Jean Rouch, Émile d´Antonio), and the reflexive documentary (from Dziga Vertov to Raúl Ruiz)."[102]

---

[101] Domenec Font, "Jean Luc Godard y el documental. Navegando entre dos aguas." *Analisis* vol. 7, 2001. www.ddd.uab.es.
[102] Ibid.

It is true that this cinema has always been imbued with a certain sense of purpose (let us not forget that Grierson suggested that the role of the documentary should be to *educate the citizen*). This idea laid the groundwork for a territory specific to the documentary and is maintained even to this day by a number of filmmakers. Grierson's philosophy belongs to a time in which the television was not as central to people's lives as it is today; for this reason it was tied to the idea of film as a tool for the ideological and educational development of individuals according to democratic and liberal principles (in the broad sense of the word). With the passage of time other values were added to this function but, for many, the documentary was never able to shake the idea that it could not be a cinema that entertained, only one that informed or, in the best of all possible cases, counter-informed. It seems somewhat unfair to attribute to the documentary something that is a part of cinema in general, as an element of communication. Even fictional cinema "educates" us (for better or worse), even when we are only looking for "distraction" or "entertainment." Yet this is only one of its qualities, to which it cannot be reduced.

Those who were most confrontational wanted the documentary to fulfill an ideological role of social transformation and assigned it the mission not only of accompanying social change, but also of trying to produce it. It sounds a bit farfetched, but this idea generated and continues to generate audiovisual work that has more in common with the leaflet than with cinema, yet which nonetheless claims a place within the documentary genre.

The diversity of documentary cinema produced more or less descriptive and declarative formulas based on the "educational or revolutionary mission" that had so long been assigned to it; later, these formulas began to come into contact with others that tried to change them through narrative modes that, without abandoning their political objectives, emphasized the need to attend to formal considerations. These changes, which I prefer to call "explorations" or "processes," only emphasized the vitality of the documentary, which, as a cinematic account, was able to experiment time and again in its attempts to take stock of the real.

Font also states: "Other rubrics that place emphasis on authenticity have enjoyed greater acceptance, though their scientific imprudence has been just as great. I refer to the categories of experiential cinema, direct cinema, *cinéma du réel* and *cinéma vérité* that gathered such force in the sixties, with the ambivalence of their attempts to set themselves apart from other types of cinema rather than restoring a clear set of objectives, defined by the strange but powerful intersection between film as a technical medium and as a spiritual state. Finally, one must not forget terms in use today, like that of the *docudrama*, which falls in line with the tendency of television to blur the boundaries between genres without challenging the consensual power of fiction; or like the creative documentary, the objective of a critique that rejects the 'laziness' of the traditional document, reaffirming the artistic character of the documentary and its status as an exercise in personal expression."[103]

For me, Font's text provokes the following thoughts: 1) the documentary is seen as a contested space that is constantly being redefined with respect to its object (the real); 2) many filmmakers experiment with multiple forms that become difficult to categorize, or, at least, all categories become necessarily *provisional*; 3) the concept of the "creative documentary" is simply an invention of critics and scholars in their attempt to convey *something that this form of cinema always possessed.*

---

[103] Ibid, the emphasis is mine.

Without a doubt, I agree with Font that the creative documentary is a cinematic form that "distances itself from the traditional document," to which the author assigns a certain "laziness," that is, techniques repeated ad nauseum that generate formal modes that nonetheless end up consolidating the hegemony of mainstream taste through television over the course of decades. Paradoxically, it is television – primarily European public television of the eighties – that contributed, through production and distribution, to the formal shift or transformation that promoted documentary cinema, the more creative elements of which had been lost.

Beginning in the nineties, a cinema based in the documentation of the real carves out a place for itself, constructing its own interpretation of the world, leaving pretensions toward objectivity and explication behind. It is an interpretation that, to the contrary, will increasingly take the form of a first-person account.

The creative documentary in Latin America

If, during the seventies, documentary filmmakers in Latin America were mostly interested in taking stock of the social and political situation, the films of the eighties are marked by progressive changes in their tone and conditions of enunciation. It is no longer as much an issue of subject as it is of form; what is said matters less than how it is said. The explicative model of the political documentary gives way to a reflection not only on cinema but also on its director. In our countries, the concept of the "creative documentary" begins to tower, as I mentioned earlier, over the panorama of documentary creation in the nineties. Nonetheless, a few films made in the eighties could be considered part of this category.[104]

---

[104] We should recall that a number of key political films of the seventies, even when they contained a strong authorial presence (*La hora de los*

I have chosen four films to discuss, all of which have narrative structures that marked a turning point in the panorama of documentaries in their respective countries and prefigured the creative documentary that took root in the following decade.[105] These are films that were made independently and produced according to different channels: in Brazil, Eduardo Coutinho's *Cabra marcando para morrer* (1984); in Chile, Ignacio Agüero's *Cien años esperando un tren* (1988); in Argentina, both Céspedes-Guarini's *Hospital Borda, un llamado a la razón* (1986) and Carlos Echeverría's *Juan, como si nada hubiera sucedido* (1984).

These films were selected because they all establish, without abandoning their sociopolitical subject matter, registers and modes of exposition that contain elements belonging to the creative documentary: a) they introduce a story as their narrative axis; b) they include the production process as part of that story; c) the filmmakers enter the story as an element of its construction; d) what is shown expresses a subjective vision of the narrated experience; e) the act of interpretation is left to the viewer. These films present themselves as open processes, and one of their novelties is that they include time as a narrative element. Let us briefly recall the synopsis of Coutinhou's film: in February of 1964, production begins on a film that would recount the political history of the leader of a peasant league in Sapé (in the state of Paraíba), João Pedro Teixeira, who was assassinated in 1962. However, the production of the

hornos, La batalla de Chile, Ukamau, México, la revolución congelada), were films with a "thesis" in that they sought to establish a closed discourse on certain political ideas within a certain ideological framework. In this respect, they differ from the creative documentary, which does not seek to be a narrative that delimits meaning.

[105] To this day, many countries in Latin America continue to live under military governments and/or those brought to power through coups d'état; others have recently begun to experience processes of democratization in the political sphere.

film was brought to an abrupt halt with the military coup of 1964. 17 years later, the director Eduardo Coutinho returns to the region to find Elisabeth Texeira, the widow of the murdered peasant leader, along with many of the other northeastern peasants that had appeared in the movie. The film is the result of that re-encounter.

Consuelo Lins writes: "That he would make a documentary was certain, but of a new kind, based on a film that was never completed, without a script or a preconceived idea. [...] In the most disturbing and emotional scene of the film, Elisabeth, in hiding since the military coup, takes her former name once again and confronts a part of her life that might have been lost. She is transformed before the camera and before the friends that sit in on her testimony; little by little, her words grow in vitality. It is no longer a matter of recounting what really happened, but rather an operation of auto-formulation, in which she reinvents herself through fragments of her life."[106]

The aesthetic and methodological process that Coutinho discovers over the course of the film would come to characterize his later work. Yet, as Lins asserts, *Cabra marcado para morrer* is a film that has an immediate effect on Brazilian cinema. A "parting of the waters," a "film of synthesis," that takes a certain type of political cinema that seeks to transform the world, typical in the sixties, and changes its course, showing other possible paths. A film that presents different elements of the documentary tradition, but in an altered, transformed, distorted form, precisely to allow for the emergence of anonymous characters and events forgotten and denied by official histories and the mass media." This "transformation" described by Lins is nothing less than the key to understanding that not only

---

[106] Consuelo Lins. "Eduardo Coutinho, cómplice de la realidad filmada" www.tercer-ojo.com.

an aesthetic change was taking place, but also a political one, which would influence documentary filmmaking from that moment on.

In Agüero's film, *Cien años esperando un tren*, the time of the narration is determined by the central conceit of the film: a film class for children. This class, which would take place over the course of several months, is a narrative thread that allows the director (whose voice appears at various points throughout the film) to enter into world of these children from the poorest areas of Santiago de Chile.

What is so unusual about Agüero's film is that, unlike Coutinho's, the subject of the story it tells is not explicitly political and yet, nonetheless, the director manages to address social inequality on the basis of an apparently trivial matter. This is a film that achieves a level of metaphor that allows for multiple readings: these impoverished children and their families begin to realize that they too can have access to knowledge meant for more elevated social strata, and that this knowledge is as critical in today's society as the ability to manipulate a medium as powerful as cinema. At the beginning of the film, they are still unaware of this, but they, and the viewer, discover it along the way; while they are playing and enjoying themselves, they are also changing the relationship that their parents have with the medium and with knowledge as a whole, in a process that allows us to be a part of the change of one and the other.

The film is made in a straightforward way and would seem to adhere to the codes of the traditional participatory documentary, as Nichols would describe it. Though its approach, like that of Coutinho, touches upon this style, the film unfolds beyond it: the cinematic approach is not concealed, a story is told and the viewer participates in it, transforming his view of the cinema and of the world of the slums. The film is at once profoundly poetic and a profound political declaration on the part of the director.

In *Hospital Borda, un llamado a la razón*, the directors present a temporally based narrative: one day in the largest neuropsychiatric hospital for men in Argentina. Through this, they are able to talk about these institutions as antitherapeutic places of internment. The camera, which we can see at various points when the process of filming is made explicit, enters for the very first time an institution that resists being captured on film. It will give an account, over the course of a day,[107] of the characteristics and consequences of the health policies to which the mentally ill are subjected in the Western world.

The film diverges from the testimonial account to present the conditions within these asylums, some of which are extant today (remember that the film is from 1985). In a register that fuses the observational and interpretive modes described by Nichols, the documentary explored the boundaries between health and illness, normality and abnormality, presenting the perspective of the patients themselves on their position as the mentally ill. This establishes a shift in roles within the documentary. A documentary typically informs, educates, clarifies, gets involved politically, generates propaganda. Here the viewer is placed in an undefined, tenuous position; one in which he is forced to identify, at times, with the "lunatics." In this way, the viewer is forced to think that anyone could cross this line: "I" (viewer) could, at any time, become "him."

This space clearly demonstrates the position of the director at the moment of filming and editing, as well as that of choosing and developing the characters of the film. On the other hand, the reflexivity (the demonstration of the shooting process) is used in a conceptual way, not only as a

---

[107] TN: Guarini uses the term '*jornada*' in this instance, which connotes not only a day, but a day of work, and, colloquially, a journey – all fitting, in this context.

matter of form. It is used to take stock of moments in which the institution resists revealing itself, resists breaking down the boundaries between inside and outside.

In the nineties, television produced a phenomenon that immediately became globalized: the hidden camera (as exposé) or the "Big Brother" style. At Borda, the camera is neither one of these things, but rather serves to take stock of the material deterioration of the institution, not to present an exposé, but as a metaphor: in our society, people are reified and become obsolete.

In *Juan, como si nada hubiera sucedido*, the shooting process becomes more complex, and film history appears explicitly in the film as the basis of an investigation: during the last military dictatorship, a young man is kidnapped from Bariloche (a relatively small city that is one of the country's most important tourist destinations), but no one knows anything about it. The documentary is constructed as an investigative report supposedly carried out by a German journalist (who acts as an alter ego for the figure of the director) and is made using two cameras (film and video), which allows for an alternation between points of view. The film plays with techniques that permit the discovery of characters and places, witnesses and accomplices (through action or the lack thereof) to the events, thus allowing a story that functions above and beyond the testimonial impulse to emerge.

There is a plot, there are characters, there are events to uncover. Intrigue shapes the storyline throughout. These narrative techniques, which would become common currency from 2000 on, have an advantage today: the agility that digital technology allows. In contrast, the films here analyzed were shot on 16mm film. This question of format is not aside the point; it means different production and shooting strategies. It also implies larger crews, more weight (in terms of the equipment) and a greater need for intervention in the shots (let us remember that 16mm film reels last only ten minutes).

From this we can conclude that, although digital filmmaking sparked and fostered significant growth in the development of the creative documentary, many of its discursive elements, stylistic practices and techniques of capturing reality were anticipated even before the use of video.[108]

The experience of DocBsAs

The creative documentary also arises as a result of the maximization of the ties between creativity and the conditions of production. This narrative tendency or "trend," which will become increasingly prominent as an effect of cultural globalization, is well suited to the needs of Latin American directors, whose conditions of production are and always have been limited and secondary to the major centers of cinematic production (Europe and the United States). In Argentina we have promoted, since the year 2000, the development of creative documentary cinema through a pioneer program in Latin America, DocBsAs,[109] which included neighboring countries its earliest projects and today also includes the Andean nations.

DocBsAs was conceived as a forum for the discussion and generation of international cooperative productions. The discussion is limited to feature length creative documentaries and includes a review of selected projects with producers working on an international level, which helps to strengthen the proposals. Essentially, participants learn

---

[108] It is worth recalling that the greatest examples of innovation in the language of the documentary are still those seen in the twenties with Vertov and Flaherty, and later in the fifties, with Rouch.
[109] The creators of which are Mercedes Céspedes, Luciano Monteagudo, and Carmen Guarini.

how to present proposals orally (*pitching*). This experience exposed me, as the coordinator of the project workshop, to numerous proposals for documentary films by directors with a wide variety of experience, who came from Chile, Uruguay, Paraguay, Ecuador, Venezuela, Colombia and Peru – even Brazil and Puerto Rico.

Over the past ten years, nearly 800 projects have passed through my hands that give an idea not only of the wide variety of subjects and points of conflict in Latin America that interest and concern the directors, but also of the different perspectives, points of views, and analysis that reaffirm the continued growth of documentary cinema. Nonetheless, from a stylistic point of view, many of these projects continue to prioritize thematic content over its cinematic expression. The possibility of a documentary's transformation into a "creative" work demands a process of elaboration that is both personal and expository, which implies a period of maturation and reflection on the language of cinema that is not always present in the projects or scripts.

In this context, the forum focuses on the importance of reworking the elements of reality that have affected each director and made him want to make a film. But a documentary film can only exist insofar as there is a re-signification of those elements presented by the real; it is through their transformation that we construct a discourse about the real.

On the level of production, the channels of diffusion and distribution within the financial systems behind the documentaries immediately come to the fore. To return to my earlier assertion, it is very difficult once a film is made to find a path to its commercial exhibition. Nearly every Latin American director has, at some point, knocked on the doors of European organizations created over the past few years as a means of supporting this form of cinema not only in Latin America, but also in countries with "at risk or emerging" film traditions, like those of Africa or Asia and the countries of the East.

In this sense, it is a miracle that many of these projects are finished and have achieved international circulation (particularly through film festivals), proving that it is both interesting and necessary to foster an awareness of our ideas beyond our national borders. In this, I share Russell Porter's opinion that a good documentary should transcend its time and place, both in the sense of its cultural specificity and in its ability to reach audiences everywhere.[110]

The creative documentary begins to work along increasingly performative lines, not only deepening the reflexive nature of these films, but also establishing an account in the first person, a *new subjectivity* that reaches its apex in the nineties. Many directors began to develop increasingly personal accounts in which their voice and image indicate an awareness not only of other ways of engaging with reality, but also of the fact that this reality is simply the result of the encounter between film and what is filmed.[111]

A few of the titles that correspond to this performative modality in Argentina are: *Jaime de Navares, último viaje* (Carmen Guarini and Marcelo Céspedes); *Yo no sé qué me han hecho tus ojos* (Sergio Wolf and Lorena Muñoz); *La televisión y yo* (Andrés Di Tella); *Por la vuelta* (Cristian Pauls) and *Meykinof* (Carmen Guarini). But also, to continue with Argentine cinema (because I know it best), films like *Botín de Guerra* (David Blaustein), *Bonanza* (Ulises Rosell), *Ciudad de María* (Enrique Bellande), *Balnearios* (Mariano Llinás), *Grissinópolis* (Darío Dorian), *Las Palmas, Chaco*

---

[110] Porter, Russell. "Sobre documentaries e sapatos" in Mourao and Labaki, *O cinema do real*, San Pablo: Cosac Naify, 2005. 47.
[111] Guarini, Carmen. "Cine antropológico: algunas reflexiones metodológicas" in Adolfo Colomberes (ed.) *Cine, antropología y colonialismo*. Buenos Aires: Ediciones del Sol, 1991.

(Alejandro Fernández Mouján), *Rerum Novarum* (Nicolás Battle) *Bialet Massé, un siglo depués* (Sergio Iglesias), *Trelew* (Mariana Arruti), *El árbol* (Gustavo Fontán), among others, are examples of documentaries in which fiction and reality are interlaced, projecting a creative documentary that is without limit.

Forms of Audiovisual Observation in Contemporary Latin American Production

Malena Di Bastiano

> *We can no longer think about the image outside the act that brings it into being.*
>
> Philippe Dubois

From its etymological roots to its specific use in the audiovisual field, observation cannot be reduced to any one thing. Differentiated from *seeing* and *looking* in that it requires a greater degree of time and attention, observation is frequently employed as an unparalleled means of obtaining information, a fundamental supplement to experimentation and, ultimately, one of the principal foundations of knowledge. The idea of observation, then, is associated with the contemplation or study of something with a certain goal in mind and carries with it, since Aristotle, the idea of control or direction.

In terms of audiovisual production, to which it is joined almost naturally, it is worth noting the different ways in which observation can occur; for example, it takes on the role of a protagonist in the case of the documentary. Bill Nichols thus speaks of an *observational mode* of representation, which he mainly describes through the analysis of North American *direct cinema* and the work of Frederick Wiseman. In general terms, this mode is characterized by the act of recording behaviors, observing others and by certain situations in which the filmmakers find themselves involved as nearly voyeuristic witnesses, without intervening. This places the attention squarely on the presence of the camera as an instrument of observation and recording at the expense of its capacity for fabrication or creation. All editorial manipulation and empathetic cues (music, reenactments, etc.) are avoided in an effort to leave the material in its raw state, or at least give the impression that it had barely been touched, as though it were arriving to us directly, or as if we had been there, observing with our very own eyes. The intention or goal of this is to identify a *what*, to foster knowledge about an object, subject, context, social condition or institution that reveals itself to us in a supposedly distanced or neutral form, as though to give us, the viewers performing the role of witnesses, space to draw our own conclusions about what is being presented.

Toward a broader understanding of audiovisual observation

There is, however, another line of thought about observation. It is a less 'justified' and more lax form, something like 'plain' observation, the central characteristic of which is to activate or mobilize a certain *reflexivity*. We will examine a number of recent Latin American productions that subscribe to this tendency; works in which observation is established not only as an act of bearing witness, but also as the first step or precondition of a creative operation. *Areas*, by Hernán Khourian (2000, Argentina), *A plomo* by Carolina Saquel (2001, Chile), *Cantata de las cosas solas*, by Willi Behnisch (2003, Argentina), *3195, 0778, 0075* and *5040* – a selection from the series *Rizomas*- by Marcellus L. (2004, Brazil), *Da janela do meu cuarto* and *Concerto para Clorofila* by Cao Guimarães (2004, Brazil), *Imagen residuo, Trans apariencias* and *Vista Interior V*, from the series *Ideogramas* by Bruno Varela (2005-2006, Mexico); and *Puna* by Hernán Khourian (2006, Argentina) employ the processes and resources of the documentary. Nonetheless, they cannot simply be defined by or inscribed within this category without provoking a certain measure of productive and necessary doubt, given that they belong to that liminal and nebulous zone that allows us to find them reviewed, placed, or placeable between the documentary, video art, experimental video and/or the video essay, fields that are themselves at odds in terms of their definition and province. The selected works require us to adopt a broader perspective on observation, in that it does not show something in the hope of offering a certain understanding of it (the *quid* of observation), but rather asserts itself as subject and principal protagonist. Placing emphasis on the formal and rhythmic aspects of observation and the observed – which are mutually implicated – independent of their referential and temporal/spatial foundations and the degree of interest this could arouse as 'content,' they ask us to *see the world anew* in a way that brings *seeing* to the fore: observation presents itself as the director's means of intervention in a world of raw material that he transforms. They work with the idea of *sight* or *vision* rather than *foresight*, that is, with the idea of creative labor *in praesentia* and with what presents itself as immediate potential rather than arriving with a fixed idea of what is sought; in this way they recover and underscore that initial capacity to cede control to events as they unfold, to what presents itself, what is seen and heard, thus becoming a superlative exercise in attention. Operating in this way, from a place more closely related to an exercise in unknowing than one in knowing, to a seeing without wanting to understand (the *ello-ver* of Francois Soulanges), these works present all manner of strategies to *defamiliarize* the mundane: perspectives that displace points of reference or debase criteria of beauty, fragmentation of the image, the distortion of camera effects or editing, accelerations or decelerations, durations that are too short, making comprehension difficult, or too long, greatly exceeding the desired effect of realism, etc. Certain images by Marcellus L. (*3195, 0075, 5040*), for example, work in this space between what the image provides and what the gaze hopes to find, between seeing and understanding, rendering our desire for understanding palpable by deferring, perhaps indefinitely, the resolution or 'clarity' that would accompany formal transparency. In this way, he calls into question the *what* of the image as an end unto itself: once we have been held up to that point, suspense gives itself over as intensity, it dismantles itself as a narrative strategy while claiming the body of time as its condition. When the moment of revelation arrives it is not able to quell the anxiety that has become, through sublimation, overdetermined; the remittance of the recognizable loses its meaning and we find ourselves compelled to withdraw into duration itself as disjoined, discontinued experience: the experience of real time (highlighted by the duration and speed of the images and direct sound) and that of our own anxiety (generated by a profound distortion of the image, generally produced at the time of shooting by effects of lighting, focus, or framing) as another, simultaneous, time that is no less vivid or real. The question of the *what* dissolves or is dispelled, it falls and recedes before contemplation itself as an event and a continuance, that is, as a transformation. The strategy of *Cantata de las cosas solas* is still more minimalist and raw: without taking recourse to the distortion of the image, which, in the case of Marcellus L. conceals a clear artistic sensibility, Benish – despite, or perhaps because of, his training in the visual arts and as a director of photography – shows us images that openly present themselves in their insignificance. It is precisely in this that the director locates meaning. Collected at random during long walks, they force something upon us that does not belong to the order of beauty. Images in which to empty the gaze, or at least in which to wonder if such a thing is possible and have the opportunity to find out. Images of lassitude. Images to empty the mind, the duration of which exceeds all justification, even on a formalist level, shattering all rhythm and cadence in order to present a time of complete suspension of meaning: a dead time made for rebirth, the recuperation of desire and of the fervor of the gaze. This same fervor appears as excess in *Puna*, which opens with the sharp movements of a camera searching frenetically for something on which to settle, come to rest, accompanied by the urgent music of a march that emphatically announces that a party is about to begin: the video has started and the camera still does not know where to be. An extremely daring image and a complex one for the viewer, in that it is the first to be seen and is no less than the image of disorientation, of dizziness: la Puna, as both a region and a film, exceeds; it demolishes all restrictions and possible expectations, demands a beginning of a different kind: one that starts in the middle, taking both the director and the viewer by surprise, urging them to adopt a different perspective in relation to it. Consistent with this is the technique of frame-by-frame recording used in several extended parts of the work, establishing another dimension, key, or perceptual regime of the visual that is fairly difficult to grasp and completely different from that to which we are accustomed; a modification comparable to that of the air on the high plateaus of the region (the same but different, of a different density).

It is a matter, in these works, of setting in motion a mechanism whereby observation is not only a resource *for*, but erected at the center *of*, the project. In this way, these works give off a certain *reflexive* character, even if this does not immediately appear over the course of a first or rushed viewing, as they seem to refer or adhere to the delight in certain surfaces or forms, beings, objects or places, in a gesture not unlike a presentation, description or even poetic composition based on these. But one must not forget that it is precisely within observation that this reflexivity locates itself. It is less a matter of *presentation* than it is the display of a certain *observational presence*, at once the allusion to and the activation of a practice, of an audiovisual mode of creation. What these works address, then, has to do with observation as a form unto itself, a structure, rather; as a form of formation, insofar as it is in the act of observing that observation shows itself most clearly.

Observation: a weighty question

With regard to conditions of production, we can establish a certain connection between the two groups known as "traditional" and "reflexive" observational works. The fact is that the development of the observational mode coincides with the appearance, around 1960, of equipment that made it possible to go out into the streets and directly record what was happening there. The works here examined employ digital video, which is light, relatively accessible in economic terms and easy to use, and while this is not a determining factor, it is a contributing one and allows, in any event, an approach that we could call personal or individual, one that always maintains a close relationship with what is happening between the camera and the director, their place *in* and *with regard to* a world. It is about getting out there, traveling, walking, seeing what a certain environment has to offer, whether it be nearby (the home garden in *Imagen residuo*, the neighborhood, province, or region - *Rizomas, Da janela do meu cuarto, Concerto para Clorofila, La cantata de las cosas solas*), or another strange or distance place (*Areas* and *Puna*).

Two of these works establish themselves in the intermediary, liminal zone represented by a window: in *Da janela do meu cuarto*, the camera-gaze is able to travel through it without a problem, without losing the position of *voyeur* that gives the work its meaning; in *Ideogramas*, Varela remains strategically in the middle of the road, taking advantage of the essence of this in-between. In this way, what emerges in all of these works is an image or delimitation of a place, underlying which is the more or less virtual, more or less implicit, idea of a certain position relative to the world. A position that is in part ethical, but above all aesthetic, that discovers itself, conquers itself, and locates itself one step at a time. "It is not in the world, it becomes with the world, by contemplating it," as Deleuze and Guattari suggest.

Areas of reference and/or belonging are, in a way that could be compared to the relationship they establish with genre and discipline (documentary, video art, experimental, but also painting, photography, music and poetry), explored, left for others, or used as platforms from which to catch a glimpse of a *rest of the world* that allows itself to be gleaned by the wanderer open to the meaning of his surroundings. A *looking from* or a *going out to look* that finds us always situated in a certain (dis)position, being that every act of observing the world, as Merleau-Ponty has pointed out, always originates from a certain place in that same world. In any event, it is a vague awareness of position, like that of an uncertain witness, or one that is tenuous enough to suppress itself to accommodate the manifestation of a presence, in the sense of the term established by Roger Munier as "that which, at certain moments, stands out among other things to a certain gaze."

A chance, then, for this presence to manifest itself *together* with that of the camera as the gaze, the protagonist, now not only as a means of restoring the world to us, of relocating us within a space or situation that it has seen on our behalf and from which the director claims to remain apart: now the camera establishes itself as an essential tool of observation and, simultaneously, of fabrication – of the image, which would not have been possible "had the camera not been there." Something arises in the process of production that, before, had not been *accessible to the gaze*. Something that we are not going to find out there, that does not really exist. *Da janela do meu cuarto* catches two boys playing in the rain. But Guimarães does not limit himself to showing us this action, rather, the image intervenes musically through the use of slow motion and the manipulation of the recorded sound of the drops of rain in relation to the movement of the bodies in the mud. Marcellus L.'s *5040* shows us a microscopic world, a surface infested with spherical, luminescent forms, green, yellow, ochre and pink reflections, like impressionist brushstrokes. Meanwhile, human voices hum in unison; murmurs as indistinguishable as that out-of-focus image. When the reflections multiply and grow ever smaller and more distant, becoming clearer as they do, the video comes to an end. In the same way, we can cite certain images in *Puna* that would be impossible to discern "with the naked eye": the wanderings of worker ants along the border, which appears as though dissolved in the eternity of time, the exaggerated colors and the brilliance of the impassive sun reflected in a glass surface; a stream that changes its course; a slow-motion image of the wind blowing through the ostrich feathers of the costume worn by man, dancing; the saturated colors of *Concerto para Clorofila* and *Imagen residuo*; the animations in *A plomo* and the photographic poses of *Areas* (the death of a sheep, suspended in time) and *Cantata de las cosas solas* (portraits). Traces that allude to forms of making appear, in their turn, in nearly all: hands, eyes, the marks of decision, and also indecision, as well as all manner of ex profeso manipulations of audiovisual material. The camera does not perform a substitutive function assigned to it by the director for our representation, but rather reveals itself as forming part of a creative act, together with an auteur, who can be found behind it – at once a tool and an unavoidable alluded-obstacle. The observation of both a person and a machine; a superposition, or rather, the absence of synchronicity.

Making through observation: from the real to the possible

With regard to observations of the world, these works do not try to maintain the innocence of the gaze or to resolve the impossibility of recording the real as it is. What interests them is less *the* real than *something* real that comes into play in the realm of immediate visibility (appearances), in the relatively printable (traces) and in the very gesture whereby the image is made. More than seeing the world or offering images through it, *stirring the murmur of appearances.*

They place us, then, halfway between that which escapes us and *that which we can control*: the trace, which both alludes to the real and allows itself to be manipulated and transformed, opening a space for the articulation of the irreversible with the unending (Soulanges). Doing what is possible arises here from an effort that makes itself felt and has to do with improvisation and the experimental and, as the word itself suggests, a weighing of or contact with the surface of things, a feeling out by means of the gaze that takes place right there, among the objects, and gradually becomes a gesture. An unanticipated gesture, just as the image it seeks (unlike what happens when a script or preconceived notion is involved) receives, and makes visible through it, in it, the silhouette and pattern resonating in harmony; *vision is inscribed in the type of being that reveals*, through which *it becomes flesh*; thought embodied in perceptible forms from which it cannot separate itself without being lost. The gesture of observing as a form of making (meta-gesture) operates in these works between the delimited and the limitless. In *Vista Interior V* (from the series *Ideograms*), Varela works with the image of the window-frame in relation to what Deleuze and Guattari call the force of *deframing* whereby the frame *opens onto a plane of composition or an infinite field of forces*, onto the gesture of the artist that is not initiated in its interior, nor does it ever remain there. From this seemingly possible apparent preamble, from this *looking out* that will never actually be realized (the camera maintains a certain distance from the window that it does not attempt to cross), arise a different type of visual inscription. Before this nearby but distant window, keeping enough distance to show himself against its light, the director proposes a series of compositions – according to criteria similar to those of sculpted reliefs – in which what one can glimpse briefly through the glass or behind the curtain comes together with that which appears in the very space that separates them from us.

It is in this apparent withdrawal of seeing, in this step backward that the images emerge. *Distance and separation establish the space of creation*, writes Soulanges. In *Trans apariencias* the delimitation is established from the outset: 80 slides, 1 carousel, 5 houses, 13 years. From this starting point, multiple possible combinations arise. The 80 images are shown two at a time, changed at different intervals on a split screen. A carousel-procession of still images, intercut, that Varela calls *coagulated cinema*. In *Cantata de las cosas* we also start out from a still image (a photo), but the image that captures it is not still – it slips along it. The body-eye of the director himself in a printed photo, the first surface to be traveled by the adult eye: the trace of the body itself and of a gaze. An-other I at which to wonder, the child-I, which in turn casts a wondering gaze toward an-other that took the photo, but whose place we now occupy (throughout the entire sequence, breathing can be heard in reverse). The starting point of a compulsive search bound to the nostalgic desire to recover something: eyes *without memory, without history, without fear*. From this point, the adult gaze, with history, fear and memory, will try, systematically, to empty itself into things. Displace itself, detach, turn, break free. Empty itself in order to recover the desire, the *insatiable, endless* fervor of the gaze of a child. "Desire, the space of infancy, how can it be given form?" asks Benisch, trying to open himself to the shapelessness of this limitless desire and recover a gaze without emphasis, without center, like a thought about nothing. A nothing that is an opening and an absolute possibility, like a blank standard without a seal, then with many: a rare event, strange, in which things are revealed. To allow things to slide along the sensuous surface of the pupil, to parade, as they do in Varela's piece, passing like time, like the trains, the clouds, and the turbid waters until something catches and awakens desire. To be ready, in this sense, is to be ready to lose oneself.

A Few Reflections on Short Film

Paulo Pécora

I.

In the nebulous landscape of a legend fueled by more than a century of images, sounds and words, a late-nineteenth century train appears in the distance, approaches the station at La Ciotat, and creates surprise, shock and panic among an audience that scrambles, knocking over chairs, to escape. The few spectators at this, cinema's first event, believe – according to those who know – that the train will come out of the screen and run them over. We are in Paris, in 1895. On the first page of a history that has lasted more than a hundred years and which many still strive to carry forward.

This first projection – or, at least, this first public presentation of the new technology – cleared a path for an art form based fundamentally on the photographic image, on light and on man's desire to live on in perpetuity. The early films of the Lumière brothers were the cry of an orphan child whose babble was absolutely free, uncontaminated. Through the lesser moments of daily French life, through the sweet smile of a baby being fed by its parents and even that gardener who is watered by his own hose, the Lumière brothers introduced a new way of observing reality and registering it 16, 18 or 24 times per second. It was the photographic succession of one single moment, which, thanks to the movements of the machine and the persistence of vision, could be repeated without end. It was the miracle of immortalizing life according to its own rhythms, thanks to a series of fixed photographic images grouped chronologically on a strip of celluloid.

Cinema was a curious child that observed and registered only what it saw around it. It documented. It would be a few years before it found itself and released the visual paraphernalia of its ego, a few more before it discovered its own narrative potential and began to feed it with rules that were often at odds with its essence, and more still before it would begin to reflect upon its own existence.

For its first twenty years, cinema had no limits or defined durations. Short, middle- and feature length films did not exist. Cinema – or, rather, visual expressions, ludic and anarchic experiences, poetry, freedom – did.

The image existed, as did the unexpected use that a few pioneers – driven by a desire for experimentation – made of it through cuts and superposition. For many of these forerunners, it was an eminently visual art form with a strong pictorial and photographic charge, influenced by avant-garde aesthetics and agendas. Images flowed unchecked, driven on by Dadaism, futurism, cubism and surrealism, while at the same time affirming that the cinema had been born to an uncertain, undefined destiny; a virgin terrain suited to all kinds of experience.

The established order did not exist; chaos was beauty, surprise and guilelessness. Despite what is said in favor of narration, many of these artists lacked any real interest in plot and believed in the audience's capacity to create a story from a succession of random images. For most of them, there was no reason to narrate, much less to entertain. It was enough to feel and communicate a singular audiovisual experience, one often tied to abstraction and the visual arts. There were others, however, who were driven by the narrative impulse. They began to explore register, as well as editing on cameras and moviolas and the distortion of time and projection speed, in order to express a sense of intimacy, the idea of the author's world, while transmitting more or less legible stories. Cinematic conventions of narration and readership were being created offhand, along the way. The filmmaker acted and the public reacted. Zones of understanding were established. Codes began to emerge.

The awareness of representation and mise en scène appeared almost on its own, and with it came the limitations and rules of planning and editing, also in their early stages. The visual scribble open to innumerable readings was replaced by the manuscript, which was most often charged with univocal meaning. The active participation of the spectator waned. Intelligible codes gathered momentum. And thus was formed a system of representation that is, to this day, institutional. They took the rebellious little boy that was cinema and they cut and styled his hair and put a uniform on him.

The girdle was cinched tighter and tighter. From different perspectives, Griffith and Eisenstein laid the foundations for a cinema of narrative and spectacle, produced on a large scale and according to formulas proven in advance, well suited for consumption by the masses. Whereas, for the American, these schematics fueled an entertainment based on newspaper serials, melodramas and nineteenth century tales, the Soviet filmmaker and theorist discovered other narrative formulas, managing to transform film into a political reflection, even propaganda.

It was in this context that the concept of the feature film, a movie long enough to narrate an entertaining story and that would, at the same time, fulfill the symbolic expectations of the audience, was born. Industry and business took over. An establishment of studios, scriptwriters, directors and stars took hold. A space dominated by prescription, stereotype and bureaucracy. The idea of the short film emerged naturally as a counterbalance, but it was forced to occupy an increasingly limited place in this model. It was destined to live, like an unwanted child, in the back rooms of cinema.

Meanwhile, outside the limits of the system, a different type of cinema lived and lives on as an increasingly prominent expression of audiovisual creativity and adventure. In this way, even beyond questions of duration, cinema takes a breath of fresh air with each sincere gesture of each creator that does not necessarily reject narration, which is now a need rather than a restrictive obligation, but that tries to reach the spectator on a more pure and spontaneous level.

All sorts of cinematic essays, protests and experiences have found a place in this democratic and diverse realm removed from the influence of the system and the institution. It is here that the short film – understood not as a genre, which is how the industry would prefer it, but as a form with its own aesthetics and values – developed and continues to do so in myriad directions. Short film is simply an institutional denomination that has been assigned to a short cinematic work, yet its specificity lies not in this most obvious physical trait, but rather in its nature as a refuge and a space of resistance.

II.

The use of photography in the cinema – understanding photography as an element unto itself and not merely as a filmic medium – is related to those first attempts to set the image in motion. I am speaking of the prehistory of cinema and of its early years, during which the scope of its technical potential was still unclear. I am also speaking of those pre-cinematic mechanisms or toys, which employed the succession of photos (or drawings, in the oldest cases) to create the sensation of movement.

The kinetoscope (or *flip-book*, in its most artisanal and accessible version, for those who sought to break a movement up into a fixed number of photographic shots) managed to allow an action to develop according to its own rhythm before the eyes of the amazed spectators. Photography in motion was the alphabet of a language that, at the time, no one really knew how to use.

The first directors were photographers who babbled cinema. They could learn to write or speak this new language freely, without any conditions or obstacles of any kind. In this way, cinema was onomatopoeia, metaphor, symbolism and any number of other forms of expression incompatible with regulations or norms of writing. Until the differentiation of shots and the different schools of editing appeared, and that which for many remained a free and emotional form of writing became, for others, a rigid and predetermined language, full of grammatical rules to follow.

This was the period that produced the great schism that would mark the history of film to come and divide its course into two distinct and opposing paths. From this moment on, cinema would be divided between those who respected the dogma (the famous Model of Institutional Representation, with its prefabricated molds for the script, editing, acting, and composition) and those who spent their lives transgressing, or simply ignoring, it. There were also less radical filmmakers who got by within the system, accepting its rules only to break or play with them. Behind the cloak of legitimacy, they trafficked in their own ideas, their own original compositional forms.

The space of the short film – the refuge for manifestations that exceed the limits of the conventional – can essentially be found in the suburbs of that extensive industrial city that is commercial film. From the periphery, it revives the primal cinematic spirit and tries to forge a path outside the norm, in the realm of free and personal creation.

Perhaps one of the greatest advantages of this *other* cinema is precisely that which many see as its principle disadvantage: its marginality. In this sense, the growing attention paid by the establishment to the more conservative examples of short film is linked to its need to project itself into perpetuity. The factory needs fuel and operators to keep functioning. And the short film, according to this economic idea of cinema, would simply be a field of indoctrination, an apprenticeship for those who aspire to join the system and continue its legacy.

In this way, rather than being detrimental, the exclusion and alienation to which the system's detractors are condemned allow them to work under no limitations other than those of their own talent, their imagination, and their access to the technology they require. Having advanced technology, however, is not necessarily a precondition of cinematic creation. On occasion, it can actually become counterproductive.

In the words of the Spanish photographer Carlos Cánovas, "technological development is coercive. Technological progress or advancement, which is supposedly liberating, imposes its conditions and its oppression. Oddly, it is not a lack of materials that leads many men who record images to use a rudimentary, primitive or simple camera. It is just the opposite: the step backwards is the fruit of a reflection generated by the opulence of the medium. By its tyranny, by the annihilation of individuality that it has come to represent. In the face of this alienation, the man who records images offers an old idea: the image is not made by the machine."

I repeat the phrase to myself, under my breath: the image is not made by the machine, the image is not made by the machine, the image is not made by the machine. And I think of that famous goat's eye cut in half by a blade, that provocative and irrational detail shot, which would not have been the same had Buñuel had access to the technology and digital media needed to create an identical image, but with a computer. The trick, certainly, would have worked the same. We would all have gone on believing that the eye cut through by steel belonged to the actress and not, as was the case, to an animal sacrificed for the occasion. Nonetheless, the strange and unreal experience of seeing an eye cut in two could not possibly have been the same. That goat's eye was the first real eye ever to be sliced open in front of the camera. It was an unrepeatable image, impossible to achieve without the same technological impediments that generated it. Never again will that same eye be sliced by that same hand, by that same blade, in front of that same camera.

III.

Its brevity, its marginality, and the use it occasionally makes of basic, elemental, almost amateur cinematic techniques are things that – far from becoming barriers – allow the short film to be what it should: a space of unparalleled freedom. There are those who think of time as a limitation, but brevity actually has an inverse effect, because it inevitably helps to shape and direct creativity. The state of grace, that fleeting and irrecoverable moment that is creative inspiration, often exists in inverse relation to the so-called limitations imposed by the lack of time and technology. The hypothesis, impossible to prove, would be that the greater the challenges, the greater the austerity and lack of resources, the greater the cinema.

"When there are no resources, you have to think about how to wrap production grounded in an aesthetic," asserts the Argentine filmmaker Gustavo Fontán, adding, "You have to get to a point where the lack of resources doesn't matter. You have to make use of what you have and not try to be like something else, because if you do, you're lost. You need to create an aesthetic grounded in the lack of resources, one whose strength is not its likeness to another model, but to itself, to what is new."

Dreyer, Bresson: poetry, frugality. A single scene of *The Passion of Joan of Arc* is enough to understand Dreyer's intentions throughout the film. Austerity. "He who can work with a little can work with a lot; he who can work with a lot cannot necessarily work with a little." That was how Bresson thought. Like him, and like many others, Dreyer narrated with a zoom lens and a gaze dazzled by detail: his camera revealed the solitary, sufficient fragment – the essence – in order to evoke the whole. He could distill entire universes into a single shot; one small gesture, an outstretched hand, a glance.

Dreyer and Bresson chose the narrative path, but they did not follow it in a restrictive or superficial way. Instead, they committed themselves to a broad and unstructured approach that took as its point of departure a cinematic consciousness attuned to the essential. They believed in stories and scripts, but they dealt in notions of beauty and resistance beneath the discrete mantle of normalcy. Their films could be understood by all, anyone could enjoy them, but their images and moments of silence provoked a profound aesthetic tremor.

An economy of resources can be inspirational to a greater or lesser extent, but it affords the filmmaker freedom without pressures of any kind, except strictly creative ones. The physical and psychological comforts of knowing that everything one needs in order to film is within arm's reach is always welcome, just as long as it does not dull the instincts and the passion stirred by the challenge of satisfying a few absolute necessities.

Yet, what are these necessities, really? They are likely neither economic nor material. The problem is not simply in finding accessible means and modes of production, because the project will always develop according to what is economically possible. It is the idea of filming with what you have on hand, of doing things in spite of it all, of feeling and being guided by instinct. It is an idea that expresses the deep, limitless creative drive through which the artist discovers the meaning of things, his reason for being.

Building on this point, the conceptualization of short film can be all-encompassing: one thinks of the costuming at the same time as the visual composition, one reflects on the acting, on the gestures and the expressions registered by the camera. One expounds on the development of a story that affects and is affected by its locations, on the scintillating camera work and the mise en scène planned out in advance; all the while keeping in mind that every gesture, every shot, every costume, every movement of the camera was carefully measured. Upon this foundation, upon this open recognition of its limitations and shortcomings, the director can move with absolute fluidity in a universe of image and sound that knows no master.

Directing is just this: letting X number of ideas, memories, images and sounds float out into a vast and churning sea and then rescuing them, drying them off, feeding them, setting them alongside one another and establishing spatial and temporal relations between them until the work begins to blossom. It is a matter of dialogue. Of being able to use subject matter, images and words in a way that leaves room for surprise, so that lovely and unexpected connections might arise, both in the shooting and the editing, both in form and content. The pieces gradually come together and an aesthetic emerges, the idea of a world.

Understood in this way, short film becomes a space of self-examination for cinema. The ideas that, for the most part, have no place in the realm of feature film – except for those defined and legitimized beforehand by the establishment – can in fact be found in that autonomous, relatively contamination-proof space that is the short. There they can announce and enact their rejection of the narrative conventions, rituals of production and aesthetic habits grounded, for the most part, in the realm of feature film. The widespread and unfounded idea that the short is some sort of preliminary stage necessary to arrive at the next level of some dubious cinematic hierarchy fails to recognize the fact that most of these artists are not interested in arriving at anything but creation itself, self-expression by means of an audio-visual text. This hierarchical conception of cinema is the result of a market system in which movies are worthwhile only to the extent that they turn a profit and perpetuate the status quo. But it denies the value of the short as a legitimate and original work of art. It marginalizes it, arbitrarily assigning it to a residual space within a system to which it does not, and does not wish to, belong: that of a conventional cinema officially regulated and controlled.

Although the space of the short is not necessarily that of the avant-garde or the experimental, its propensity for reflection and self-awareness allows one to imagine, at least, the existence of a wide range of other possible cinemas. It is a space without borders or established rules, where filmic alternatives, which tend to be independent (in the sense that they are produced at the margins of or outside the system), militant (as ideological reactions to the *establishment*) or avant-garde (to the extent that they question institutional modes of representation), are able to coexist.

It would be worthwhile at this point to recall the definition offered by Javier Hernández and Pablo Pérez with regard to this other type of cinema: "We understand the cinematic avant-garde to be a combination of aesthetic proposals that represent an alternative to those of the institutional model; this presupposes the coexistence of formal experimentation, the return of an active spectator, the explicit engagement of the technical and linguistic mechanisms that make representation possible, the challenges of metafiction, shattering the illusion of identification, working with subject matter that breaks with tradition, and all this without losing sight of financial independence and the ideological use of the material at hand."

IV.

At the outset, cinema could have gone in any direction, not only a strictly narrative one. Instead of a story or novel, a short- or feature film, cinema could have chosen to be poetry. A space well suited to dreams, the strange, the enigmatic. To the beautiful, the unexpected, the spontaneous. But for the most part it chose the path of bureaucratic convention and official norms, leaving no room for metaphor.

We can understand the avant-garde as a crack in the artifice of the conventional, one which crosses its uniform surface and leaves it to crumble into pieces. It directly threatens narration and the referential nature of the figural image.

The disorientation caused by a film-poem of light and texture, the optical pleasure of the moving forms, the valorization of the gestalt, just like so many other things that touch on the experimental, are often directly linked to the artist's need to break with a certain established political order and, especially, with the aesthetic and linguistic models upon which it feeds.

Yet this resistance can take hold in narrative film, as well. There is generally a solid core to the narration, a space from which the story is structured: the rigid articulation of the script. For some directors, however, the script is just one among many useful, though not absolutely necessary, tools. Those who understood it in this way opened up a rift through which the extraordinary, the purely cinematic, the magic that can only exist in the unexpected and the spontaneous, could work its way in. In both their filming and editing, this type of director tried to generate a space for the gradual or sudden appearance of truth.

And I think once more of Fontán: "To direct in this way is to take a political, an ideological, position. What does it mean to make film from the periphery? To adopt a peripheral position, to make an extreme choice. We cannot go on generating conventional responses. The ideal is a heterogeneous array of individual quests and aesthetics."

The Mise en Scène of Early Short Films

Daniela Goggi

— Where are most short films produced?
— In film schools.
— What kind of short films?
— Narrative.
— Who makes them?
— Students in filmmaking programs.
— Under what conditions?
— As the practicum for their course on directing.
— Do the students have any thematic or generic guidelines to follow?
— Generally speaking, no. They just need to stay within the time limit, since the materials for the production are provided by the school and need to be shared.
— Why are they asked to make short films?
— Through the process of making a short film, they are able to make the transition from theory to practice; the idea of mise en scène, which had been abstract, should become concrete at that point, and all its elements should be moving together in a cohesive way.
— Are there other reasons, aside from these formative exercises, to make short films?
— Certainly, but not many. The cost of a feature-length film is due in part to the extra time it takes for shooting and post-production; making a short film, relying on the help of a cast and crew made up of friends, is a compromise but at least it is somewhat accessible. It can also be a means of

securing financing for a feature based on the story and the aesthetic proposal that appear in a condensed, low-budget form in the short film.

— Can you give an example?

— Yes, Paz Encina; her short film *Hamaca paraguaya* from 2000 was not only an admirable work unto itself; it also allowed her, five years later, to make the feature film of the same name. Also Diego Lerman, who, in *Tan de repente*, develops the narrative at the heart of his short film *La prueba*, which was based on a short story by César Aira of the same name.

— Could you say that, for a filmmaker with access to the resources to produce a feature, directing short films no longer makes sense?

— You could say that.

— There aren't any directors, locally, who have made a short film after the commercial release of a feature?

— Not many, but again I can cite Lerman and *La guerra de los gimnasios*. Beyond the local, David Lynch is still making short films. He puts them up on his website or you can see them on youtube.com. Godard has made short films. There are also movies that are compilations of shorts and short features, like *Bocaccio '70, New York Stories, Lumière et Cie; Paris, je t'aime*, and the Spanish *Hay motivo.Motivo*.

— On the other hand, don't you sometimes get the feeling that certain movies are just short films that have been stretched out or supplemented in order to reach the standard length of a feature? Narrative themes that could have been developed perfectly well in a short film?

— In film, commercial guidelines generally determine the conventions and characteristics of the product, such as duration, and not always with a negative effect. It is likely that, without these guidelines, a filmmaker might take less time to develop his narrative or, on the other hand, much more.

The cinema is born as short film. The first stories of cinema were told in this format. The Lumière brothers' first shorts lasted less than a minute.

The evolution of cinematic language begins with the short films of the Lumière brothers, Méliès, Porter and Griffith. The duration of these early motion pictures – especially those of Lumière and Méliès – was not the choice of their directors, but a limit imposed on them by the length of a roll of film.

Until the technique of editing was developed, the length of the shot was that of the take, and this was another limitation.

These days, without these material limitations, minute-long movies continue to be produced; they are commonly called minute videos or minute films.

There are festivals of minute video, video poems, experimental video, short film festivals; film schools require the production of shorts or minute videos to graduate; commercial breaks on television are a string of shorts ranging from 30 seconds to one minute in length, trailers last about a minute, a minute and a half, innumerable music videos last around three minutes or however long the song is; most recently the proliferation of home videos posted on youtube.com, etc. etc.

Why does this format withstand the test of time?

The first answer that comes to mind is that it is a good tool for learning, for developing skills.

A platitude: for those who work in film, each movie – short, mid-length, or feature – represents an apprenticeship in a variety of technical details that, with luck, will be put into practice in the next movie; I should clarify that the word "apprenticeship" is used neither in a pejorative sense nor to place emphasis solely on the educational.

In the 1990s, film schools began to open in Argentina, through which passed the majority of the directors of the so-called New Argentine Cinema, which no longer seems so new.

Until the nineties, then, directors learned from watching films, making shorts or documentaries, working as part of the crew on other directors' shoots, working in advertising; any means was a useful apprenticeship in technique and the aesthetics of composition.

Generally, when one speaks of short film, one tends to mention the work of the great directors, the precedents for or origins of their feature films; the short films that are screened are those that have won international awards. Whatever the case may be, it is rare to get the chance to see "unsuccessful" or "bad" short films outside a teaching or learning environment, that is, a film school.

Drawing on my experience as an ex-student and current instructor of film, remembering and watching the evolution of the projects, but also having participated in different roles during the production process of shorts and feature-length films, it occurs to me that everyone goes through the universal history of mise en scène before reaching, ideally, their own style.

Sadomasochistic enumeration of all that doesn't work, sort of works, or ends up seeming rudimentary or trite in students' first shorts, in which it is very common to see traces of early film – clichés and tics that are repeated year after year as though they were genetically ingrained:

- poor continuity (unintentional);
- the scale of very long or wide angle shots – wide shots can be reassuring when it comes to defining space;
- ellipsis is generally used to move from one scene to the next, and especially from one set to the next;

- camera movements that follow the movement of the characters and barely have any other purpose;
- shots that are shots only to the extent that they contain the action of a character; the frame is almost never empty because the function of the shots is simply to transpose the script;
- detail shots that emphasize the relevance of an object to the dramatic action, despite the fact that the object was clearly visible in the previous shot – the fear of a narrative element being overlooked demands an *insert*;
- the diffusion of perspective by an overdetermined, omniscient narrator that seeks to provide greater narrative clarity;
- a camera height that matches the height of the characters
- the use of normal lenses, even though advertising and music videos encourage the use of wide angle;
- continuity problems having to do with the actors' lines of sight – instead of maintaining continuity with respect to the camera, they do so with respect to actual physical space;
- the soundtrack is generally limited to one music track that is heard throughout the short, like the pianist or organist that used to accompany silent films;
- limited, ineffectual or casual use of the space outside the frame or glances off screen, immediately neutralized by a reverse shot;
- shots of extras simply because they appear in the script – the classic shot of the waiter who appears to take an order and is never seen again;
- titles and credits in white against a black background;
- etcetera.

After making these short- or minute- movies that allow audiovisual techniques to be put into practice; as they advance in their training, whether because they recognize in their work certain traces of early film, or because they begin to think about the aesthetics of representation, students tend to enter a phase of excessive respect for the classics and adherence to cinematic conventions generally considered to be purely academic – anything having to do with the normative grammar of editing, the move from an establishing shot that presents the entire set to a medium shot of the character, a naturalistic action, a dose of information, etc.

During their "traditionalist period," in which the students adopt the narrative and compositional conventions of standard cinema, they work on focusing the point of view in relation to their protagonists, using cross cuts as commentary, presenting a central conflict. The setting is a dramatic entity that should offer information about the characters, subjective shots allow the viewer to share in the perspective of the character and his perceptions, flash-backs offer new information about the characters that has a causal relation to present events, lighting effects reinforce or punctuate the tone of the story, fades to black underscore not only the passage of time, but also the suppression of information.

Generally, by testing and employing these resources, one often appeals to genre narrative. This is the case in a number of detective or suspense shorts made in film schools, about things like robbery, murder, kidnapping, rape, revenge, drug deals, etc. By working according to the logic of a genre, certain production challenges arise that threaten the verisimilitude this type of short requires. For example, it is very common in short films to assign an atemporal framework to the action.

Atemporality: it is impossible to deduce when the action takes place; it could be in a past or in a future, but it is obvious that it is not inscribed in the present. The idea that it is "a" past or "a" future is stressed here because if it were "that" past or "the" future, it would not be atemporal and would require the reconstruction of an era (in the case of the past) or the representation of a determined collective imaginary (in the case of the future).

This atemporality is often determined by the challenges of production. The problem is most clearly seen in the sphere of art direction. Atemporality allows the combination of a fedora from the fifties, a *wincofón* playing a theme by Astor Piazzolla, a crystal chandelier from the twenties, a Tramontina fork and other elements from different eras that would only be found together at a pawnshop... and student films, in which the participants get the objects they need from their various relatives.

What is defined as atemporal, then, in short film is actually – in the vast majority of cases – pastiche. The limitations of production create a sort of autonomy of representation in the short film: what is seen has less to do with the real, historical world than it does the world of the short film itself.

If the logic of genre film privileged certain types of heroes according to their success with audiences and established norms to avoid disappointment (the *happy ending* of romantic comedies, the clear resolution of the mystery in crime dramas, the triumph of virtue in melodrama, the victory of the just and the restoration of order in westerns), the short film had its own evolution and established its own conventions.

If the shorts produced in the various films schools of Buenos Aires (FUC, CIC, ENERC, UBA) were examined side by side, it is quite possible that – beyond certain common features – differences or traits characteristic of each program would begin to emerge.

An example: prostitutes. (I'll save the vagrants, the beggars, the crackpots, and the loners for another occasion.) The prostitutes in short films tend to be gorgeous, very young, and dressed to the nines; they may be standing on a rundown corner in Constitución, but they do not deviate from the stereotype of red fishnet stockings, intense red lipstick, vinyl miniskirt, stiletto heels and a designer purse – they smoke and wait in frame for about five seconds before a client invites them into his car.

The problem could be explained in part by the tremendous influence of Hollywood and its peculiar sense of realism, which turns Meg Ryan into a housewife and Bruce Willis into a self-defense serial killer...

The *flashback* – according to the most specific definition of the term, masterfully applied in traditional cinema – could be defined as a jump into the past executed mentally by a character, a subjective and diegetic memory. A conventional example: close-up on the face of a character, cut to a new scene in which a different dramatic situation is developed, cut back to the character's face. The temporal jump is rendered subjective and the different temporalities are clearly defined.

This type of *flashback* has recently appeared more often in short films than in features. In fact, in contemporary cinema the flashback no longer represents a jump into the past, but rather a commentary on the story. As such, it is more difficult to assign to it a specific temporality.

Some endings are repeated year after year in short films: the death of the protagonist or a shot in which a character wakes up with a start or to the sound of an alarm clock.

These endings are more common in the so-called "traditionalist period" of the study of mise en scène than in the "early period" of filmmaking; the closure of the narrative becomes the responsibility of the character, as though the director was not entirely satisfied with the outcome of story or the resolution of the central conflict.

Dialogue is an essential means of providing the viewer with information. The limited timeframe of the short film forces the director to take advantage of any tool available to make his intimations.

In some cases, problems with the dialogue can be attributed to a lack of faith in the image; for example, when a character calls his friend/girlfriend/cousin/etc. by their name: "Hi, Laura." Why does the dialogue need to present a character as he or she would appear on the first page of a script? The same thing happens when presenting family relations: "How was your day, mom?"

An adult male sits at a table, a young man arrives and opens the door with his keys; casual body language, glances exchanged without a trace of eroticism; as the story develops, it will already be understood that they are father and son, or of some other blood of political relation, whatever that may be.

The voice-over is another crutch frequently used in early shorts. Used as an internal monologue, it often ends up as a running commentary on the character's actions and not as a fluid consciousness that works according to free association. In some shorts, the internal monologue occurs in a moment of solitude for the character, which he uses to summarize what has happened to him over the past few years, which is not only excessive but also unbelievable, as though the character were unfamiliar with his own personal history and had to tell it to himself as a narrative.

The point of view shot, the fascination with viewing the scene through the eyes of the character, is yet another resource that appears systematically in short films. Mitry, in *The Aesthetics and Psychology of Cinema*, suggests that the use of point of view – by attempting to replace the character with his perspective – more often than not creates distance rather than closeness. In some short films one can even see an attempt to turn the camera into a character in search of a "realism" that is, in itself, impossible. For example: blackouts to indicate blinking, sunglasses placed over the camera lens when stepping out into the street, etc. The radical nature of Robert Montgomery's point of view work is unmistakable in his early short films.

The next step in the student's evolution through the history of short film composition is the "modern," which adopts a variety of aesthetic proposals: neorealism, the *nouvelle vague*, independent American cinema, the Generation of the 60s in Argentina, Antonioni, Fassbinder, Tati, Lynch, etc.

(A quick clarification: the different stages of representation that I have been discussing do not always occur in the same order. It is worth noting, however, that this evolution takes place over remarkably little time in the students.)

Traits that emerge during the stage designated as "modern" include the dissolution of the central conflict, non-naturalistic modes of representation, a concept of verisimilitude that differs from realism, a greater awareness of the mechanisms of enunciation and an open acknowledgement of this fiction (glances at the camera, the camera appears on screen, etc.), cuts that break continuity, music that interrupts the soundtrack, occasional parodies of the conventions established in traditional cinema, performances that do not seem organically related to the tone of the story, the insertion of posters that make reference to advertising, literature, silent film (intertitles), etc.

The narrative often appears in a more minimalist form; or perhaps it would be better to say that the events of the story are more trivial, more mundane, more disorganized and that a relationship of cause and effect is not established between sequences. The subject matter of the story is condensed to fit within a limited timeframe: one night, a party, a morning, a date, a romance that only lasts a few days, a class, waiting for a bus, a road trip, the moment a couple ends a relationship, a memory, etc.

Certain figures appear with regularity in these short films: ambiguity, the open ending, an explicit disinterest in narration, and a blind faith in visual devices. I would like to emphasize that these figures are, in certain cases, grounded in a conceptual error. Ambiguity should always be a product of a compositional manipulation and not of narrative indecision.

I remember something Jorge Goldenberg once said to a student about an ambiguous, open ending. Goldenberg asked the screenwriter, "and what do you think happened?" pointing out that even what is meant to be ambiguous should be thought through; that it is a construct and the director/screenwriter needs to have a clear intention in order to construct it. Otherwise there is no way to plan the mise en scène.

The non-narrative is difficult in film. What chance of not being figurative does cinema have? A black screen, after a hundred years of film, reads as the negation of the image, but this is also a form of narrative. Aumont – referring to Metz – indicated that a detail shot of a weapon does not simply present a weapon; it comes across as "here is a revolver," which immediately generates questions.

Allusions in this type of short film refer back to auteur cinema. The female characters with their little bobs à la Anna Karina. References to other films are made in dialogues and through the physicality of the actors. The image bears a nostalgic relation to its referents.

A few conclusions can be drawn from this brief inventory of formal, thematic and generic approaches that frequently appear in early student short films.

The first is that the students have a tremendous capacity for reading images in the audiovisual formats they consume daily – animation, music videos, TV series, commercials, movies, experimental films posted on the internet, images of themselves and others taken by webcam, video recordings made on cell phones, home movies, etc. But when the time comes to manipulate an image, they experience something like the transition from understanding a foreign language to actually being able to speak it for the first time.

Second conclusion: the short film is a very difficult format; the shorter the film, the more difficult its mise en scène becomes to manage. The evidence of this can be seen in the failed short works of good feature film directors, or those who can not claim lack of experience; an example of this is Spike Lee's short film in *Lumière et Cie*.

And the last: if the inventory of all that comes into play in short film is so varied and makes reference to so many distinct moments in the history of cinema, it means that this continues to be an area of experimentation.

The Audiovisual Arts in Argentina: Possible Horizons[112]

Mariela Cantú

The opportunity to reflect on audiovisual production is always an attractive one, particularly in Argentina, a country in which this multifaceted topic is frequently relegated to broad conceptual frameworks. Given the extensive panorama that this scene presents to us, we will propose several possible critical axes. In the first place, we believe that the perspective generally held in our country with regard to film – which is, within the grand scheme of the audiovisual, the most widespread and recognized discipline – tends to limit itself to a quantitative approach, that is, how many films are shown in theaters, how many people attend the screenings, and how much money is made. For some, these are the only parameters that justify the support and distribution of national productions. We disagree with this approach, as we believe it is of the utmost importance to observe the minor points and the minor productions that, though they may be far from major investments, manage to propose a cinema of quality, an auteur cinema that places itself in opposition to dominant narrative structures and forms. Let us add to this idea the fact that Argentine cinema, for a variety of reasons, has poor attendance figures on the local level.

---

[112] An earlier version of this text was presented with Jorge La Ferla at the conference "¿Un Lugar Bajo el Sol? Los espacios para las prácticas creativas actuales," organized in August 2006 by the Cultural Center of Spain in Buenos Aires.

At the same time, it is essential to take a broad view of audiovisual production, in the sense of understanding the vastness and complexity of the field and considering other practices in addition to film; though they may not be as visible, this does not make them secondary. On the contrary, it is vital that they be taken into account when the time comes to establish policies about the support, study, distribution and conservation of the visual arts in their totality, in all the forms they take.

With regard to this issue, it is worth emphasizing that the axis of cultural patronage presents a troubling panorama as the first decade of the third millennium draws to a close, both in Argentina and in Latin America. The audiovisual flows of spectacle, consensus and political manipulation have been condensed to fit into just a few hands; those of major corporations that control production/distribution/consumption and those of entities in the form of foundations that promote the visual arts in order to improve the corporate image of their own ventures and reduce their financial responsibility. On the other hand, public institutions tied to the State use their budgets, the majority of which ends up paying salaries and benefitting friends and clients, in the service of manipulations driven by partisanship and favoritism. These processes are clearly the result of the same government policies that brought about the destruction of the patron Argentine State in the final decades of the twentieth century, a government that had managed to distance the country somewhat from the stark class divisions that dominate the entire Latin American continent.

In the case of cinema, these complex adjustments result in an almost exclusive concentration on the distribution of movies in multiplex theaters – the majority of which are made in the United States according to the Model of

Institutional Representation[113] and the uniform emotional canon established by an industry in Hollywood that has not, since the eighties, produced anything particularly challenging. This certainly has an influence on our local production, the most extensive in Latin America, which finds itself greatly hindered by the lack of followers among the public, making it difficult to compete in our own market. On the other hand, the disappearance of independent film distribution is dramatic in its own right, and translates to a difficulty in showing titles produced in this country and to the increasingly limited importation of high quality, independent foreign auteur cinema.

Historically, the cinema has presented itself as the wellspring of all audiovisual media in Argentina; perhaps this is why it tends to be the privileged mode of expression when it comes to audiovisual patronage. Despite this image, which plays a pronounced role in its branding outside the country, Argentine visual production is in a precarious situation and the policies that regulate it are very shortsighted. In the context of our country, we are not able to identify a serious position with regard to cinematic production because the unquestioning acceptance of the often-repeated euphemism "New Argentine Cinema" seems to have done away with any chance of examining this new phenomenon, which is actually very difficult to define, as the field it claims to encompass is not a stable one. In this sense, though certain interesting filmmakers have been able to step onto the scene with their first film, the monopoly established by INCAA[114] over the funding of new work unquestionably endangers the production of creative, innovative projects

---

[113] Burch, Noel. *El tragaluz del Infinito*. Madrid: Cátedra, 1987; "Pré-cinemas: O cinema das origens" in Pré-cinemas & pós-cinemas, Arlindo Machado (ed.). San Pablo: Papirus Editora, 1997.

[114] National Institute of Film and the Visual Arts, www.incaa.gov.ar

by noteworthy directors, who are forced to navigate endless obstacles and work their way through a complex system of competitions and presentations in order to make their films. This question is not only relevant on a financial level related to the management and allotment of funds, though it is true that INCAA has become the only means that many have of making a film. The problem is much greater than financial support in and of itself, and is not likely to be solved by distributing more credit. As we mentioned, one runs the risk of understanding the current state of Argentine cinema solely in quantitative terms, without also considering what type of cinema is being furthered by these policies.

This is how a push for the production of quality auteur cinema in Argentina is still the subject of debate; anything that could be considered experimental in film and, similarly, projects in other electronic and digital media, fall outside the purview of the INCAA's calls for proposals. Nonetheless, we should point out that in 2006 two theaters screened Ernesto Baca's film *Samoa*, an unprecedented event in that it was a project based purely on an expressive quest, part of which was shot on medium-format stock. And, on the other hand, there was Paz Encina's *Hamaca paraguaya*, an Argentine co-production of tremendous expressive and compositional value, which was widely praised at the most important film festivals in the world. We will return to this film later on.

Added to this state of affairs is a critical perspective that tends to accord prestige to audiovisual works only insofar as they relate to cinema as an absolute point of reference, certainly a questionable approach. In the first place, because many of Argentina's most renowned audiovisual artists have started to work from a place of experimentation, even in other media such as video, for example, in the case of Esteban Sapir, Fabián Hofman, Mario Levín and Eduardo Yedlin, among others. This is, without question, not simply the result of the financial challenges involved in film, but rather the symptom of an attitude toward the audiovisual that seeks to distance itself from the formulas and rules of efficiency. In the second place, because it is no longer possible to insist on a nostalgic purity of these media, given that the arrival of digital technology has almost entirely displaced pure filmic work; there are no longer processes of production that do not pass through other formats, particularly digital ones. Yet these varied non-filmic processes adapted spontaneously through production have not been met with any reflection on the creative possibilities of the admixture of the photochemical, the electronic and the digital, which proposes a different set of productive, conceptual, expressive and narrative mechanisms distinct from those of the ideological institutional model.

Although this history may still remain unwritten, we should recall that our country boasts a long and prolific trajectory in the visual arts, particularly in experimental cinema, video and digital art; unfortunately, it is one that has been largely ignored not only by the institutions responsible for promoting audiovisual art, but also by academic studies. We should, however, mention a few notable exceptions, such as the Fundación Antorchas,[115] the CCEBA,[116] the Rector

---

[115] Particularly in their grants and materials for research in the audiovisual arts, in addition to the organization of forums, conferences and seminars for the development of directors, which took place in the cities of Bariloche and Colón. For further information, see Castilla, A. "Al borde del río o del lago. La experiencia de análisis de proyectos en los Talleres de Colón / Bariloche" *Hacer cine: producción audiovisual in América Latina*. Buenos Aires: Paidós, 2008.

[116] The Spanish Cultural Center in Buenos Aires was one of the first centers dedicated to the promotion of video art in Argentina, particularly through the organization of exhibit Buenos Aires Video, which was born at the old site of the Institute for Ibero-American Cooperation. This event launched the consolidation of one of the most important video libraries in the country, as well as the publication of two anthologies on video,

Ricardo Rojas Cultural Center,[117] Fundación TyPA,[118] the FNA,[119] the Goethe Institute,[120] the cultural branch of the French embassy[121] and the French Alliance,[122] MALBA,[123] MAMBA[124] and the Telefónica Foundation Space,[125] to name

---

based on the works shown there. This space, then, is one of the greatest collections of video art in all of Argentina.

[117] This organization is part of the University of Buenos Aires (UBA), and is where the Euro-American Exhibitions of Film, Video and Digital Art are held, and where more than fifteen internationally recognized books on the subject were published between 1995 and 2002. The Franco-Latin American Festival of Video Art also takes place here, at which dozens of artists, scholars and cultural figures from around the world, including Tania Blanich, Pierre Bongiovanni, Alain Bourges, Robert Cahen, Carlota Álvarez Basso, Jean-Louis Comolli, Philippe Dubois, Anne-Marie Duguet, Jean-Paul Fargier, Sandra Kogut, Lev Manovich, Antonio Muntadas, Francisco Ruiz de Infante, Eder Santos, Peter Weibel, Siegfried Zielinski and others gave talks and led classes and seminars. See www.rojas.uba.ar.

[118] Theory and Practice of the Arts (TyPA) has taken up the work of Antorchas in its promotion of auteur cinema and the continuation of the workshops in Colón, in the province of Entre Ríos. See www.typa.org.ar.

[119] The National Arts Fund is active in the promotion of the audiovisual arts through a wide variety of grants and subsidies for works, publications, etc. Visit www.fnartes.gov.ar.

[120] See www.goethe.de/buenosaires.

[121] La cual, a partir de la gestión del recordado agregado cultural Aldo Herlaut impulsó la difusión de las artes mediáticas en nuestro país, estando en el origen de la conformación de las Muestras Euroamericanas de Cine, Video y Arte Digital.

[122] In addition to their seminars, screenings and exhibits, the Alliance offers a remarkable media library. www.alianzafrancesa.org.ar.

[123] The Buenos Aires Museum of Latin American Art (MALBA) contains its own film wing, a film library and its own archive. It offers audiovisual exhibits of the highest quality, among which can be counted shows dedicated to the work of Fluxus, Glauber Rocha, Abbas Kiarostami, thirty years of videosculpture in Germany and one on Andy Warhol, to name just a few. Visit www.malba.org.ar.

[124] The Buenos Aires Museum of Modern Art, www.aamamba.org.ar. The site of important exhibitions of the work of prestigious international media artists, and the organizer of the MAMBA/Telefónica awards, the only event of its kind in Argentina.

[125] The EFT is an important center for the documentation of media art and consultations on audiovisual media; it also boasts a media lab. It does

just a few of the most notable centers dedicated to the promotion of the arts and experimentation, both in their relation to science and technology as well as through festivals, exhibitions, publications, workshops and roundtables, among other activities. It is worth noting that many of the institutions that promote these types of activities are foreign or privately run, filling in for a State that lacks this type of undertaking.

This was the context within which Paz Encina's *Hamaca paraguaya*, a work unlike any other in Latin American cinema, was made in 2007. The director had no way of gaining access to credit from official Argentine organizations, as there was no institution in Paraguay – her native country – that could organize a co-production.[126] Because of this, the film needed to find alternative methods of financing, a process which many filmmakers must go through in Argentina. Beyond the well-deserved distinctions and recognition the film has received, we believe it is worth celebrating Paz Encina's approach to the audiovisual: "I have never thought of film in terms of the market. I am a bit radical in this sense. For me, it is all or nothing. I know that it is not going to be a box-office hit, and that it is destined for the festival circuit. Or maybe I am wrong, and it ends up like *El sabor de la cereza*, which started out as a curiosity".[127]

The panorama of the production and distribution of experimental audiovisual works becomes even more complex in fields like video or digital that, despite their extensive use in our country, are not as widely studied or

---

a tremendous job with regard to the exhibition of work, the publication of catalogues, the organization of workshops, seminars, etc. through the efforts of its coordinator, Alejandrina D'Elía. www.fundacion.telefonica.com.ar/espacio.

[126] http://www.sklunk.net/Hamaca-Paraguaya-de-Paz-Encina?lang=fr
[127] http://www.clarin.com/diario/2006/10/31/espectaculos/c-00403.htm

do not benefit from the policies of financing and support we mentioned earlier.

The field of video art began to come into its own in Argentina in the late eighties, despite early experiments in the sixties. This first phase, realized by those in the visual arts, focused on the artistic exploration of the electronic image, adopting the technology of television but proposing a deviation from its commercial or corporate use.[128] During the nineties, an original and radical body of Argentine video art that continues to this day was formed, which makes it possible to speak of a history nearly thirty years long. This is why it is so unsettling to observe the lack of attention that plagues many institutions in the context of this phenomenon, and which translates most obviously to the absence of archives, research, financing and distribution for these works of electronic art. We should recall that the most complete and best-maintained collection of Argentine video can be found at the Videobrasil Cultural Association[129] in São Paulo, Brazil. The big exceptions are the National Fund for the Arts (FNA), with its grants and incentives, and the awards given out annually by the Museum of Modern Art (MAMBA), together with the Telefónica Foundation Space (EFT).

Digital art, in turn, still finds itself in an early period of development in Argentina, though we can identify a number of notable artists who stand out in the field, such as Iván Marino, Marcello Mercado, Mariano Sardón, Mariela Yeregui and Marina Zerbarini, among others.

In the context of the audiovisual arts, the case of Brazil is paradigmatic for its geographic proximity and the way

---

[128] Alonso, Rodrigo. "Arte, Ciencia y Tecnología, sus vínculos y desarrollo en Argentina." *Cuadernos del Centro de Estudios en Diseño y Comunicación, Universidad de Palermo*, 20. Buenos Aires, 2006.

[129] Associação Cultural Videobrasil, www.videobrasil.org.br

it has managed to foster policies of recognition, a sense of history, systematic reflection, as well as support and exhibition for works of video art, video installations, bio- and digital art, and so on, which are able to find a place to come together and be seen at public universities, certain private institutions, and at numerous venues and events. Among these, worthy of mention is the Videobrasil Festival, perhaps the most important in the world in its field, along with the memorable international symposia on digital art Emoção Artificial I/II and the historical screening of Brazilian video *Made in Brazil*, organized and produced by the Banco Itaú Cultural Center,[130] which has dedicated an entire specialized area to the subject.

Many Argentine artists, scholars and directors have had the opportunity to share their work because of these events. For the same reason, we should mention the first *workshop* for video creation in Buenos Aires, organized by Eder Santos and produced by the CICV, the International Center for Video Creation, in collaboration with the French Embassy in Argentina and the La Ferla School at the University of Buenos Aires, in 1991. And one absolutely must mention the workshops on video art run by Micky Kwella, the director of Berlin's Video Fest, at the Goethe Institute of Buenos Aires in the mid-nineties.

In Argentina, there are no museums or public centers dedicated exclusively to technological, photochemical, electronic and digital audiovisual art, in all its variety and complexity. In a broad sense, we should recognize that this is not only related to economic, architectural or technical limitations, but that it also implies a need for organizations with teams trained in archival work, curatorship and the production of audiovisual works (subjects marginalized in Argentina) examined through the dedicated practice

---

[130] www.itaucultural.org.br

and tremendous efforts of teams who are, in this way, able to influence the direction of research in their field: research into the implications of audiovisual installations, for example. Nonetheless, we should mention the EFT, MALBA and MAMBA[131] as three shining examples of how to handle audiovisual work in an artistic and institutional environment.

For all these reasons, we believe that although the range of policies of support should include financing, exhibition, collection and archival work, this backing should not be limited to sums of money or adequate technological resources. Rather, it should be accompanied by access to meaningful instances of study and reflection that would allow a high level of creative and conceptual development, articulated with academic thought on, and artistic praxis of, the entire spectrum of audiovisual media.

For this reason, we believe also that teaching and research on the audiovisual arts in Argentina is another vital element in the articulate, coherent and intelligent advancement of the audiovisual. We feel that it would also allow the cultivation of directors who explore other media and other paths, unlike those established by traditional cinema studies that are so in vogue at the majority of innumerable film schools throughout the country, starting with the officially founded ones.

Film continues to be the privileged object of study in our schools; even when other fields or media do appear in the lesson plan, they almost always take second place to the subject of film. Yet this is a paradoxical situation, particularly in the public universities of a country like Argentina, in which many of the free programs or schools that teach

---

[131] Will soon reopen its doors in San Telmo, which has meant a series of refurbishments to the building that left MAMBA without a fixed location since 2005.

audiovisual do not possess the equipment necessary for a legitimate course of study. As we recall, the price of film stock and photochemical processing tripled after the economic debacle of 2001. This causes video to supplant cinematic production on an unprecedented scale, yet in such a way that video came to see itself as film... made with an electronic image.

Unfortunately, this lack of awareness of the diversity of audiovisual media denies the possibility of original, artistic productions – despite the fact that any student today could write, produce and edit his own material with the aid of a computer and pair this process with extensive study of and a serious approach to the different kinds of production made possible by each technique, including film hybrids. The distribution of works is thus another relevant issue, given the restrictions that the dominant market logic imposes on the circulation of all audiovisual products that do not meet the institutional commercial or corporate parameters established by INCAA.

In Argentina, we are still far from finding an ideal space in which to cultivate the production and promote the creative distribution of experimental or auteur audiovisual works. Nonetheless, we continue to believe, despite the prevalent demagogy, in the importance of a hopeful and emphatic discourse on all that is yet to be done but is currently very difficult to find.

For these reasons, we insist not only in the creation of new channels of production and distribution by, at least as a first step, in the recognition of those that already exist. This implies, on the one hand, the revalorization and even recycling of spaces, doing away with the unrelenting desire to think of new buildings and new financial investments. It also means the recognition of a great number of practices that do not require concrete physical space, yet that could nonetheless foster study, financing, collection and instruction, such as personal and institutional networks, as well as networks among universities and educational centers.

We understand that there is also a great deal of virgin territory in our country, overlooked even by the patrons of culture, that are concentrated with the greatest energy in urban centers, particularly in Buenos Aires, which appears still to be the space of validation par excellence. Because of this, we also suggest the need to abandon the capital cities – megalopolises like Buenos Aires, São Paulo, and Mexico City – in order to encourage projects from the margins, with models different from those established by those monumental cities with millions of inhabitants. In this sense, the San Luis Cine project, with everything interesting and grotesque it has to offer, demonstrates another space for the production and revitalization of film outside and independent of INCAA, in the abandoned center of the country.

It is the challenge of the entire audiovisual field and of cultural administrators to educate themselves and to foster new debates and new ideas about these questions, beyond the notions of film, the culture industry and New Argentine Cinema – notions that currently, tenaciously, hold the discussion of all media captive. In this way, we believe it is possible to foster an opening onto the limitless dimensions of the audiovisual within the terrain of convergences that is the only possible space for its existence. "To imagine culture as that account, that imminence of something not yet occurred, that collapse of something it may yet be possible to avoid. To relate the potential experience of others. To relate with others," in the words of García Canclini.[132]

---

[132] García Canclini, Néstor. *Latinoamericanos buscando un lugar en este siglo*. Buenos Aires: Paidós, 2002.

Also published by Fundación TyPA:

▶ *El museo en escena. Política y cultura en América Latina*, 2010, edited by Américo Castilla. Fundación TyPA and Editorial Paidós.

▶ *HACER CINE. Producción Audiovisual en América Latina*, 2008, edited by Eduardo A. Russo. Fundación TyPA and Editorial Paidós.

▶ *Idea Crónica. Literatura de no ficción iberoamericana*, 2006, edited by María Sonia Cristoff. Fundación TyPA and Beatriz Viterbo Editora.

www.ingramcontent.com/pod-product-compliance
Lightning Source LLC
Chambersburg PA
CBHW031249230426
43670CB00005B/107